FOREIGN DEVILS
HAD LIGHT EYES

FOREIGN DEVILS HAD LIGHT EYES

Dora Sanders Carney

A Memoir of Shanghai 1933-1939

VIRGO PRESS

Canadian Cataloguing in Publication Data

Carney, Dora Sanders, 1903-
  Foreign devils had light eyes

ISBN 0-920528-26-0 (pbk.)

1. Carney, Dora Sanders, 1903-   2. Journalist -
Canada - Biography.   3. Aliens - China - Shanghai -
Biography.   4. Shanghai (International Settlement) -
Description.   5. China - History - Republic -
1912-1949. I. Title.

PN4913.C37A3   1981   070'.92'4   C81-094200-3

10 9 8 7 6 5 4 3 2

Second printing, January 1981
Published by Virgo Press *(a division of Panama Press Ltd.)*
              103 Church St., Ste. 209
              Toronto, Ontario
              Canada, M5C 2G3

First Published 1980 by
Dorset Publishing, Inc.

Design by Anodos Graphics
Cover illustration by Steven Vero
Book illustrations by Pamela Patrick & Josephine Patrick
Typeset by Virgo Typesetting
Manufactured in Canada

Some of the photographs included in the book originally appeared
in *National Geographic* magazines 1930-1940 and other periodicals
of the time.

To my husband,
Jim Carney,
who taught me so much.

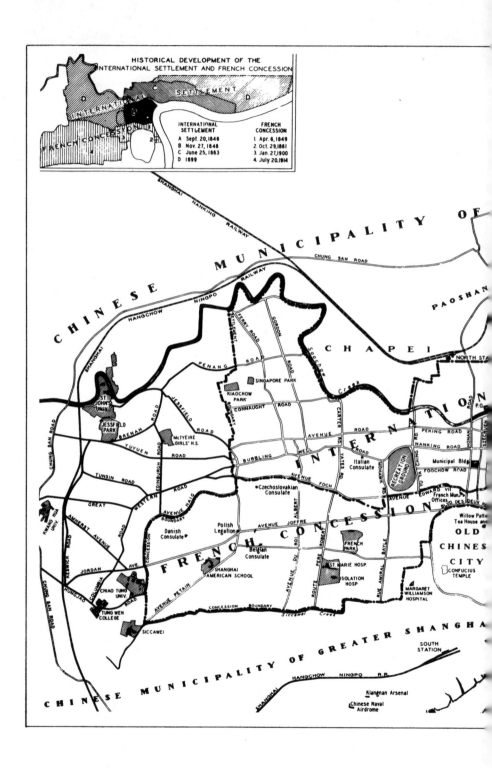

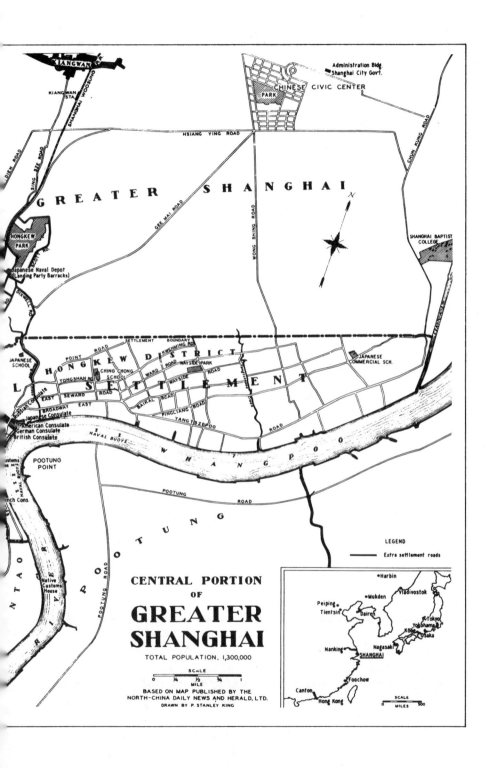

KIANGWAN

KIANGWAN STA.

KIANGWAN PARK

Administration Bldg.
Shanghai City Govt.

CHINESE CIVIC CENTER

PARK

HSIANG YING ROAD

G R E A T E R   S H A N G H A I

N

SHANGHAI BAPTIST COLLEGE

HONGKEW PARK

GEE MAI ROAD

WONG SHING ROAD

Japanese Naval Depot
(Landing Party Barracks)

SETTLEMENT   BOUNDARY   ROAD

JAPANESE COMMERCIAL SCH.

JAPANESE SCHOOL

POINT   ROAD

L HONGKEW DISTRICT

CHING CHONG SCHOOL

WAYSIDE PARK

WAYSIDE   ROAD

TONGSHAN RD.

S E T T L E M E N T

WARD   ROAD

BAIKAL   ROAD

EAST   SEWARD   ROAD

BROADWAY   EAST

PINGLIANG ROAD

YANG TSZEPOO   ROAD

Japanese Consulate
American Consulate
German Consulate
British Consulate

NAVAL BUOYS

W H A N G P O O

POOTUNG POINT

POOTUNG   ROAD

P O O T U N G

Customs

NAVAL BUOY

R I V E R

French Cons.

N T A O

Native Customs House

POOTUNG ROAD

LEGEND

_____ Extra settlement roads

CENTRAL PORTION
OF
**GREATER
SHANGHAI**

TOTAL POPULATION, 1,300,000

SCALE
0   ¼   ½   ¾   1
MILE

BASED ON MAP PUBLISHED BY THE
NORTH-CHINA DAILY NEWS AND HERALD, LTD.
DRAWN BY P. STANLEY KING

Harbin

Peiping
Tientsin

Mukden

Vladivostok

Dairen

Tokyo
Yokohama
Kobe
Osaka

Nanking

Nagasaki

SHANGHAI

Foochow

Canton

Hong Kong

SCALE
0   500
MILES

FOREWORD
AND
ACKNOWLEDGEMENTS

THIS NARRATIVE IS NOT intended as an historical treatise. It is instead the simple record of simple people caught up in a great international experiment.

Some of the characters in this book are real. They possessed characteristics too fine, I feel, to be tampered with. Others are fictional composites created to represent special points of view. Any resemblance such characters may have to real persons is purely coincidental and unintentional.

In writing this book I am indebted to my husband and also to our children who opened stores of knowledge, old and new; to my sister Byrne and brothers Jack and Wilfrid; Shanghai friends now living in Canada, for their encouragement and generous sharing of their experiences; and to Mr. Patrick Orr, student of Chinese culture, for intelligent and helpful criticism.

Others who have contributed, unknowingly, are Professor O.E. Clubb, U.S. Consul General in Peiping until Sino-American relations were broken off in 1950, whose book, *Twentieth Century China* (Columbia University Press) painstakingly unravels China's confused political emergence; Eleanor M. Hinder, formerly of the Shanghai Municipal Council staff, who recorded *Life and Labour in Shanghai*, 1933-1941 (published by the Institute of Pacific Relations in 1944); Sir Reginald Johnson, tutor of the boy Emperor P'u Yi, by his fascinating summary of the end of the Dynastic government, *Twilight in the Forbidden city*; Finlay Mackenzie, author of *Chinese Art*, (Spring Books, London); and H.L. Mencken's *New Dictionary of Quotations*, Alfred A. Knopf, Inc.).

Quotations in Chinese are Romanized in accordance with a system used in *An English-Chinese Vocabulary of the Shanghai Dialect*, prepared by a Committee of the Shanghai Vernacular Society and recommended by the Shanghai Municipal Council to members of their staff working with the Chinese population. One exception is the quote which heads the first chapter where the Vocabulary's "le", translated as "come", is spelled "lay-lay." This is done to enable the reader to pick up the sound of the oft-used summons as spoken by Shanghai Chinese who frequently repeated final syllables for euphony and emphasis. The Vocabulary was printed at the American Presbyterian Mission Press in Shanghai originally in 1889. A copy of the Second Edition, issued in 1913, is in the possession of the author.

My thanks also to Dorset Publishing Inc., whose vision and understanding have made the production of FOREIGN DEVILS HAD LIGHT EYES a broadening and enjoyable experience.

Dora Carney
Vancouver, B.C.
March, 1980

ALL MEN
WITHIN THE FOUR SEAS
ARE BROTHERS

-Chinese Proverb

1

LAU OO LI
LAY-LAY

BY NOON THE CITY LAY in sight—Shanghai, in 1933 the world's largest city, Queen of the Orient, Vice-pot of China!

"Most wonderful city in the world," said Jim at the rail beside me.

We were on the *Empress of Russia*, one of the CPR *White Empresses* that crossed the Pacific regularly every two weeks before the Second World War. I was on my way to Hong Kong, secretly planning to break off an engagement the Family approved but I did not. The Family felt that at the age of twenty-nine I should be married. Otherwise, in the 1930's, current opinion was that I would be left on the shelf, a spinster. Under pressure from the Family I had accepted, after first refusing, a proposal from a family friend in England, who was now employed in Hong Kong. The lure of travel was tantalizing and I was beginning to make some mark as a freelance writer in Toronto. Surely a trip to China, even if it ended in a broken engagement, would provide material to bait the hooks that would catch the freelance cheques! After persuading the Family to avoid publicity I left Toronto quietly with a suitcase and portable typewriter on the understanding that my major luggage would follow "after the date was set".

I was resolved that it never would be. I did not feel like a spinster—word of grim portent—and the shelf seemed a very comfortable place to be.

Now, for instance, there was Jim on one side of me, Ellis from Hong Kong on the other. Tall, red-headed and jaunty Irish, Jim was on his way home after his second Long Leave from the Shanghai Municipal Council, whose service he had joined after four years with the Canadian Infantry in World War I. Since we had first met, three days out from Vancouver, Jim and I had spent most of the daylight hours together, many of them sitting on a huge coil of pleasant-smelling rope in the stern of the the Third Class deck. Third Class passengers were all Chinese of the coolie class and the coil of rope had been like a desert island. We had much to talk about. Although our backgrounds were different—mine was "professional English" and his Irish peasantry, descended from the Vikings—our ideals and attitudes were much the same. He was a grand story-teller and I an avid listener.

Ellis, in the Hong Kong Civil Service, was smooth and dapper and pleased with himself, the sort of man I did not like. Throughout the voyage he had hung around the fringes of of my friendship with Jim, openly licking his lips in anticipation of future conquest. "I don't mind telling you," he had remarked to Jim within my hearing moments before the *Empress* turned from the broad Yangtse Kiang into the Whangpoo River for our first sight of Shanghai, "I'm looking forward to the two-day trip to Hong Kong after you leave the ship!" He seemed quite sure that I would fall into his lap like a ripe plum. He never went down among the coolies on the Third Class Deck.

I asked Jim, "You've been here for nearly twelve years and still find it wonderful. Why?"

"You have to live here to find out," he said. "I'm not very good at describing such things."

"Proper sink-hole if you ask me," remarked Ellis. "Built on a stinking bog to start with. Hong Kong all goes up. Blue sea. White sands. Rules and regulations. No Chinese allowed to live on the Peak."

"Rules and regulations in Shanghai, too," said Jim, "since Chiang Kai Shek has taken over. But his regime is so new there aren't facilities yet for enforcing them. Outside the Settlement, that is. We have a good police force in the International Settlement. It *is* true it's built on a swamp, but look at it!" Domes, spires and tall rectangles, dazzling white in the sun, pearls on the horizon like the magic city of a child's fairy tale. "It all rises and falls with the tides. Foundations on floating rafts and cornices specially designed to allow for the movement of the walls. That's why no building is more than ten stories high—the rafts can't carry the weight. Quite an achievement for the foreigners. They're the ones who built this city, not the Chinese."

Jim and I were on deck soon after breakfast when the *Empress* moved across an almost straight line in the sea and the brilliant blue water we had known for fourteen days turned coffee-coloured. "Now you're in China," he announced, although there was no land in sight. "This brown in the water is clay brought down from the very heart of China by the Yangtse Kiang, the Big River. You won't see blue water again until you leave China."

When land finally showed itself it was flat and low, actually a dyke, I was told, built to keep incoming tides from invading soy bean and cotton fields planted behind it. Only an occasional scrubby bush showed on the bank—the River's other bank was out of sight.

Ellis had joined us. The lunch gong sounded as we turned into the Whangpoo, but very few passengers went below. Red and black river steamers passed close to us and faces crowding the rails grinned at us. High-pooped junks, square sails mended with brown patches, dipped and bobbed over the waves, and faces on the decks grinned up at us. Families in small jerky sampans craned their necks, grinning at us. As we approached the city, river traffic increased and swift junks skimmed across our bow like moths, breath-takingly close. Ahead in the curving mid-stream was a line of low grey warships.

"There they are," Ellis exclaimed, "watching like slavering wolves. The great extra-territorial powers—Americans, French, British, Japanese, Italian, Swiss. We have only the British in Hong Kong."

"They never interfere in the affairs of the Settlement except in an emergency," said Jim. "Before the War there

3

were Germans and Russians, too. They're here as a reminder that peace must be preserved. They're the powers who conceived the idea way back in the 1850's—long before the League of Nations—of an International Community governed by its own Municipal Council, which I work for. Not the French, of course: they always want to run their own show, so they have their own Concession still, just ahead. But the Council and all the consulates and the Central Chinese Government work quite well together."

Suddenly I knew that I did not want to go to the well-regulated colony of Hong Kong and the Suitable Marriage the Family approved. Instead I wanted to explore this unique international experiment, the only community of its kind in the world. I fled to my cabin and sat on my bunk and thought about it. The arguments seemed obvious, but how could I change my papers and plans on such short notice? I rang for the cabin boy and asked him to find Jim and tell him I wished to see him. Jim came quickly, for he was in his own cabin packing to disembark.

"I've decided to go ashore here and find out more about this International Settlement. Do you think I can do that?"

He jumped up and down like a small boy, all smiles, then sobered. "It won't be easy—there isn't much time. But give me your papers and start packing. I'll find the purser and see how we can fix it."

Later, when I knew more about passports and visas and immigration laws, I wondered how the change had been effected so rapidly, but Jim's two leaves had taken him twice around the world on British, Greek and Dutch vessels. At the time the only miracle seemed to me that I had my suitcase ready when, almost as soon as the ship's engines slowed to dock, muscles appeared at the cabin door to carry it ashore; my typewriter was always classified as hand baggage and had to be carried by myself. The muscles were Chinese, bare to the waist above short shabby cotton pants and bare legs. They were already laden with several bags but were absorbing my suitcase also when Jim came pushing through the crowds that milled in the corridors waving my papers above his head. The ship quivered with a high rhythmic chanting. He shoved the papers at me, shouted "See you on the tender," and hurried towards his own baggage.

My suitcase had vanished and I was actually leaving this ship which had been my link with home. It was too late to change again. All my belongings had gone. Holding my cloche on my head with one hand and clutching my purse and typewriter with the other, I plunged after them.

Our ship was docked against one shore of the busy Whangpoo River but we had to disembark through the Customs House on the other side. This meant we had to cross by tender. There was no problem about finding which way to go, for everyone was excitedly going there too. Soon we were sitting in rows across the deck. There Jim joined me and our row heaved this way and that to make room for him. He and I were both highly nervous and made small talk.

As we edged across the river I noticed that a devoted young couple, whom everyone on the voyage had assumed were engaged, now ignored each other, sitting well apart without even looking at each other. I made a comment. Jim shrugged.

"That's the way it is. She probably has a husband meeting her or he a wife." He added fiercely, "What's wrong with that?"

"Nothing, if that's how they want it." Then the words rushed out. "Have you a wife meeting you?"

He raised his right arm in the air. "By my strong right arm I swear: I have not." Silence. Then he said, "There may be a woman, though." Well, of course, I was nearly on the shelf and he was older than I. There was bound to be a woman. He went on talking. "It was none of my wanting. She chased me for two years before I went on leave. Her husband is a big shot and I was afraid of a scandal. So I told her, divorce your husband and I'll marry you. But she wouldn't do that—I think because he earns a big salary and I don't. She's older than me, too— has two daughters at school in the States. I didn't want to come back to it."

"Well, tell her you and I are engaged. That'll fix her.

We can always say it's broken off, later."

He shook his head. "She told me if I came back with another woman she would throw herself into the Whangpoo. That would really start the fireworks. I'd probably lose my job and have to leave Shanghai—there'd be nothing for it but the Foreign Legion. I don't want to involve you in anything like that. My one hope is that her husband has been transferred to Singapore and she may have found another interest. But she *is* quite capable of coming up here to meet me."

I slid my hand under his big warm palm. Problems, problems! How many more on the tender were chugging across to problems?

Ellis, his face flushed with joy, breezed past. "Have a gay time!" He was heading for more joy in his few hours ashore. His problems were all in Hong Kong. I hoped there were several.

"The Chinese Customs do this alphabetically," said Jim, "so I'll be through before you are. I'll make it as quick as I can and come and help you. When you know the ropes it sometimes makes things easier."

I sat on my cabin trunk with suitcase and typewriter at my feet. I had nothing in the hold: most of my luggage would have come later, in the event of marriage. All was a quiet bustle, a murmur of many languages, the ever-present monotonous singing—but nothing to suggest that a woman had rushed to one of the wide openings in the walls and thrown herself into the Whangpoo River.

When Jim reappeared he had two friends with him. Peter, tall, dark and handsome, was English. Basil, short, round and grinning, was from Australia. The two went off in search of a Customs official and Jim told me quickly, "She's here and she won't let me go. She has an apartment furnished, right down to sterling silver. I told her I'm definitely *not* interested but she said she'd phone me later."

"But she didn't jump into the river! Don't worry about her. We can handle her—if you want to."

Basil and Peter came back, each with a Customs officer, and my three pieces were chalked without being opened. Arrangements were made for them to be delivered to the Astor House Hotel and we headed for the

opening to a street called "The Bund" which ran beside the river.

"You staying at the Astor House?" queried Peter.

"She is. I'll be at the Navy Y. She'll be working, she's a newspaper woman." I felt the two men eyeing me covertly, for in 1933 newspaper women were the forerunners of emancipation. The term was an exaggeration and I felt embarrassed: after all I had only written advertising copy and a few magazine articles, and I had never worked on a newspaper. There were no schools of journalism then and newspaper offices were the best training grounds for would-be writers.

There was no time to explain, for the Bund was a hurly-burly of movement and bewildering noise. Cars tooted, street-cars clanged, bicycle bells shrilled continuously. Chinese with hand-carts and baskets swinging from shoulder yokes peddled their wares, runners pulling rickshaws, and well-muscled men pushing wheelbarrows pursued their way with heedless indifference. And always there was the monotonous chanting that took hold of one's senses and dominated all other sounds.

I said, "Surely this is the singingest city anywhere!"

"It's the carrier coolies chanting to keep their loads

light," Jim explained. "They all do it—rickshaw coolies, wheelbarrow coolies, everyone. Without it the Devils would sit on their loads and make them heavy, especially the nastiest, the Old Fox."

"Lau Oo Li," supplied Basil importantly. It seemed to mark him as a Chinese scholar.

"That was the first Chinese phrase I mastered," said Jim. "I was posted as a guard for the Sisters in the psychiatric ward of their big hospital here. Wasn't much to do so I studied Chinese. The head matron was a real tartar and the Chinese staff were afraid of her. Whenever she appeared in the distance I heard them warning each other 'Lau Oo Li Lay-lay!'—'The Old Fox comes!'—and they would all start to look busy."

Somehow we stemmed the current of sound and movement and crossed from the Bund's river side to the pavement below the tall white buildings.

"That would be a good motto for me," I said, with a bravado I certainly did not feel. "Watch out, Shanghai! Lau Oo Li Lay-lay!"

The three men laughed. On the corner a very small Chinese man in faded blue cotton clothing and high-crowned straw hat drooped indifferently beside a bucketful of large yellow chrysanthemums.

Basil said, "Buy her some flowers."

"No," said Jim.

Tall, dark and handsome Peter said, "Then I will."

"You'll do nothing of the sort," said Jim. He gestured

to the small Chinese. "How much for all?"

The Chinese slid his eyes laconically over the three men and replied, "Tlee doll-o."

"No," said Jim again. Then he explained pleasantly, "I live this side. I no belong ship-side tourist. Here!"

He held out a single bill and the small Chinese swiftly pushed it under his hat. Then he scooped all the flowers from the bucket, wrapped the wet end in a sheet of newspaper, thrust them into my arms and scuttled around the corner with his empty bucket.

With her arms full of shaggy yellow suns Lau Oo Li layed-layed along the Bund to conquer Shanghai.

2

DON'T LOOK
FOR FIVE FEET ON
A CAT

-*Don Quixote*

MY ROOM IN THE Astor House had a high ceiling and two tall narrow windows hung with long strips of flowered cretonne. It was on a level with the roofs of buildings across the street, and the broad upper wings of a low pagoda posed against the sky beyond them. From the city street four stories down came the hum of traffic, the sound of bicycle and street car bells and the eternal chanting of the coolies. I could hear too the cries of boatmen poling their craft on near-by Soochow Creek.

One of the buildings across the street must have been a banana warehouse, for a never-ending line of small bent figures moved, chanting, from the creek to the building bearing green and yellow bunches on their backs. Whenever I looked out my windows, as I often did, it seemed that the sun was striking at different angles between the buildings on the blue-clad figures and their green and yellow burdens.

A round table and wooden chair stood in front of the windows of my room. In one corner was a dresser with a big round mirror and beside it a wooden wardrobe in which to hang my clothes. A flowered easy chair invited laziness before a small black fireplace kindled by a slight Chinese boy who entered with his own key and without knocking. Between the bed and the corridor was the bathroom. There was running water for sink and bathtub, but in the toilet there was a bucket.

I rang the bell and asked the Chinese who answered it

to bring me vases for the chrysanthemums. He wore a white coat and black trousers which marked him, I thought, as being above the coolie class. I shook out my meagre assortment of clothes and hung them in the big wardrobe. Then I sent a cable to Hong Kong and sat down to finish a partly written letter home. It had to be an explanation and was not easy.

When the telephone shrilled harshly I jumped to my feet, then froze, remembering it would not be for me. Jim had told me he was taking a room down the hall for two or three nights and had arranged with the desk clerk that if a woman phoned him the clerk was to let the phone ring in his room and then transfer the call to mine. We had agreed that this was the best way to help him in discouraging his predatory admirer.

Jim had said he needed this moral support. He was sure she was capable of destroying herself as she had threatened: I, never having met her, was sure she would not. "People who talk about it do so as a gimmick. They don't go through with it."

"They do in Shanghai. It happens. When I first came ashore I joined the Police Force. Discipline was strict. We single men slept in barracks. Fellow in the next bed to mine was involved with a Russian woman who said she would kill herself if he left her. He didn't believe her and one night she managed to get into the barracks and shot herself at the foot of his bed in front of all of us. There was a fearful flap about it. The Authorities frown on such goings on. He had to leave the Force."

Now when the phone had rung three times he tapped on the door, removed the receiver from its hook with one hand and groped behind him with the other. I moved forward and held the groping hand. He took a deep breath and then spoke into the telephone. "No. I've told you, I've always told you, I don't want it and I'm not going back to it."

A voice quacked over the telephone. Jim's grip on my hand tightened. He said, "I don't want you to do that and there's no point to it. It wouldn't help anyone."

I whispered, "Think of her daughters."

"Think of your daughters. It wouldn't be nice for them."

I found myself on the verge of laughter. This matter-of-fact understatement was so typical of Jim.

The telephone quacked again, then silence.

He hung up. "I think she knew you were with me. She said she'd call later—that means about midnight. We can't pull this stunt then. You're going to be drawn into it. She's probably phoning everyone I know and everyone she knows about you right now."

"Look," I suggested. "Let's be normal about this. When she calls you again ask her to meet me. Tea or something tomorrow. She may be curious and accept."

"A drink before dinner at the Palace. She's not the type for tea. What will you say to her?"

"Nothing special. I'll just act dumb. It's no use me trying to be glamorous or sophisticated, I don't know how. But I can act dumb easily: I just say as little as possible and make my eyes big and round—it's one of the advantages of having blue eyes. And you act devoted. That'll baffle her. She'll wonder what you see in me—maybe she'll think you're too stupid to be worth it. Two stupid Canadians!"

"Doesn't sound too difficult." Jim was always so ready to accept any suggestion that he was nothing much. He had told me his Irish farmer father had drilled this into him and his brother when they were boys. To me it was one of his great attractions. He sat down on the bed and asked, "Why are you doing this for me?"

I sat on a chair by the window. "No ulterior motive— don't worry. I've just always despised predatory females —and men, like Ellis—and like to make them look silly."

"You'll get lots of opportunity here. We'll try as you suggest. Meanwhile, can you meet me in the lobby in, say, half and hour? I have a surprise for you."

The surprise was a small maroon two-seater with a rumble seat.

"Why didn't you tell me you had a car?"

"I didn't want you to like me just because I had a car. Besides it's foolish, really—there are no motor roads here, nowhere to drive. Three miles out to the airport, that's all. But it's handy for getting around, faster than the bus, safer than the public rickshaws, and now I can

The Public Gardens, in the corner where Soochow Creek joins the Whangpoo River.

show you the Settlement. Aren't you going to get in?"

We turned back over Garden Bridge. I said, "As we walked across earlier today I was looking down at the small crowded boats. There were children playing in them and women doing housework and hanging out laundry, and on one of the boats I saw a potted red geranium. I suppose that's why it's called Garden Bridge?"

I thought I was being humorous, but he answered soberly.

"It's called Garden Bridge because of the Public Gardens here in the corner where the Soochow Creek joins the Whangpoo. Didn't you see them? Didn't we point them out?" He drew up to the curb and stopped the car where the sidewalk was flanked by a high white brick wall. Across the Bund, beside the river, was a triangle of green grass, shrubs and benches behind an iron fence.

"This is the Central District of the Settlement,—it used to be the British Concession. The British Consulate is behind this wall on our right. The Astor House is in Hongkew, which used to be the Japanese Concession, and the Japanese Consulate is opposite the hotel on the creek mouth. Further up the river, ahead of us, is an old walled Chinese city called Nantao, a fishing community

which has been there for centuries. When trade with China first opened up not quite a hundred years ago, early traders, their agents and the troops sent here to protect them had to live in Nantao. But the Chinese and the whites didn't like the way each other smelled. The Chinese said the white men reeked of whisky and tobacco smoke, and the whites couldn't stand the smell of Chinese cooking or the fact that all the household waste waters were thrown off the balconies into the narrow cobbled streets to trickle down to the river. So the British asked for a bit of land where they could build their own community and the Imperial Government at Peking contemptuously gave them a no-good tract of swamp between two creeks, Yang King Pang and Soochow. It was only for a hundred years, but the foreigners built there anyhow and soon other nations followed with similar concessions."

I saw it happening as he told it and was enthralled. Once again we were together as we had been on the coil of rope, throngs around us, but no one really near us. I was very aware of his sexuality, and he was always alert for any opportunity to implant a kiss or assert himself, yet I always felt safe when he was around: he was the essence of protection. I forgot my broken engagement and the fact that night was shadowing this Sin City of the World and that I was alone in it. I was reliving history with someone who was as interested in it as I was.

"And this was their park. A nice place to walk and watch the river traffic."

Jim said, "At first the Chinese Government forbade any Chinese to enter the foreign community, but this had to be changed because Chinese tradesmen needed to come in to deliver their goods; the whites wanted servants and there were Chinese who wanted to work for them. But there's a particularly virulent type of catarrh endemic among the Chinese here. They're always clearing their throats and spitting out wads of phlegm and clearing their noses with their fingers—the streets are a mess. You have to watch where you step. The whites reserved their park, or Garden, as they called it, for themselves and no Chinese were allowed to enter it,

View of the Bund – about 1889

until 1928. I was here then, when all the parks were thrown open to all the nationalities—except the Race Course."

"Why not the Race Course?"

"The Race Course is private property, bought by members of the Race Club and maintained by them. Fabulous sums of money were spent not only to buy the land but to remove the graves that were on it to another location. Everything is played there—tennis, cricket, polo, soccer—with the race track around the outside. All kinds of people mingle at the Race Course—we have fifty-five nations living side by side in the Settlement, and you'll find them all enjoying the Race Course, except the Chinese."

"Because of the catarrh?"

"That and other things. Their approach to sanitation is different from ours."

He had started the car and we drove on to Nanking Road.

"Da Mo Loo," he announced happily as we swung around the corner between the Cathay and Palace hotels. "That means Great Horse Road. Then we have Second Horse Road, which is Foochow—Nanking Road is main street to the whites, but Foochow Road is main street to the Chinese. Then there are Third and Fourth and Fifth Horse Roads; they were planned for carriages, not cars."

For several blocks Nanking Road was a crowded

15

midway of flashing neon lights, fluttering banners, jostling Chinese pedestrians all over the street and vocal vehicles. I was so terrified of an accident that I was unable to speak, but Jim, threading his way carefully through the traffic, kept on his travelogue.

"Had a friend in the police doing patrol on foot here one night, when he found a goose wandering about. He tied a string around its neck and kept it with him. I met him about two A.M., and the street was empty then, and he was pacing along with the goose waddling behind him. Never saw anything funnier."

I managed, laughing, "What did he do with it? Take it home for dinner?"

"No, he let it go at the end of the patrol. Said it was good company. Sounds crazy, eh? They're pretty brave fellows the police. Year or two ago, there was a circus camp on a vacant lot somewhere behind your Astor House and a tiger escaped and was wandering around the Settlement. General alarm went out and everyone who could make it was out hunting for the tiger. Then a rickshaw coolie walked into Central Police Station with his shoulder all torn and bleeding and said he was sleeping between the shafts of his rickshaw down on the Bund somewhere when a big cat scratched him. Friend of mine named Conning went out with an Indian Sikh to try and find it. Conning had a great big luscious steak on the end of a rope, hoping to coax the tiger out of wherever it was hiding. They found it finally, holed up in a summer house in the Public Garden. Conning threw in the steak, hanging on to the other end of the rope and was trying to coax the tiger to come after it when the Sikh pulled out a revolver and shot the tiger over Conning's shoulder. Quite a shock to Conning, who didn't know the Sikh was armed.

"In those days, just after I came out here, our police weren't armed. But one night one man on patrol saw an armed man robbing a Chinese. When he saw the policeman the robber ran away, but our man went after him. The robber turned and shot him in the stomach, then went down a dark alley. But our man followed on hands and knees, spilling blood until he died. The Chinese was quite an influential merchant and he went after him

Public Gardens on the Bund, with summer house where the tiger was shot. Behind in the centre is the Cathay Hotel and tower.

when he saw him crawling away like that. He told the story. After that our fellows were issued with guns, and so they should be."

There was less traffic by the time we reached the well-lit oval of the Race Course. Trees edged the side of the road along the Race Course wall. On the other side were tall western-style buildings, a large movie theatre, the main YMCA building several stories high, and beside it a block of apartments, each with its own small balcony. Beyond the Race Course the street straightened again but was now called Bubbling Well. Soon we were standing beside the "bubbling well", enclosed in concrete in the middle of the road. A street light above it shone down on the gurgling water.

Jim commented, "Probably marsh gas."

On the left was the big foreign cemetery behind iron palings, on the right a Buddhist temple, The Temple of the Tranquil Repose.

"This has been a holy spot for centuries," said Jim. "There's a bronze gong in the temple which the monks say was in a temple on the same spot 1800 years ago. For a few coppers they'll let you swing the beam that sounds it—we'll do that one day. This is the edge of the Settlement," he said as we got back into the car. "I'll take you now along Avenue Haig which is the boundary with Chinese territory. But the population has grown so much, especially the Chinese in the Settlement, that the Council has recently bought strips of land twenty feet wide, cleared them of graves and paved them, and won

17

jurisdiction from the local government over the houses built along them. They're called the Outside Roads. Funny thing, most of the big houses in the Settlement are occupied by rich Chinese, and the wealthy foreigners live along the Outside Roads."

The Yang King Pang had been a water highway like Soochow Creek and had been important in old China because it was so near the walls of Nantao. When the French asked for their Concession, a year or two after the British, they managed to win a 99-year lease on the dryer land between the creek and the walls of the city. The Yang King Pang, muddy, smelly, crowded with river life, then became the boundary between the British and French, traditional enemies and trade competitors. However, the two Concessions later co-operated in capturing the water of the creek at their boundaries and leading it to the Whangpoo River through a hugh culvert which was covered over and finally paved. This important street was six traffic lanes wide and named Avenue King Edward VII.

For dinner we went to a small crowded Russian restaurant on the north or French side of Avenue Edward. The proprietor, Jim's friend, greeted him with much pleasure and sat with us as we devoured big bowlsful of rich, steaming red borscht. He was a distinguished-looking man, educated and mannerly, and a survivor, Jim had told me, of a Bolshevik firing squad. The bullet that struck him passed through his head from side to side just above his eyes and the two scars were plain to see. When he regained consciousness, on this side of death, he found himself in an open grave full of bodies. He stayed there until after dark, then made his escape across Siberia and finally to Shanghai. Now he was one of the stateless Russian community who were not recognized by any homeland.

After borscht, which took a long time, we continued down Avenue Edward to a wide square where the six-lane highway met another wide street, Tibet Road.

"The streets in Central District are named for places in China—Nanking, Foochow, Peking, Tienstin—but the French streets have the names of famous French generals. The exception to the place names is Avenue

Edward VII, but that was a major piece of engineering and the name gives the period when it was done."

The intersection of the two wide streets formed a large open space that seemed to be filled with people, many groups laughing and talking in the middle of the traffic lanes.

"This is a favourite place with the Chinese and it's always crowded," Jim said. "On that corner is a big foreign movie theatre, the Nanking, and nearby is a popular cabaret, the Casanove. Our friend Ellis is probably there now. Opposite is a new apartment hotel, opposite that a temple and then the famous Great World, the Da Se Kah."

"Is that a newspaper?"

"No! An entertainment centre, mainly for the Chinese, though anyone can go. Theatres, puppet shows, wrestling, sing-song girls, games of chance, food shops. Families can spend the whole day there." I did not dream that four years later in this square of family fun I would narrowly escape death by bombing.

While Jim drove, I told him about the bucket in my bathroom. He was casual about it. "That's right. The old Astor House still sells its night soil. It's big business in Shanghai. Tank barges haul it up the creeks at night to fertilize the fields outside the city. We call them the honey barges."

19

We turned into the French Concession, drove slowly along Avenue Joffre past very small dress and millinery shops still open for business. "Little Moscow. These little stores are kept by Russian women—they have a flair for clothes. Many of them are former aristocrats, refugees from the Russian Revolution."

We passed the sprawling Canidrome. "Good fun," said Jim. "You can have dinner and dance between courses or go out and watch the greyhound-racing, outlawed in the Settlement."

"Why is it outlawed?"

"It's supposed to be cruel because the hare is mechanical and the dogs never catch it. Though I saw them catch it once when something went wrong with the mechanism. They had a grand time pulling it to pieces. But I think mainly it's a Chinese ruling, part of Chiang Kai Shek's effort to curb gambling among the Chinese. The British go along with it, but not the jolly old French."

Past the tall building where the tall men from northern Spain entertained with their fast national game, Hai Alai, we came at last to the Rue des Deux Republiques which skirted the wall of old Nantao. This took us to the French Bund, which led us back to King Edward VII's Avenue. Here on the boundary was a large bronze angel on a high pedestal, wings spread, back to the river where the warships slept in line: the Angel of Peace. Jim stopped beside it.

A very large, round late October moon hung in the sky, flooding the river with light.

I said, "It's a sort of miniature of the big international world the League of Nations dreamed about. 'The most Wonderful city in the World.' "

"That's the way I see it. There's nothing like it anywhere else and never has been."

We pressed hands, shoulders, lips. Jim asked, "What now?"

I had to make him understand my 1933 point of view. "I think you're the best friend I've ever had."

"I don't want to be a friend. I want to be father and mother and brother and sister and—"

"I don't want to be anything but friends until we've known each other at least three months."

"Three months!" he yelped. Then, "Well, that's two and a half months for us. We've known each other half a month already."

"I'm absolutely determined not to be dependent on any man. First thing I have to do is get a job. I had one at home and I'll try and find one in Shanghai."

"I have a job, but I suppose that's not the same thing."

"You're right. It's not. Whatever we do in the future, I don't want anyone to be able to say I did it because—because—"

Jim supplied, "For a meal ticket."

"Exactly. So now we go back to the hotel and first thing tomorrow I look for a job."

He was silent for some time, saying at last, "I have things to do too, but not about my job."

"Don't worry too much. We'll handle her."

The moon still had something to say and we handled that too. Then we drove back to the Astor House, where Jim dropped me at the door and drove off to park the car. I went up to my Victorian room alone for my first night in Shanghai.

At about two in the morning, I was awakened by the stealthy opening of my door. By the dim light which came through the windows, I saw a small shadow slip in and glide to the bathroom. There was a stifled clank of buckets, one withdrawn, one replaced, and then the bedroom door closed again.

I heard wheels rumble on the carpet of the hall—stop—rumble on again—stop—rumble...

Soon there were small wagons clanking softly on the cobbled street, the louder sounds of tanks being loaded into barges on Soochow Creek. To the subdued chanting of coolies poling their laden craft upstream I went to sleep again.

3

EVEN
A FOOL CAN
BE USEFUL

-*Danish*

THERE WAS NO JOB for me in Shanghai.
The huge, sprawling city was fully staffed in every corner, brimming over with workers of every description, tightly regulated, protected and controlled.

Three firms might offer the kind of work I had done at home, two advertising agencies and the English language morning newspaper. I went early to the closer, small agency. The owner, a tall, rather sad American with a mop of shaggy white hair, interviewed me kindly. He had a small business, he said, for the foreign population in Shanghai was relatively scanty. He could foresee no openings but would try and think of something.

At the second agency the offices were larger. It was named Baker's Agency for its owner, an Englishman, and had branch offices in Sydney and London. I was told that Mr. Baker was in conference but his assistant, Mr. Barson-Brown, would see me. Blonde and well-tailored, Mr. Barson-Brown seemed interested. He studied the few work samples I had brought with me, asked many questions, sighed and shook his head. He, too, was staying at the Astor House and suggested a cocktail before dinner some evening when we could talk further, but he felt duty-bound to tell me he could foresee no hope and his advice was to take the first ship home.

The editorial department of the newspaper was housed about four stories up in a white stone building on the Bund. Windows overlooked the busy Whangpoo and there seemed to be a pleasant camaraderie among the staff. I longed to work there. The editor gave me a book to review and his secretary, Ruth, took me to lunch.

We walked about three blocks up Nanking Road to an American-owned bakery called The Chocolate Shop. With small tables and tiny shaded lamps it could have belonged on any street in London, Toronto or New York. I chose tamales as the most foreign-sounding item on the menu.

Ruth told me that in canvassing for a job I was doing something that was never done by white women in Shanghai. English, Australian or American women who worked in the Settlement were signed on "at home" and came to the Orient under the auspices of the firms employing them.

"Because no white women ever come here looking for jobs there just *aren't* any," she said.

"But I don't want a big job, a career or anything, just enough to keep myself while I look around. I can proof-read, or lick stamps or serve in a store,—*anything*."

"Our proofreaders are very special people and those jobs are reserved for men. They have to be, because the typesetters are Chinese who have no idea of the meaning of the letters they set. Being a proofreader is almost like being an assistant editor. You wouldn't walk in asking to be an assistant editor."

(I might, I thought savagely, but did not say it.)

Ruth continued, "All clerical work, stamp-licking and so on is done by Chinese men. This is according to treaty, the Land Regulations, which cover all kinds of things to protect the interests of the Chinese. Nobody dares to break the Land Regulations. Only Chinese women, for instance, can serve in the foreign-owned department stores. It's part of the licensing arrangements. Over in French-town some Russian women have their own stores, but there's always a man in the background who pays the rent. You see, the whole set-up is different from at home. Here we are in a foreign country. On paper we're signed up on four or five-year contracts and if anyone leaves, we're replaced by another girl from home.

"You're trying to do something that just can't be done," said Ruth. "Mr. Lewis, our editor, asked me to explain to you. We are trying to help you."

"He gave me a book to review."

"Yes, but the only payment he can give you is the book itself. All money transactions go through the accounting office. It is strictly regulated."

Rules and regulations, Ellis had said.

I walked with Ruth back to the newspaper building and then went on to the shipping office to check sailings home. The next sailing was in about two weeks time and was the more expensive southern sailing with a stop at Honolulu. I did not make a booking.

Afterwards I walked back to the Astor House where a message from Jim said he would pick me up at about five-fifteen. Meanwhile I began to read the book to be reviewed. It seemed a silly thing and badly written yet had found a publisher and presumably made money for somebody. For a few minutes I stood at one of the two tall windows, tempted to hurl the silly book into the green and yellow rhythm of the banana market. Instead I laid it respectfully on the table, lay down on the bed and went to sleep.

I did not have to "act dumb" during that hour in the Palace Hotel bar. I felt very dumb indeed, depressed, forlorn, plain—in fact quite stupid.

She was a pretty woman, perhaps 44, expensively dressed and perfumed, with kid gloves, little feet in exquisite shoes. We were introduced and bowed politely and then she and Jim began chatting about mutual friends— what had happened to this one and that one while he had been away. Nothing for me to contribute to that.

I sat sipping a lemonade—nothing alcoholic! It fit in with the dumb act, but it was not a concession: I was unaccustomed to alcoholic drinks, especially in the afternoon. The lemonade was actually genuine preference.

I remembered the Somerset Maugham stories about the tropics and women in their forties with too many servants and not enough to do who liked to attach good-looking young men to themselves to bolster their self-confidence. This made me sorry for her. Resolving that if ever I lived in Shanghai, I would not have servants like everyone else because, thank goodness, as a Canadian I knew how to do my own work, and feeling quite bucolic, I interrupted a flow of words to ask her if she had any children. She seemed surprised to see me there and said that she had two daughters, both at school in the United States.

"Oh? Are they old enough to leave home?"

"Yes, both in their teens and anyway my parents live near their school." She added, looking down at her glass, that she had married very young. Complete and absolute silence. Jim's hand came sliding under the table and covered mine on my lap and I smiled at him, then saw the expression on her face as she caught the smile.

No effort at all!

Jim asked, "How's Willie? I hear he's transferred to Sydney. Doesn't he mind you being away like this?"

Oh, no. She had told him she wanted to do some shopping. A pause. Perhaps I would like to go shopping with her?

Oh, thank-you very much, I'd really like that! Learn all I can about the city, I thought. I might get some free-lance articles that would sell at home. My spirits began to revive at the prospect.

"Tomorrow?"

"Not tomorrow," Jim said. He explained to me, "Basil wants you to go to tea at his house and meet his wife and kids."

The next day, then. She told Jim, "I'll ask Katie to come with us—she knows the Russian shops so well. Then we'll have tea at her house and perhaps you'll come there from the office?"

It was so normal and undramatic. When we all rose on a common impulse she refused Jim's offer of a ride, saying she had one or two things to pick up and would take a taxi.

Said Jim in the car, "You did that beautifully."

"I did nothing. If I appeared satisfactorily dumb, I'm sorry, it's just the way I am."

"I saw her looking at us. She couldn't make you out at

all. That's why she wants to take her friend Katie along—to get her opinion of you. How did you get on at the paper?"

I told him all about it and it took a lot of time. We had dinner at a quiet little place not far from the Bund. Because it was early for dinner the place was almost empty. Only one other table was occupied. Three men sat there leaning forward, talking earnestly in a language we did not recognize. There was no music, but the dance floor in the midst of the tables was shining and the tables all ready with damask and bright cutlery. Waiters in black suits with white shirt fronts and napkins folded on their arms moved about quietly.

Suddenly on the edge of the dance floor appeared a large fluffy black cat. A white triangle spread from his throat over his chest and he stood still under one of the lights, tail upright, and seemed to be making an inspection. Jim said, "Mein Host."

With stately dignity the cat moved forward, placing each foot with almost tender care. He passed the table where the three men sat, still absorbed in conversation. But just as he was almost out of reach, the man with his back to us reached backwards without looking down, caught the cat's tail and swung it back as far as he could reach. The talk went on, the cat stood still, tail down, curled tip expressing irritation. Then Mein Host raised his pennant and began his tour once more. Again he was caught by the tail and brought back, again stood still, expressing annoyance with exquisite manners, again moved forward.

Not one of the men, not one of the waiters seemed to notice what was happening. Jim and I laughed and laughed as the absurd unscheduled "floor show" was repeated four, five, six times. The cat never changed the direction of his tour; the timing was almost mechanical. Then an orchestra came in and began tuning their instruments, diners were seated at the tables. The mood changed, the cat vanished. We danced and talked and danced again and thought of free-lance articles that might be written. Jim suggested one about the Chinese devils.

"I think the Chinese are rather fond of their devils. It's

so convenient to shift blame onto them when things go wrong. Ask a wheelbarrow coolie how he came to upset his load. He doesn't say 'I didn't watch where I was going.' He says a devil came by. In Chinese mythology devils were always supposed to have blue eyes. That's how the earliest traders, nearly all English or Scottish, earned their nick-name, Foreign Devils. They were blue-eyed trouble-makers, who had their uses all the same."

Towards midnight we drove back to the Astor House. As a final comment on the job situation, I sighed, "Perhaps I should have gone on to Hong Kong," and Jim popped out his "No."

I knew he was right. All around us the "proper sink-hole" as Ellis had called Shanghai, The Vice-pot of the Orient, was enjoying another night of iniquity. But surely well-regulated Hong Kong could not provide such genuine entertainment as we had had. Rules and Regulations would never allow a cat on a cabaret floor.

Come to think of it, even the Land Act, had its writers thought of it, might have something to say about what kind of cat would be allowed.

The comical episode had banished gloom. I vowed to myself that I would find a job in Shanghai.

Next morning I stayed in my room and wrote my first freelance article about Shanghai, which I delivered to the editorial office of Ruth's newspaper. I called it:

A Visitor's Impressions of Shanghai

To the newcomer, landing all unprepared in Shanghai, the city presents at once a most exhilarating and bewildering experience: exhilaration in its almost futuristic intermingling of nations; bewildering in a terrific sense of activity over what turns out to be a modicum of work done.

With columns in the paper every day about the disarmament conference, the League of Nations, the spread of nationalism, the threat of war, it is thrilling to an outsider to walk into Shanghai and find so many peoples living more or less harmoniously together; flags of many countries fluttering

within a few blocks of each other; a council of several nationalities co-operating for local government; meetings at which dark-haired and fair-haired, Nordic and Slavic and Latin and Mongolian discuss with a common quaintness of broken English their common problems.

In the country which I know best there is a national snobbishness that is very deeply rooted. People from other countries are not merely different but decidedly inferior. It is a distinctly missionary spirit that admits a foreigner to our social clubs—the kindly tolerance of a good Christian who is not afraid to mingle with those lower than himself.

But here in Shanghai there is a pride in internationalism. No doubt Old China Hands will laugh at a newcomer's enthusiasm but one's impression of Shanghai is like a snapshot album of the future. If this camaraderie of nations can exist here, why not in other places? Why doesn't all the world know about Shanghai?

Shanghailanders themselves, of course, are far too busy to tell the world. I never knew a city so full of busy people. The streets are thrumming hives, rickshaws darting in and out, bicycle bells ringing and ringing and ringing, motor horns tooting and tooting and again tooting. Everyone is in such a hurry—to get where? What for?

It isn't as if things were done more quickly in Shanghai than elsewhere. Indeed I have been warned that "Everything moves slowly here."

It is not as if there were more work done. Foreign men do not tend furnaces, or take out ash, or put up screen doors in their spare time. Foreign women don't do housework or cook, or sew. Their children are at school or with the Amah. The gardener attends to the flowers. I would like to stay for years and years in Shanghai and learn this art of being busy without apparently doing anything.

I would like to solve a few of the city's many mysteries. What lies at the head of Soochow and Hongkew creeks? Where do the rickshaw coolies get their hats? What is the name of the perfumed

Foochow Road – always thronged with shoppers of many nationalities.

white lilies on very long pale green stems?

It would be nice to understand why, when the American and Chinese dollars are rated roughly one to three and it costs the equivalent of five American cents to send a letter into Shanghai, I have to pay twenty-five Chinese cents to send a letter out?

What is the meaning of the portraits carried through the streets in sedan chairs by bearers wearing red clown hats led by a bare-headed man with a red umbrella, open in the shining sun?

Who are the austere bronze figures on the gates

Seen from the Chinese District of Pootung, river craft on the Whangpoo with the Bund on the opposite shore.

of one of the buildings on the Bund?

Why, in a city of many languages, should one be so firmly corrected for saying "o" instead of "naught" and "lunch" instead of "tiffin"?

Is it really true that you can tell a bad dollar piece by blowing on the edge and listening or is that just a Tall Tale for Tourists?

Maybe after two or three years there would be

no more romance for me in the big brown sails moving slowly up the Whangpoo or the sky-blue sampans kicking up their red heels in the creeks. Perhaps it would no longer amuse me to see, beside a block-long excavation piled high on either side with earth and broken asphalt, a sign no bigger than a pocket handkerchief labelling the activities "road work".

Maybe after a year or so I would not stand and listen to the music in the streets of Shanghai—the chanting of the carrier coolies, and songs of the street pedlars and reiterant melodious calls of the newsboys.

But in place of these, a "griffin's" pleasures, I would gain a lot in self-respect. I would face the Chinese with assurance and dare to fling back bogus coins instead of pretending to myself that they will make interesting souvenirs. I would gather up and throw down handsful of coppers with a fine indifference as to whether I was cheating somebody or being cheated. I would walk brazenly into small shops and buy delectable underwear for less than half the price asked.

And I should get over in time, I hope, this wistful, very childish yearning for the friendship of policemen and bus conductors.

As payment for this piece of writing I received from the newspaper in due time sixteen proofs of my story. These were not recognized Shanghai currency, so after folding one to send home to the Family and adding another to my work samples I stowed the remainder away in my cabin trunk.

4

TRUST EVERYBODY,
BUT THYSELF
MOST

-Dutch

BASIL DID NOT OWN A CAR but had a private rickshaw, very clean and polished, shiny black with copper mudguards over the big wheels. The Chinese who pulled it was well-dressed in black tunic and tight black pants, white socks and black felt slippers and black skull cap. Basil insisted that I ride in this and for himself hired one of the public rickshaws always clustered near the Astor House front door.

I had already learned that a rickshaw was summoned by calling "wang ba-tso!" Jim said this meant yellow wagon because the public rickshaws, owned by one central company and rented to the runners, were always painted yellow. The yellow was so faded and discoloured by dust that it just looked dirty and the runners were dressed in threadbare suits and a variety of hats ranging from the old hard bowlers preferred by English business men to ladies' brimmed straws complete with flowers. They also usually wore toothy grins, and Jim exchanged sallies with them in the patois of the streets, in which he was fluent.

There was another difference between the public rickshaws and this private one of Basil's. Under the back seat Basil's had a metal leg which kept the rickshaw right side up when not held by its runner. With the "yellow wagon", should the runner let go of the shafts, the weight of the passenger tipped the rickshaw backwards: the shafts pointed skyward and the unfortunate passen-

黄包車

ger was prone on his upper spine with his knees in the air, often imprisoned there by his own packages while his runner engaged in furious argument with whoever had collided with him. The safety leg on Basil's carriage made this impossible.

There were also springs under the seat so the ride was most pleasant. Basil's runner was strong and kept up an easy rhythmic lope, avoiding accidents with the grace of a dancer. Basil, however, seemed to have the narrowest escapes. His rickshaw bumped into pedlars and a bicycle and swerved away from cars by hair's-breadth margins. Once they careered into a crowd at a corner and stopped with three other Chinese and a Sikh policeman between the shafts with the runner.

My lithe "chauffeur" seemed to have one eye always on the other rickshaw. When the pile-up occurred he stopped and we both watched, exchanging smiles, as Basil stood up, shouted something and the tangle of bodies extricated themselves, the crowd laughing heartily. Then away we went easily again, one, two, three, four, one, two, three, four, 'til we turned from the busy main thoroughfare to the quiet of a residential street.

Postal addresses here had both street and lane numbers, for between the streets was a network of narrow lanes between high fences of woven bamboo. We stopped beside a gate. Beyond it was a pocket-size garden and then a house in a terrace of houses that might have been on any of a thousand streets in England. Inside there was a narrow front hall, stairs going up, a sitting room with a small fireplace burning coal that smoked vaguely and double doors opening into a dining room with oval oak table and mirror-backed buffet.

Short, round Basil had a tall, gaunt, very quiet wife. Only four of their seven children were present, along with two big friendly dogs. A Chinese 'Boy' in long white coat served us tea with small hot scones and jam.

Basil and his wife were doubtful that I would find a job in Shanghai. They suggested that I marry Jim at once, implying that it was inevitable. Basil said Jim was a nice boy but lonely and needed a wife to keep him out of mischief. It wasn't exactly what I had in mind as marriage.

His wife Edith thought perhaps that being a Canadian, I should contact a Canadian who headed the Shanghai office of a Chinese department of the national government. Being government, of course, he could only employ Chinese, but they must know all kinds of people in the Settlement who could be helpful. They looked up the address in the telephone book and then Jim arrived and we had more hot scones and jam.

"I don't understand it," said Jim. "It doesn't make sense. If you're short of money, I have money."

"It isn't that. I have enough at the moment. And I couldn't take yours, anyway. You don't take money from a man you aren't married to any more than you eat with a knife or wipe your nose on your coat sleeves."

"I damn well would," said Jim, "if I had a running nose and no handkerchief. I just don't see it. If I find a girl I want to marry, why can't I spend money to keep her around until we can marry? Why do you have to go home?"

If I could get a job it would all be so simple.

A note to the Canadian in the Department of the Chinese government brought a prompt reply. He and his wife called at the hotel in their chauffeur-driven car and took me home to tiffin. They also brought me a large bouquet of home-grown sweet peas although it was December. The sweet peas, they explained, were grown in their own greenhouses. Gardens and greenhouses were tended by two gardeners.

"We like to grow the flowers we loved at home," my hostess said. "Sweet peas and nasturtiums have always been my favourites, and it pleases the gardeners to grow them for us the year round. They are very clever and I think it is so sweet of them."

They lived in a large Tudor-style house in the country outside the Settlement on one of the Outside Roads. House and land belonged to the Chinese government but were under the jurisdiction of the Settlement because they fronted on an Outside Road. A short drive led to the front door between hedges of shrubs that opened to vistas of lawns and gardens like an English country estate.

Host and hostess were very kind, insisting that I feel their home was my home and that I come out whenever I felt like walking in the gardens or browsing in the library. A phone call would summon their car to bring me out. They were, however, pessimistic about a job. The Department employed only Chinese, of course, and everything else in Shanghai was negotiated under contract, the best ones signed at home. Vacancies to be signed locally were quickly filled by residents who had lived in Shanghai for years and had pipelines into all the offices.

As I put on my coat to leave, in a bedroom of deep-piled carpeting and satin eiderdown, my hostess said impulsively, "I think you are very brave to do what you are doing but as a fellow Canadian I feel I should warn you. Even if you find a job—you might as a governess or something—Shanghai is a terrible place to be poor in.

You have to make all your pleasures and everything costs money. Perhaps you should go home."

"But the Settlement is so interesting! There are so many different kinds of people."

"But you never meet them," she replied. "Everyone sticks to his own kind. The Chinese live by their own culture; we have the English Country Club and our culture, the French have theirs, the Americans, the Swiss. The only people you ever mix with are your own Club members."

Later I asked Jim about his Club. He said he had none except the Rowing Club, which he had joined so that he could use the swimming pool. "As a Canadian I guess I could join either the American or the Country Club, but I can't see the point of it. If I had wanted the companionship of only my own countrymen, I'd have stayed home. A lot of my own countrymen I don't like anyway."

"At the Rowing Club do they row?"

"I think so, sometimes, in Soochow Creek if the tide and the time is right."

I drafted a cable saying I was coming home to the job that had been promised me there, but I did not send it. Not quite yet.

I had hoped that in the Russian dress shops I might find a job as an assistant, but this proved another dead end. Katie's chauffeur-driven car delivered us to Avenue Foche in the French Concession, then followed at a convenient distance as we walked on foot in and out of the tiny shops. At each one Katie, who had been Katya before her son was born, exchanged sharp cries with the women proprietors and disappeared behind a curtained door. We other two tried on hats or held garments against ourselves from scanty stocks, not more than a dozen or two in each store. Once we were invited behind a curtain into a sitting room and served very sweet tea from a samovar. Nobody bought anything or tried to sell us anything. Katie's car took us back to her two-storey apartment where we admired her baby, and then Jim arrived to drive me back to the Astor House.

"If you belonged to my faith," said Jim, "I would say

see a priest. He would tell you to accept money from me."

"What faith? You don't go to church."

"Yes I do. I've been to lots of churches, Catholic, Russian Orthodox, Presbyterian, Greek, Anglican. I must say I like the Anglican best. I can understand it and there's lots of singing."

There was an imposing red brick church in the centre of Central District, every brick expensively imported from England by parishioners seeking to uphold their traditions, just as I was. I went to the adjacent offices to find some help in unravelling my confused ethic about borrowing money from Jim. A secretary said, "Please wait," and I waited for a long time.

At last I was shown into the office of a well-polished man who was obviously very busy with many papers on a large desk.

He nodded to a chair and when I was seated said, "Ah yes, you want a job?"

"Well, yes—"

"Not going to be easy," he said. "We might find a spot as a governess or companion, but when people offer jobs in their homes like that they usually want someone with good solid references from home. Where are you staying?"

"At the Astor House."

"Oh dear," he exclaimed. "Expensive, much too expensive. We should be able to do better than that." He touched a bell on his desk and asked the grey-haired lady who entered immediately to tell Mrs. Thompson she was needed. "You come from Canada," said the minister. "I was in Canada once, gave a lecture at some university there. Nice place, very nice place." Mrs. Thompson entered breezily, a rather short woman with a very wide grin and a very large nose. She had pulled her hair back in a bun from which a few wisps of graying blonde hair had escaped.

The minister said heartily, "This young lady needs a boarding house. See if you can fix her up." He nodded to me. "She'll fix you up."

I had spoken exactly six words in an interview over

which I had agonized for hours.

Mrs. Thompson ushered me down the corridor to a room full of empty wooden chairs.

"I know there is no vacancy in the place where I stay," she said, "but there is another place I'll sound out for you. Just sit down."

I waited until I felt she had had time to get securely hooked to a telephone, then quietly let myself out of the room, down the nearest staircase, out of the building, and walked back to the Astor House along the bustling Bund.

One concrete thing came out of this. Jim and I agreed that the Churchman was right—the Astor House was too expensive. In a small apartment I could surely economize and last longer financially than in the hotel.

Jim had moved as planned to a room on the sixth floor of the Navy YMCA on Szechuan Road. "Very monastic. No women allowed above the first floor, no phones in the rooms and the elevators go off at eleven. If I'm not back by then I walk up five flights of stairs."

I said it sounded safe and he replied it did not have to be safe. "She is still around but I assure you I see nothing of her. I know now she'll not kill herself."

"So we don't have to be engaged anymore."

"Better leave things as they are," he said. "It'll save a lot of gossip."

I told him that I would like to live the way the Chinese lived, perhaps in a boat on Soochow Creek. He said *no*.

"Of course, I forgot. The Treaty—"

"More than that. For one thing, no facilities: no running water, no electricity, no sanitation. And the mud at low tide—whew! It stinks. Besides, it's not the Settlement way. It's international—everyone lives as he does at home—subject to Municipal By-law."

Jim said he thought he knew just the place I'd like. "It's small, rather Spanish. I've always thought it the best place in Shanghai but it's always been full up with a long waiting list. You might be lucky. Let's drive there now— I'll show you."

"What about those houses where Basil lives? Does anyone let light housekeeping rooms?"

"Forbidden under By-law. If some landlords got hold

The boats in Soochow Creek. One can imagine the condition of the water after all these people have washed and thrown their refuse into it. Clock tower in the background is the General Post Office.

of a house like that they would subdivide the rooms by putting in extra floors half-way up. Those two front rooms would make four units. The landlord would live in the kitchen. Upstairs are probably three bedrooms. That makes six more units and two small rooms in the attic. Then there would be a loft over the front hall for a single man or a couple with no children—he could get thirteen rentals and he would too, without the By-law."

"But I don't want a boarding house! I want to do my own cooking whenever I feel like it. But I hate those big apartment blocks with long corridors smelling of other people's dinners—"

It was a small narrow building, two stories high and no more than twenty feet wide. Jim said there were twenty-eight suites, fourteen on each floor, each opening from two full-length balconies, connected at both ends by stone stairs. The suites overlooked a vacant building lot, so there was a nice sense of airiness about them. We went to the office of the owner, a Chinese businessman named Perkins Yue.

He was very scrubbed, very dapper, very courteous—and very sorry. Everything was booked up, and he could see no vacancies in sight.

"I like to deal with Canadians," he said, "although I have not known too many. I happen to be a Chinese but I was raised in a British company."

Jim seemed in no hurry to leave. He spoke of his recent visit to England and music hall shows he had seen in London. The two men reminisced and laughed together and then Jim asked what rental the one-room suites were commanding now. Perkins Yue told him and again regretted that none were available. Jim went back to London.

After some time, Mr. Yue said reflectively, "There might be one flat I could get. It is rented by a young Australian who has lost his job and is behind in his rent."

"I'll pay his back rent," said Jim. "Perhaps he will sell us his furniture too and that will help him to get back to Australia. Poor kid. I know just how he must be feeling. Do you know how to get him on the telephone? See if you can get hold of him and sound him out."

Mr. Yue's eyes went very round as he looked at Jim across the desk.

Before we left I had paid two month's rent and what seemed like a very small sum for the young Australian's bed, table and chairs. It all represented about two weeks' worth of bills at the Astor House.

Perkins Yue was all smiles. He promised to see personally to the cleaning of the apartment and said I could move in on Monday.

At the desk in the hotel lobby were two messages. One was from the owner of the small advertising agency, a shaggy-haired American who had reminded me of Mark Twain. He now wrote suggesting I try writing a Tourists' Guide. "Tell them about typically Chinese things to buy and where to buy them and sell space to the firms you mention."

The second message was from the kindly Canadian who headed a Chinese department of government. "I think you should see Miss Phyllis Ayrton, Secretary of the Chamber of Commerce, the only woman in the world, I think, to hold such a post. I have a great respect for her." She sounded formidable but I telephoned at once and was given an appointment for 11:30 next morning.

That evening Jim and I stayed at the Astor House for dinner. The gentle Swiss headwaiter found us just the right table, and stayed around to make sure all was well for us. A dark-haired young woman passed and the waiter looked after her admiringly. "She's a beautiful yodeller."

"Yodel? Where do you yodel?"

He said, "The Swiss community often goes out at night to the downtown business area. The tall buildings are dark and the streets empty like the canyons in the mountains at home. We yodel to each other from street to street."

He drifted away, leaving us happy. That sort of story was exactly Shanghai's charm for us. At the same time, however, I admitted to feeling scared.

"Of living alone?"

"No. Silly things, like—where will I buy my food?"

"Easy!" Jim was triumphant. "We have very fine markets in Shanghai. There's a good one only three or four blocks from where you'll be living. But Shanghai's biggest—one of the biggest in the the world, I guess—is Hongkew Market, a short walk from this hotel. You should go and see it before you move. Why not tomorrow morning? I wish I could go with you but it's impossible. I have to be at my own office early tomorrow. But don't get there later than six o'clock! Everything will be closed up and hosed down by eight."

He drew me a map of how to get there, and before he left that night he gave me a silver dollar and asked me to buy myself some flowers from him. The dollar was worth about thirty cents in Canadian money. "And if you need any help with the hornrimmed woman give me a call at the office!"

5

ONE PACE
BEGINS A JOURNEY OF
A THOUSAND MILES

-Chinese

AFTER IT CROSSED Garden Bridge the International Bund became a street named Broadway. The river curved away to the right with a street called Whangpoo following it to accommodate wharves and warehouses. Where Whangpoo Road left Broadway the Astor House was on the left. On the right, on the lip of the creek where it joined the river, were the Japanese and Russian consulates.

Broadway continued into the heavily industrialized districts of Hongkew, Wayside and Yangtsepoo. These had been the Japanese and American Concessions. After the union of the Settlements the Americans moved across the Creek into the Central and French Concessions, but the Japanese still lived in Hongkew. Hongkew, Wayside and Yangstepoo districts were heavily populated with Japanese, Chinese and Asiatic Indians. Records show that an average of 700 persons lived on each acre of land.

On Broadway, immediately behind the Astor House, began the Indian silk shops. Before six o'clock in the morning the fronts that protected them by night were rolled back, and bales of rich fabrics glowed in deep jewel colours. No stores in the Settlement were so reminiscent of Ali Baba's cave of treasures as these Indian silk shops. The gleaming silks and satins were so much more vibrant than the tempered tones in the Japanese stores just beyond them or the delicate hues in the Chinese stores on Nanking and Yates Roads in the Central Districts.

The silk merchants, I had been told, were among the wealthiest men in the Settlement, although they lived in comparative austerity above their stores on Broadway. Most of them were Parsees, descendants of Persians who fled to India in the 8th Century to escape persecution by the followers of Mohammed. There was a Parsee Temple on Foochow Road (Number Four Horse Road), which ran parallel to Nanking Road in Central District.

Like the bearded, military Sikhs who helped the police maintain order in the Settlement, the Parsees were bitterly hostile to the Muslims, and there were many Muslims in the Settlement. The Council handled this situation by encouraging the Muslims to work, and therefore live, in Yangstepoo, on the far edge of the Settlement on the way to the Yangste Kiang River.

During his early years in Shanghai, Jim had made friends with a night watchman at the Parsee Temple and had even been allowed to take off his boots one very early morning and proceed to the sacred inner sanctum to see the Light That Never Went Out.

The small, glowing, Indian shops, the wide, inviting Japanese stores with the sound of geta clicking so busily against the pavement—and then the market. You couldn't miss it. It covered an entire block of several acres and was built of concrete, open on all sides between stout concrete pillars supporting the second floor. The movement, the dust, the noise and the smells were bewildering. Jim had said, "All the landladies in the city with their money bags and cook boys will be there bargaining like mad," and there they were, pushing and jostling and shouting in several languages, none of them sounding English.

So many nations of the world were there, wearing their different clothes, buying their different kinds of food, to be prepared in so many different ways!

On one outside corner was the poultry, all of it live—Nobody in Shanghai buys a dead chicken because how did it die?—hens, roosters, guinea fowl, geese, thrusting

their necks from their crates, voicing their comments or protestations. Not far away, fruits and vegetables were piled high in baskets large enough to hold men. Pyramids of similar baskets, now empty, gave evidence of the quantities of these foods which had already passed into the hands of Shanghai residents that early morning. Carrots, onions and cabbages dangled in chains from overhead wires; vivid green spinach and other leafy stuffs made miniature mountains.

Under lights on either side of a wide centre aisle slabs of meat and curtains of fat hung from large hooks slung from the ceiling. Broad blades on short handles flashed with incredible speed while the Chinese men and women wielding them talked incessantly with the customers. Next were piles of pink shrimp and live crayfish crawling over each other and stretching their claws up the sides of wooden tubs. Tons of fish, big and little, were cleaned, scraped, skinned and chopped. Some fish swam in tubs of water, gaping round mouths at the surface. An eager vendor snatched one by the tail and dangled it, flapping, in my face. I fled around the corner.

Here seaweed and pickled turnip gave off that sour saltiness peculiar to Japan, and sure enough all the customers were in kimono and geta. Geta are raised wooden soles worn by Japanese on the streets, under the "tabi" or toed socks worn inside houses. A few steps further, Asiatic Indian women in draped saris surrounded vats where spicy steam rose above hot bean oil.

Suddenly I was standing by huge hot griddles where live eels wriggled on the hot surface and customers complacently devoured slices of those already cooked. In my hurry to get away I bumped into people blindly, saw a staircase, climbed it quickly.

There was less confusion in this, the Chinese section of the market. I wished that I knew how to cook the balls of white curd, bean cakes floating in brown sauce, rows and rows of leafy vegetables, green and white and creamy yellow, the glazed ducks hanging by their feet, the ginger, mushrooms and water chestnuts. Conversation was quieter, too, and ceased altogether as I came along the aisles. The brown eyes stared in open curiosity. I seemed to be the only white person on that floor and,

Hongkew Market.
The character
in the centre was
known as 'Fatty',
a popular fruit &
vegetable vendor.

feeling that perhaps I was breaking some rule or custom,
I went down another flight of stairs and found myself
among the flowers.

Ah, the flowers! They spoke my language. Displays
reached to the ceiling, effectively shutting out the rest
of the market. There were flowers I knew and many I did
not know, serene and exquisite and sometimes enchant-
ingly fragrant. I showed my silver dollar to the smiling
flower seller and pointed to this and that as long as he
seemed willing to keep on adding to the bouquet. Neither of us found it necessary to say anything but we
smiled at each other continuously.

Back at the Astor House the room boy looked injured
when I asked again for containers for my flowers. What
he finally brought was not adequate and I searched the
room for suitable vases. A large jug holding water by the
wash basin in the bathroom was set in front of the win-

dow to display the blooms with the longest stems. The
toothbrush holder held the scabious. Just before he finished wrapping paper around my purchase the flower
seller had reached under the shelf he used as a counter
and brought out a bunch of parma violets which he
tucked among the other flowers like a baby kangaroo in
its mother's pouch. These went in the drinking glass on
the bedside table. Then I went down for breakfast.

Later that morning as I dressed for the Chamber of
Commerce interview I made a small corsage with some
of the parma violets and pinned it to my coat lapel. If
Miss Phyllis Ayrton proved nice at all I thought I would
give it to her.

She was a small neat Englishwoman with straight gray
hair cut in a boyish style and very blue eyes. There was a
sense of quality about her and somehow she reminded
me of a piece of blue and white Spode china my mother
cherished at home. We sat in a big room overlooking the
Bund and the river, and furnished with the traditional
long Board Room table and heavy-set chairs. There was
a desk in a corner and filing cabinets but we sat at the
table as though we were presidents of this or that Company.

Miss Ayrton had read the *Visitor's Impressions* and we
talked of many things, including my morning's impressions of Hongkew Market. Impulsively I unpinned the
parma violets and gave them to her then and there. She
went and found a small glass of water, put the violets in
it and set them on the long Board Room table in front of
her.

We discussed the shaggy-headed American's idea of a
selling sheet for tourists. She said she knew him, he was
a kindly man, but she did not think the selling sheet a
good idea for me at any rate.

"You do not know the city or the Orient well enough
to be an authentic guide. But there must be a job somewhere in Shanghai for a girl like you."

She never once suggested that I should go home to
Canada but told me to talk things over with Louie Stops,
who shared her apartment and was editor of Shanghai's
Financial Times.

"She knows all the businessmen. Don't worry, we'll fit you in."

She telephoned Louie and I was shaking hands with her in fifteen minutes.

If Phyllis was Spode china, Louie was Crown Derby, warm, vibrant, skirt and sweater clad, with iron-gray waving hair and laughing brown eyes. That interview ended with an invitation to dinner that very evening. "And bring this Jim of yours with you." She didn't say it but her manner implied that she and Phyllis had better have a look at him.

They lived in a penthouse on top of a ten-storey building one block away from the Bund. Their windows and a simple patio on the roof of the building commanded a wide view of the city and the river. A Chinese Boy of vast dignity came in by the day to do the housework and cooking, but at night they were alone with their tail-less cat.

"He's not a Manx but an Accident," Phyllis explained.

He was a problem, too. He dreamt of romance and liked to go out at night, but there were no alleys ten stories up for him to prowl. He stalked along the low parapet around the roof, calling plaintively into the abyss below and now and then stretching a paw over the side as if calculating a dive. Even nine lives could not have saved him if he had tried it.

To cool his ardour and save his life, Louie told us, every night after the Boy had gone home Phyllis chased the Accident around the rooms of the penthouse. Louie described it with relish and gesticulations, the fat, tail-less cat and slight, academic Englishwoman rushing down the hall and back again, skittering on the scatter rugs, scrambling over the chairs and back of the chesterfield, into the bedrooms, into the bathroom, down the hall again and back. At last, exhausted, both sank down and settled themselves for the night.

Louie, Jim and I laughed and laughed, but Phyllis sat composed and smiling, as though Louie were describing something she did that was very clever.

After the delicious dinner, we sat deep in the flowered slip-covers and sipped our liqueurs and coffee. Louie told us she had always dreamed of retiring to Canada and raising baby pigs and tomatoes. When a young woman, she had satisfied some of her craving for travel by accepting a post as a governess with an aristocratic Russian family. On their country estates she had met baby pigs and fallen in love with them.

"The gardeners, too, grew the most wonderful tomatoes in the greenhouses. I have always thought if I raised tomatoes I could eat all I wanted and feed the rest to the baby pigs."

Said Phyllis, "Trouble is, babies grow up."

"Then I'd sell them."

"What kind of bacon would they make raised on tomatoes?"

"I'll figure that out when the time comes."

The Russian revolution drove her family of aristocrats across Siberia and Louie came with them. Somehow they brought funds for a new beginning. The family stayed in Harbin but Louie, with money sewed into the hems of her skirts and underclothing, came to Shanghai.

Phyllis, pouring the coffee, smiling fondly, maintained her blue and white reserve.

It was Friday morning, and I was pretending to pack my things although it could have been done in half an hour anytime, even fifteen minutes if not too carefully folded. I was restless and perhaps a bit homesick, for home now was at least a month away.

When the telephone rang I answered it quickly, sure that now it would be for me—the lady from Singapore was no longer a menace.

The voice was Louie's. She had made an appointment for me to see Mr. Fred Baker, owner and president of the advertising agency where I had been interviewed by Mr. Barson-Brown. She and Phyllis had spoken of him briefly at the penthouse dinner when they were discussing the possibility of a job for me in Shanghai. He was a brilliant man, they agreed, talented in many different ways, an artist, writer, almost a genius in sensing business trends. Born poor, he had made and lost two fortunes and was on his way to making a third. He had been married but was now a widower and the target, gossip said, of many women, both married and single.

"We grow three crops of cotton every year, around this area," Phyllis said, "and the trade figures are phenomenal, but our best crop is gossip. Would you agree to that?" she had asked Jim and he had laughed and agreed that apart from the tragedies sometimes involved it was more entertaining than all the music halls of London.

On the telephone Louie stressed that I was to see this man and no one else. "If you see Barson-Brown don't be waylaid. Fred is expecting you and the sooner the better."

I tried to telephone Jim to pick up a little moral courage but he was not in his office. The day was cold and wet and all things considered it seemed better to splurge on a taxi than to walk a few blocks or take a rickshaw. We had only to cross the Garden Bridge, turn right one block and then turn right again. I felt very gauche and unsophisticated.

The door to Mr. Barson-Brown's office was closed and I hoped fervently it would remain so as I approached the reception desk. I was shown to a room where a thin woman with strange opaque dark eyes played her fingers skilfully over her typewriter. That was another thing I couldn't do, I couldn't type like that. Actually, what worried me most was my hat. Was it tipped enough? Should I have pulled it to the left instead of to the right? Finally I was shown into the great man's office.

As a target of romantic gossip he was most unglamorous in appearance. He looked like what he was, the middle-aged product of an English industrial town. He ruffled briefly through my sample folder, then said he was more interested in what I could do for him than what I had done for someone else. We spoke of layouts. I told him I could draft layouts and knew something about type faces but couldn't draw for nuts. He grunted, "I want you as a writer." Then, "I hear you are on the verge of getting married."

This infuriated me. It was one thing to be entertained by gossip, but I did not relish being its target myself. I said stiffly, "My personal life has nothing to do with my work."

"Are you on the verge of getting married?"

"One is always on the verge of being married or not

being married."

He looked angry, then laughed. "Will you sign a contract?"

"Not to get married?"

"Not to have children while under contract."

"For how long?"

"Six months preliminary, then three years."

Six months could solve a lot of problems. "Yes, I'd like to, thank you."

We discussed salary. He took some forms from a drawer, filled in names and figures and pushed it across the desk with a pencil.

"Sign along there."

"I should like to read it first."

"Sit over there and read it."

"I would rather take it home."

"You want to show it to your fiance."

"My father is a lawyer and told me never to sign anything without reading it carefully. I would like to read this at home where I can concentrate."

"Bring it with you Monday morning when you report for work. Give it to Michael Barson-Brown." He grinned and stood up. "He will give you some small accounts to start with." We shook hands and my grin was much wider than his.

My feet seemed to bounce as I went downstairs and I grinned through the streets to Louie's office. She clapped her hands. "It worked!"

Then she told me that "Mike Brown" was due to go home on leave and sign a new contract and was holding out for a very large pay raise before agreeing to come back. She read my contract all the way through and said she could see nothing wrong with it.

"But there wouldn't be. You don't have to worry about Fred Baker. He is extremely honourable. I'll phone Phyllis. She'll be glad."

I bounced back to the Astor House and this time Jim was in when I telephoned.

"Look," he said. "Can you meet me in the foyer about six-thirty? And I suggest you have a rest this afternoon. Tonight we really celebrate."

6

THERE IS A TIME
TO FISH AND A TIME
TO DRY NETS

-Chinese

ALTHOUGH THERE WAS A BAR at the Astor House, many people drank their before-dinner appetizers in the lounge-like lobby, served by Boys in short white tunics over long black gowns. The first thing I saw at 6:30 was Mr. Barson-Brown standing by a pillar, holding a glass of something green. I turned another way but he caught up with me quickly and said just behind my shoulder:

"That was a pretty sneaky thing you did."

I turned and looked at him. "I think it was rather sneaky not to tell me there was a job going when there was."

He widened his pale blue eyes at me. "There was no job! That was *my* job."

I widened my eyes at him, with, I felt, better effect.

"Why, Mr. Barson-Brown! I could never do your job! I'm just going to help Mr. Baker with the copywriting while you're away."

"Is that what he told you?"

"Well, actually he didn't mention you, except at the end. I've only learned since I saw him that you're going home on leave for six months or something. He said I was to see you on Monday and you would give me something small to start on."

Michael Barson-Brown said, "I will give you nothing. Tell that to Fred Baker. I will not help you at all or tell you anything whatsoever."

"When do you sail?"

"I'm telling you nothing." He took a sip of his green drink and walked away, and I looked after him, reminding myself that he could also be called Mike Brown.

The celebration began with dinner at The Jinx, a small place kept by a German on Bubbling Well Road, specializing in beef and beer. It was a good place for talking, especially in the early evening when most of the tables were still empty. The waiters, who all looked as though they or their ancestors had come from central Europe, kept a discreet distance.

I told Jim all that had happened that day, including the recent encounter with Barson-Brown. He laughed about that, saying he guessed I'd given him something to think about. "You could probably do his job better than he can, and he knows it."

"Of course I couldn't! As Phyllis said, I don't know anything about Shanghai yet!"

Jim laughed, too, at my rejoinder to Fred Baker that one is always on the verge of being married or not being married.

"What made you say that?"

"It just seemed a good thing to say."

"You couldn't have said it to a better man."

I had brought the contract in my purse. Like Louie, Jim read it through and said it seemed safe enough. By the time we surfaced from my affairs we were halfway through the meal and The Jinx was coming to life. In two or three places on the dance floor other couples were leaving wide spaces around British sailors who were dancing in a sort of winged-heel ecstacy. They were marvellous dancers, and Jim explained that after being at sea for weeks with no music but a mouth-organ or pipes, they loved the sound of a real orchestra. The orchestra played up to them, too. The bottoms on their sea-going trousers flared and fluttered as they twirled and toe-tapped deliriously and alone, pretty Chinese dancing partners floating after them in butterfly silk dresses, always nearby when wanted but never in the way. Professional entertainers often seemed an anti-climax after the British tars had held the dancing floor.

At our next stop, the Hai Alai arena, there was no food

and no music except the hard rhythm of balls colliding with walls and racquets and human voices surging and moaning as the fortunes of the Hai Alai players waxed and waned. The arena was semi-circular, narrow, and bright light focusd on the courts below.

The Hai Alai players were Basques from northern Spain, tall, dark and handsome, wearing full-sleeved white silk shirts open at the throat, wide bright satin sashes and dark tight-fitting trousers. They played with tremendous vigour and speed, standing with their backs to each other as they swung their smashing racquets. Spectators laid their bets on the sashes although many fans called their heroes by name.

Encouragement, vituperation, delight or anguish were voiced in Spanish, Portuguese, Russian, French, German and English in all its dialects. Excitement ricocheted as the balls flew back and forth and women ooh'd and eeeh'd, thrilled or sobbed as the virile gladiators whirled to victory or went down in defeat. I found Hai Alai in Shanghai a brilliant, exhausting and somehow savage experience. A few well-dressed Chinese were in the audience but the game did not seem to be popular with the general Oriental population.

The Canidrome was the only stadium licensed for dog racing in the whole Shanghai area and it was in the French Concession. Jim said he had been checking his local history, for he remembered when he came soon after the end of the First War there had been several stadiums.

Chiang Kai Shek was the first man to succeed in unifying China, liberating the people from the corrupt and generally harsh rule of the local provincial War Lords. Among the reforms which he and his Kuo Min Tang, or Central Government, tried to institute was the suppression of gambling which, Jim said, "Had the Chinese by the throat."

The Chinese had been delighted with the racing whippets which the white men imported. They bet so wildly and lost so much money that the reforming new government outlawed the sport in Chinese territory and persuaded the Municipal Council to ban it in the Settlement. The independent French could not be persuaded.

Hanging baskets dripped flowers under the lights of

the Canidrome Grandstand. Chinese boys in neat monkey-jacket uniforms rushed up and down the terraced aisles with betting slips, answering fluttering hands, shrill calls and waving handkerchiefs. Chinese, Japanese, Europeans, Indians in every conceivable costume filled the seats with twittering excitement as bells rang and trumpets sounded and shouts and cheers blasted through the surfing sound of many languages.

The race track itself was a ring of light around a dim green oval. Above and beyond it the night sky was a black dramatic background for two neon advertising signs that blazed on and winked off, blazed and vanished continually. The slim cream or gray dogs were paraded, each wearing a bright silk coat and led by a trainer in matching jackets and jockey cap and white riding breeches. When the dogs were shut into their starting kennels they set up their own excited clamour as bells rang in all parts of the Grandstand and people quietened and sat forward in their seats.

A white electric hare popped out of its barrow and backed into place. Then away it went, down the track, once around and as it passed the starting kennels the doors flew open simultaneously. The dogs fell absolutely silent and came out like streaks. They flew around the course in seconds, the hare popped out of sight and the race was over.

Leads were snapped to the dogs' collars, the winners paraded, cheered and clapped, the confetti-coloured crowd scattered to dance floor, bar or betting wickets and the turmoil and the tension began again.

"There's one night club I would have liked to take you to," said Jim as we drove away from the Canidrome. "That's old St. George's, now closed down. It was kept by a man named Fredericks, don't know where he came from, may have been Germany or Greece. He and his wife started a small place in Hongkew. It did very well and he bought this old Chinese farmhouse right across the street from the bubbling well and the Temple of Tranquil Repose. It was a typical well-to-do Chinese country house, though a bit out of repair. There was a wing for the man and his wife, a wing for the concubines where he had the dining and dance hall, and a wing for the kitchen staff, all built around a central courtyard where he kept his animals. St. George's Farm, he called it. He had a water buffalo and a couple of sheep there, I forget all the animals,—oh yes, a camel, and I think a lion once, and a great big Tibetan dog. He was my favourite."

"Quite a combination, a night club and a zoo! And quite a corner that made it—the Temple on one corner, the cemetery on another, the night-club zoo on a third. What was on the fourth?"

"There isn't a fourth exactly. Great Western Road comes in there, and Yu Yuen Road, and Jessfield, and a little further on Avenue Road. These are all Outside Roads. It's quite a busy corner. In times of unrest the British army usually has an armoured car there. One or two armoured cars can control all the approaches."

Since we could not go to old St. George's we drove into the parking lot of the Del Monte. The time was two in the morning and the lot was scarcely one-third full. The place did not wake up until three or four o'clock, Jim explained, and later breakfast was served for those who wanted it. Strings of lights stretched across the lot from the eaves of the building like the ribs of an umbrella, glinting on the trees that edged the short driveway and illuminating the sharp features and bristling beards of turbanned Sikh watchmen. There was no cover charge at the Del Monte but it was well disciplined, well run and possibly Shanghai's most famous and best loved night club.

All the dancing partners were white and usually Russian. In evening gowns of gleaming satin or pastel chiffon they sat at little tables edging one side of the small dance floor and sipped clear tea or fruit juice. The Del Monte's dancing partners never drank on duty.

I was not wearing evening dress and had not even thought of it until I met the supercilious survey of that glittering array of lovely ladies. Under their critical appraisal I felt dowdy and dishevelled, wondering uneasily if my slip was showing or one of my stockings had snagged and run. When the dance ended and we sat down again at our table I surreptitiously explored my legs with my finger-tips and checked the straightness of my stocking seams. I asked Jim, "Should I fix my lipstick?"

He only laughed. "Feeling outclassed? I've heard that Del Monte girls have that effect on outside women. How do they do it?"

"They sort of look at one."

"Well, they don't like you being here, you know. You're bad for their business. Look, there's Bert, one of the men I work with, and his English wife. Do you mind if they join us?"

Soon we were six, for pretty Katie appeared with her American husband, Orville, and he ordered drinks all round. Millie and Bert, like us, wore daytime clothes, but Orville was in a tuxedo and Katie outshone any of the dancing partners. They were friends of hers and she twiddled her fingers and waved and smiled. She whispered to Orville, who went over and brought one of the girls to our table. Katie introduced her.

"This is Natasha, my very dear friend." Natasha drank a ginger ale, chatted and joked happily, but Millie stiffened and looked disapproving. A stranger bowed to Natasha, who danced away with him. Orville quickly filled her empty chair with another friend of Katie's. Millie sat silent and grim-lipped. When the new girl joined the dancers Orville and Katie quickly followed her.

"I call that very poor taste," said Millie.

"Why?" asked her husband. His face was flushed and he seemed ripe for a fight.

"It was hardly the thing to do," said Millie, "bringing them here to the table with us."

"Why not?" demanded her husband. "They were very pleasant girls." Millie was biting her lip.

"You were lucky it was only two," said Jim. "Orville might have brought all seven of his ex-wives over."

Millie said sharply, "That wouldn't have been very funny."

"You jealous?" enquired Bert.

The atmosphere at our table was growing decidedly heated, and Jim and I, of one accord, rose to dance. The dance floor was so crowded now that couples were shuffling shoulder to shoulder. We lost ourselves somewhere in the middle. Talking is easy under such circumstances when you are imprisoned in the middle of a mob and merely moving from one foot to the other. I asked, "Has he really had seven wives?"

"Eight. Katie is his eighth. He got them all from the line-up there and returned them quite happily when he wanted a change. I suppose he gave each a nest egg. But now Katie has given him a son and I think she feels herself secure."

"Did he really marry them?"

"Absolutely. He makes a moral issue of it. What I think is funny is Millie's outraged virtue. Bert was on leave the same time as I was and it was then we met Millie and her family. Highly respectable, I might add, and Millie was so prim and unapproachable we nicknamed her The White Lily. But old Bert got around her somehow. They ran away one night and didn't show up for three days. It caused quite a flap in the hen coop. Something religious, I think,—he didn't belong to the same church and they were afraid the family would not allow the match."

"But they did get married."

"Oh my, yes. With all the trimmings."

When we returned to our table Millie and Bert were sitting close together, holding hands, I suspected, under the table. We did not see Katie and Orville again.

Del Monte's had a good floor show and it was nearly four in the morning when we left. The small maroon car moved along narrow streets where low balconies jutted over the curb-like sidewalks and small store fronts were covered with locked iron grilles. Jim parked and locked the car and led my wearying high-heeled feet down a long cobbled alley walled on both sides with woven strips of bamboo. Dim light gleamed behind one section, and peeping through chinks between the woven strips we looked at a Chinese cobbler's shop. Kerosene lanterns hung from the overhead bamboo poles over which rush mats were thrown to form a roof. By the light of the lanterns several Chinese—adults, old people and children—were busily making and mending cotton slippers.

"Chinese territory," Jim commented. "In the Settlement such a building and such work hours would not be allowed. People at home talk about the exploitation of the Orientals by the whites, but no white man has exploited the poorer classes of the Chinese as the Chinese have.

"There are lots of things to see in the Settlement you won't like," he told me, holding my elbow as I staggered over the cobbles, "but the Council can't do anything about them because they weren't given jurisdiction in the original Land Regulations. Now the Government won't extend the Council jurisdiction—they don't want the whites to gain any more power."

We reached a doorway with two huge eyes painted above it lit by two electric light bulbs shaded from below. The eyes were black and long-lashed, shadowed seductively with green. They glanced sideways above the edge of a fluted fan. The name of the night club was Chorny Glasee, Black Eyes, understandable in any language.

Beyond the door we found ourselves in a whitewashed corridor. On a row of hooks along one hall a few men's hats and coats hung. Against the other wall the guardian of the coats sat at a small table with a man friend, both of them spooning soup from small bowls.

At the end of the corridor a small dance hall was decorated to resemble a coconut grove. Pillars, or rather posts, whose function we felt was to hold up the uncertain roof, were covered with an artificial bark and long green leaves hung down between them. The floor was laid with wide uneven boards with no pretense of polish, and hard knots protruded in places. An orchestra of three—piano, violin and traps—sat under another larger painting of Black Eyes.

Several young sailors sprawled at some of the tables, three or four frankly sleeping. Men with glittering eyes discussed intensely some matter of no concern to the rest of us. A few mixed groups, evidently continental Europeans, were talking and drinking and shouting with laughter. Behind the piano on plain wooden chairs sat five plain women, square shouldered and square hipped. Four wore white blouses and dark skirts; the fifth had a long dress of sleazy gray rayon banded at the hem with red. A shaggy red artificial flower was tucked behind one ear.

Although we were not thirsty Jim suggested that we split a bottle of beer. He said we were supposed to order something, but the coffee would be nauseous and the spirits poisonous. "In a place like this, never drink anything but beer. The spirits are cut with raw alcohol and could leave you blind by morning."

The orchestra began to play. Everybody danced except ourselves, the sleeping sailors and the men with the glittering eyes. Some sailors danced with each other, some claimed the girls in white blouses. When all were in their seats again the woman in the sleazy dress stood up and sang a song in a hoarse frog-like voice.

The orchestra then played a sort of reel and a man from one of the tables was pushed forward by his friends and began to dance alone. A girl from another table jumped up and joined him. They danced together shyly, without looking at each other's faces, watching only their feet. We wondered if they spoke the same language, but they danced together beautifully while the orchestra played with a merry abandon and one of the guests, a big man, beat time with one hand on the table-cloth and occasionally shouted encouragement. When it was over we all clapped vociferously, then all but the sleepers and the talkers tripped over the knots in the floor.

"There are dozens of places like this scattered about in the alleys," said Jim. "Cheap, free and easy. If you want to get drunk, get drunk. Nobody cares."

Perhaps that is the sadness of a place like the Settlement, I thought. Where so many people follow their own codes and there is no standard public opinion, if someone follows the 'wrong' code, nobody cares; there is certainly freedom but I felt vague and unconvinced and did not try to voice my feeling.

Light still gleamed through the bamboo wall. Peeking through the chinks we saw the cobblers, wrapped in rags and coats, sleeping on the floor where they had been working.

"How about breakfast?" Jim demanded as we headed back toward the Bund. "I'm hungry as a she-wolf."

"It's only six o'clock and the Astor House dining room doesn't open 'til 7:30."

"I'll show you something."

We went to The Kitchen on Broadway, a small place

slipped into an area no bigger than the small stores surrounding it. One long counter stretched from front to back facing a row of old-fashioned coal burning kitchen stoves, their cooking tops cleaned and polished to a high gleam. On each stove a kettle steamed but there were no other cooking utensils. As we perched on high stools our breakfast was cooked before our eyes: bacon, eggs, hot cakes and toast sizzled in moments on the hot surfaces, tended by cooks in white aprons, bristling moustaches and white chef's caps. Smoke and steam escaped in vents along the wall, and the aroma was enough to give a stuffed hog an appetite.

7

WHO
DOES NOT VENTURE
HAS NO LUCK

-Dutch

As I APPROACHED THE OFFICE, contract in hand, on Monday morning I was greeted by the sound of many voices. I had checked out of the Astor House, leaving my luggage with the hotel office to be picked up during the day. At the moment Baker's Agency seemed my only home, and I felt rather like a swimmer in the ocean clinging to a piece of spar and approaching a life raft.

I appeared in the doorway to a sudden silence. Between me and Mr. Barson-Brown's closed door was an office desk surrounded by six Chinese coolies in blue cotton suits. There was also an imposing-looking Chinese businessman wearing a long silk Chinese gown, an enormously fat white woman, and several other people. Fred Baker's personal secretary, Mrs. Chandler, was telephoning from the reception desk but almost immediately hung up the receiver. Her dark opaque eyes were on me as she said,

"Mr. Baker won't be in today. He says you will just have to make what arrangements you can."

"Isn't that just too nice!" ejaculated a tubby bald man with heavy black eyebrows. "Always there's trouble, he isn't coming in. 'Sort it out yourselves,' he says. 'Don't ask me!' Ain't that just lovely!"

I found my voice. "I would like to see Mr. Barson-Brown."

"That's the trouble," said the fat woman. "Mr. Barson-

61

Brown would not like to see you. Fred Baker says to put a desk for you in Mr. B-B's office, so they do. Mr. B-B says, take it out, so they do. And Mr. Baker has a headache, so he says, and isn't coming in." She looked as happy as if she had swallowed a porpoise whole.

"And ain't that lovely," repeated the bald man. He turned away and went down the corridor that led to Fred Baker's office. The six coolies all began to talk at once to the dignified Chinese man, who listened with a bland composure.

Now a slim Chinese woman who wore a gown of exquisite styling and quality began to speak volubly in Chinese. Her face was badly scarred from small-pox, but she had an air of elegance and authority. First she seemed to scold the coolies, who again fell silent. Then her words flowed like a mountain torrent around the dignified Chinese gentleman.

Mrs. Chandler rested a boney hip on the reception desk and watched and listened with a slight cynical smile.

"Don't mind me," said the fat woman, apparently to me although I *wasn't* minding her. "I don't belong here. I own the lending library on the street level and I'm just a friend of Fred's. Tra-la, everybody. Have fun." She edged past me and through the door. The stairs creaked as she went down them.

Now the woman with the pock-marked face was conferring quietly in English with a tall lean man whose expression surely could never be anything but anxious. Their conversation obviously concerned me, so I waited. At last he nodded and went away. She turned to me.

"Don't worry. We will find a place where you can work until this is straightened out. Would you like to come to my office until we think of something?" She led me to a small partitioned cubicle beyond the reception desk and disappeared.

The office relapsed into normalcy. Voices murmured, typewriters clicked, steps sounded softly in the corridor, but no one came near me. I thought about Fred Baker and his headache. Was it real? Or was it just his way of avoiding foreseen trouble? If avoidance, was it cowardice or was it cleverness? I decided it was cleverness. It made Mr. Mike Brown look rather foolish. His employer did not have the time to worry about his injured feelings —the situation Mr. B-B had created was so unimportant that the office staff could handle it alone.

I heard the Chinese woman say sharply, "Don't be silly!" Then she was issuing vehement orders in Chinese again. Her voice was almost strident when she spoke Chinese, but beautifully modulated when she spoke English. I found her vastly intriguing.

The six coolies began a chant to keep the devils from burdening their heavy load and bore my desk past the open door. I heard them strenuously manipulating it through an opening that was almost too narrow, then chanting it away through an inner office. My unknown hostess returned, sat at her desk and faced me.

"I am sorry you have encountered this trouble," she said in a refined, and gentle voice. "Unfortunately Mr. Baker and Mr. Brown are engaged in an altercation regarding Mr. Brown's contract renewal. He is to go on leave and expects to return at a much higher salary, which Mr. Baker does not wish to pay. Of course you could not know this." It was a question, and she waited for an answer.

"I knew nothing of it when Mr. Baker engaged me and I can't see how it concerns me, anyhow."

"My name is Mrs. Hamilton. I am the office manager. We have found a place for your desk, not very nice but perhaps less embarrassing for you than if we try to force you into Mr. Brown's office against his will. Come with me and I will show you."

We went into the corridor, through a doorway and across a large windowless room where Chinese men in western-style suits were carefully comparing galley proofs with sheets of typewritten copy. In another partitioned space, also windowless, four desks were tightly crowded. Three were littered with account books and newspapers. One was bare: mine.

"Please come to me," said Mrs. Hamilton, "if you have any problems."

"I was supposed to give this to Mr. Barson-Brown."

"Your contract. I will look after it."

She spoke peremptorily in Chinese to three young

men who appeared in the doorway. They wore long dark gowns and small silk caps topped with round buttons as black as their eyes. Without introducing us, Mrs. Hamilton vanished and the three young men sat wordlessly at their desks and began to measure newspaper advertisements, make entries in their books and add figures. Two of the men had Oriental newspapers, the one next to me the English daily which had published my Impressions.

I opened one drawer of my desk. It was empty, so I put my purse in it, took off my coat and hung it over the partition, placed my hat on the bare desk top and sat down. In another drawer were pen, pencils, a ruler and a stack of paper. Behind a cupboard was a pop-up typewriter. After managing to get it to pop up, I put some papers in it and began fooling around with nursery rhymes:

Mary had a little ad,
About an inch or so.
When people wanted what she had
It told them where to go.

I filled in the time with this nonsense until the young man next to me laid aside a sheet of newspaper. I asked him in English if I might borrow it, and he pushed it to me promptly. By noting pencil marks he had made I learned the names of some of our clients and began making a list of them.

After lunching alone at the Chocolate Shop I roamed the downtown streets looking for firms we represented. The Shanghai Power Company occupied a fine corner building with wide display windows: they were featuring electric stoves. Whiteway Laidlaw was the big English department store on the corner of Szechuan Road and Nanking. More or less opposite was Hall and Holtz, purveyors—no other word would do—of men's quality clothing. Up the street was Brewer's Books, with a five-foot thermometer out front advertising Stephens Inks and registering the temperature in both English and Chinese. The Shanghai and Hong Kong Bank stood on the Bund, stone lions crouched at the entrance, immovable, indestructible.

I felt I knew something about our business when I

Nanking Road, the main street in Shanghai for whites.

went back to the Agency and decided to learn more about the office. Beyond the proofreaders' room was a print-shop housing several linotype machines. The tall lean man I had seen in the morning occupied a corner office and was obviously in charge. He saw me through the glass partition and almost smiled.

The bald man with heavy black eyebrows was on the telephone in an office next to Fred Baker's. Stacked against one wall were display cards used in buses and streetcars and on top of a filing cabinet was a drawing I had seen enlarged on billboards.

Next to the bald man, in a pleasant room overlooking Szechuan Road, was the dignified Chinese. His office contained several chairs, and a Chinese painted scroll hung between the two windows. A short corridor connected with Mr. Barson-Brown's office. Off this corridor, in a small area that had doors opening in each direction were the reception desk and switchboard where Mrs. Hamilton worked liked a dynamo.

Between the proofreaders' room and Fred Baker's office sat the secretary, Mrs. Chandler, fingers flying on her typewriter. She stopped work when she saw me peering in.

"How you doing?"

"Fine, thank you. Exploring a bit."

"Of course. Come in a minute. Mrs. Hamilton and I

have been talking. We think if you looked through the files you could learn a lot. I could help you."

I could have hugged her but merely outlined what I had done that day. Her telephone rang and she answered briefly, glancing at her watch as she replaced the receiver.

"It's nearly closing time and someone has called for you. We'll start the files tomorrow morning."

The "someone" calling was, of course, Jim, come to drive me to my new home, a distance of about two miles diagonally across Central District. Earlier in the afternoon one of the Chinese chauffeurs employed by the Council had picked up my suitcase and typewriter and delivered them to the new address. Jim had some boxes from the big cafeteria and delicatessen store, Kiesling's, on Bubbling Well Road.

"I thought you wouldn't want to be bothered shopping and cooking until you knew more about the kitchen arrangements, and it seemed cosier to have a snack right at the apartment than to go out. Kiesling's make the best food; got some pork pies—yum! yum!—and other things. Hope I'm invited!"

"Hope I am! *You* bought the food."

My apartment was one room, really, about twelve by twenty feet, with a five foot strip partitioned off one side to hold bathroom, clothes closet and tiny entrance hall and kitchenette. It was in the middle of a row of similar flats on the first floor with garages below. There were three windows, all in the wall opposite the entrance. The smallest of them was in the bathroom, the other two in the main room, all looking onto a paved court which provided access to the garages. Beyond the court soared a typical block of second-rate city apartments.

I thought my kingdom charming, opening as it did directly out of doors. It was spotlessly clean, plainly but adequately furnished, and I had bought new towels for the bathroom and kitchen at Whiteway-Laidlaws.

We did have a cosy meal with a bottle of wine and full discussion of the momentous day. Jim knew the fat woman, whose name he said was Alice, because he had borrowed many books from her library.

"She gets a grant from the Council and then of course we pay rent for the books we borrow. Gossip has it that she located there because she's had her eye on Fred Baker for years but he isn't having any. Imagine getting linked up with that! You haven't seen anything until you've seen her getting out of a rickshaw backwards."

Jim told delicious gossip.

"I hear Fred Baker has a new one now that he picked up on the streets of London. She's staying at his house on Hungjao Road and all the old biddies are in a flutter because they're afraid he's going to marry her. So far she's kept out of sight and they've been able to ignore her, but if he marries her, what then?"

"I wonder if he thought that was what I was talking about when I said people are always on the verge of getting married or not getting married."

"I'm sure he must have thought that was what you were getting at. Imagine if the wedding comes off! From the sidewalks of Piccadilly to the high courts of Shanghai! They'll have to take some notice of her because he's one of the leading lights of the community, a member of the Rotary Club, and all that."

"Poor Alice."

"Don't worry about her. I'm sure she hasn't given up. She was up there this morning to get an eyeful of you. She must have enjoyed the situation."

"I thought she looked as though she'd swallowed a porpoise, comfortably."

"Give her credit. She could swallow two or three."

Afterwards we did the dishes and then Jim left for the Navy Y.

Next morning when summoned to Fred Baker's office I was able to tell him that I was quite happy where I was with the three Chinese. He said he was looking for some house ads, very short and semi-humorous that people could turn to for a morning smile. I typed up the nursery rhymes and took them to him rather diffidently. To my surprise he laughed and said they were exactly what he had in mind—could I do some more?

After checking some of the files with me, Mrs. Chandler took me to lunch and gave me further insight into the people of the office.

Mrs. Hamilton, she said, would never be my friend socially. She was full-blooded Chinese of aristocratic family, and after her husband's death she had reverted to the old Chinese custom which did not allow friendship with foreigners. Her father had been very wealthy and educated his daughter in England. She had married a Scotsman and borne a very blonde daughter who also married a Scotsman and had two quite blonde children, one of them with red hair.

Mrs. Chandler's opaque oriental eyes looked straight at me across the table as she said firmly, "I am an American. My father and my grandfather were both American although neither my mother nor myself has ever been there." She looked down at her plate and added, "My grandmother also was full Chinese. But I have not red hair."

Mrs. Chandler often joined me for lunch, although Mrs. Hamilton, whose elegant composure I so deeply admired, never did. However, my friendship with Mrs. Chandler did not develop beyond the point we reached on that first day. She never invited me to her home and was always unable to accept invitations to mine. I learned from others that her husband was an American tobacco salesman, away for long periods of time travelling in the interior of China, and that they had no children. The barrier between her and myself lay somewhere in her strange, opaque dark eyes, reminiscent of the Chinese but lacking their pure brightness. Whenever I met those eyes of hers I had a guilty feeling, as though I were personally responsible for her inherited misfortune in looking like a grandmother whom she resented.

Jim said he had known many Eurasians during his years in Shanghai and had found this quality of resentment in many of them. He said they seemed to him to be people at war within themselves as if the two races within their genes were eternally in conflict.

In Shanghai nationality wrapped us like a cloak. Jim and I were more than white, more than British: we were Canadian. Some countries automatically conferred citizenship on the wives and children of their nationals, but this did not affect nationality. Often, too, the father disappeared before or soon after the baby's birth. The child would then be raised in the family of the mother, endowed with her traditions but never fully accepted by her people. Nor would such a child be accepted by its father's people.

Among all the cultures and backgrounds that mingled in the foreign community of Shanghai, the Eurasians particularly seemed to have no place. Many of the men who worked with Jim had Eurasian wives, but I found no friend among them. Perhaps I was afraid of them: they were thought to be unpredictable. At any time, in any place, an Eurasian woman could precipitate a scene that was both shocking and embarrassing. She would begin screaming invective against anyone who annoyed her, pouring out a vocal stream in a voice as shrill and harsh as that of a coolie woman on the streets of the Chinese sector.

And they did strange things. One Eurasian wife, passing from pretty girlhood to plump womanhood, indomitably attended all the men's stag parties, sitting out the evening on a chair in the hall or in the store below the restaurant, waiting to take her husband home. Another woman was not at home when Jim and I arrived for dinner, although she had telephoned me to confirm her husband's invitation. Our host, who was slightly drunk, explained that his wife had been called away by an emergency, and took us out for a dinner which none of us enjoyed.

Jim said that he knew only one Eurasian man with whom he had been able to form a friendship. He was a man who spent a full year in every five at a monastery somewhere in the Yangtse Gorges. In the quiet routine of monastery life he said his two natures, Oriental and Occidental, came to terms with one another and he was able to accept himself. He was a happy man, and I sometimes wonder if, perhaps, this deep-rooted personal acceptance is the foundation of all happiness.

8

TAKE THE WORLD
AS IT IS, NOT AS
IT SHOULD BE

-German

THE BUBBLE BURST on my second day at Baker's agency. The young Chinese whose office I shared were bookkeepers, called "shroffs" in Shanghai. They worked quietly, spoke softly to each other in lilting Chinese and never interfered with me.

Suddenly, this morning there was bedlam. Settling-up time was upon us. Bills had gone out, cheques were coming in. Dozens of shroffs representing our debtors and creditors crowded the office, all talking vigorously, until one by one they were singled out and dealt with by Mrs. Hamilton.

They pressed beside me, staring peering over my shoulder to see what I was doing. They picked up my pencils and ruler, thumbed and played with the brush eraser. Some put their faces only inches away from mine and grinned impudently. They sat on my desk, backs turned, rumps wrinkling the papers I was working with, and they talked and talked and talked. Their chatter was a hailstorm of sounds beating on my head. Towards noon the babble suddenly became too much for me. On the verge of hysteria, I scribbled a note to Fred Baker, saying that until proper office space was available I would work better at home, gathered up my purse and papers and rolled away in a rickshaw.

The rickshaw seemed particularly shabby and dusty, the Shanghai streets incredibly overcrowded and dirty and my self-esteem was badly tumbled. I saw myself de-

flated to the level of a Chinese coolie woman, living in one room with cockroaches—I had seen a few in my kitchenette—and who-knew-what other bugs—having to shriek to make myself heard, and I was never good at shrieking. Inside the small, stuffy flat I threw purse and papers on the pint-sized table, lay down on the bed and cried for home.

Then I got up and washed my face, made myself tea and a piece of toast and went back to work.

The telephone rang. It was Fred Baker. He said nothing about my panicky departure and I learned later that this was typical of him. To Fred what was done was done, and his only concern was what to do next.

"Michael Barson-Brown is leaving us tomorrow. He sails next morning on eight months' leave. You can have his office on Monday morning."

"But I don't want his office, Mr. Baker."

"Why not? He won't be in it. He'll be away for eight months, possibly longer. It's the only place where I can put you. I could put a desk in my office but you wouldn't like that—my phones are always ringing and people coming in and out. You'll be better in an office of your own. We'll have your desk moved in and his removed. It'll be all ready for you by nine o'clock. Meanwhile work at home. I'll see you on Monday."

"Thank you, Mr. Baker." What else was there to say?

So now I had an apartment, and a job, and the chair where Michael Barson-Brown had sat during our first interview when I had timidly asked for a job and he had told me positively that there was none.

Shanghai newspapers appeared in many languages. Through our office advertisements were placed in nearly all of them. Some came from overseas and had nothing to do with me. Local copy was prepared by me in English and then translated. The dignified Chinese, Mr. Choy, was in charge of the translators. He was a wise and scholarly man and would stand just inside the door of my office, refusing to sit down, and instructed me in Chinese custom, literature and legend.

All final proofs came to me for okay. Wording had been checked by the translators but I was responsible for general appearance. All the hazards that exist in any advertising agency existed in Shanghai—cuts could be run upside down, a line or block of type poorly spaced—but there was also other details to be watched.

Where a human face appeared in the picture, two drawings had to be made, one with Occidental features for English, American or Russian papers, another with Oriental features for the Chinese and Japanese. Sometimes even these had to be touched up, for the two nationalities were quick to spot racial differences. Costumes too had to be watched and adapted with as little expense as possible. I found that there was a small studio inhabited by three Russian artists between Mr. Choy's office and that of bald-headed Morse Friedman.

Chinese and Japanese written characters were basically the same picture language and had similar meaning although they represented Chinese words to the Chinese and Japanese to the Japanese. In 1933 in Shanghai a Chinese and a Japanese who could not speak each other's language could read the same newspaper.

Selling approaches to the different peoples were also varied. In selling an electric stove, for instance, cleanliness was an important factor for English-speaking and Japanese customers but had little to do with appeal for economy-minded Chinese and Russians. Speed and no wasteful ashes brought a better response from them.

The Japanese liked everything modern, but the Chinese clung to their traditions. For the Telephone Company Mr. Choy and I designed an ad which was used both on display posters and, greatly reduced, on round bamboo and paper fans distributed free during the hot weather. For English and American customers, a slim figure of a girl was shown with a Caucasian face and long ruffled Empire-style gown. In the Oriental version face and hair were changed, and the gown redrawn as kimono and obi (the broad Japanese sash) or long Chinese gown made fashionable by Madame Chiang Kai Shek. This gown had for many years been worn by men and its adoption for women was synonymous with Western women going into slacks.

For Western and Japanese customers the copy suggested the time saved by using the telephone and the

warm intimacy of the human voice. For the Chinese a flight of bats was added in the background, for in local Chinese beliefs bats were "good joss" and brought important news, hopefully good. Chinese copy was prepared by a young man called 'The Poet' after long interviews in my office with Mr. Choy interpreting. (The Poet sat down but Mr. Choy stood, benign and dignified.) In the end I was given an English translation of the poem prepared with great care by a Chinese language student at Lung Wha University:

> As world civilization reaches a higher level, electrical science progresses by leaps and bounds. News of the universe reaches our ears, places thousands of miles apart seem to be in the same house. Using this medium to converse is like having the ability of Chow Yen Tse and even beating the skill of Pi Chang Fong.
> The telephone saves time and money. Please try.

Mr Choy explained that in Chinese legend Chow Yen Tse could hear conversations thousands of miles away and Pi Chang Fong could travel vast distances in a few minutes.

Life now began to take on a definite pattern. Jim introduced me to a grocer—called Compradore in Shanghai— a few blocks from my apartment on Avenue Edward VII. His name was Ho Li, but when he became a Christian he adopted also the name Moses. I refused to believe this until I saw the name in large letters above the neat emporium. HO LI MOSES.

He stocked no fresh fruits or vegetables, but all kinds of wine and liquor, rice, dried beans and canned goods, including canned butter from Australia and canned Edam cheese from Holland. As I prowled the shelves I heard Jim challenge Mr. Ho.

"How fashion your name Moses because you Christian? Moses belong number one Jew man."

"Sure," beamed Mr. Ho agreeably. "I belong Number One Clistian."

He spoke excellent English except for his trouble with r's. Standing in front of the large bin of rice I asked if he

kept natural or unpolished rice. He did not understand and we both tried to explain. He looked very puzzled.

Jim said, "Not white rice like this. Brown rice."

"Oh yes." Ho Li broke into smiles. "I know what you mean! Dirty lice!"

He said he did not sell it and did not know where it could be obtained in Shanghai.

Ho Li had an assistant who would deliver an order any time in exchange for a small reward. I could phone from the office and whatever it was I needed would arrive at the apartment soon after I did.

Phyllis Ayrton and Louie Stops came for dinner, stipulating that the meal must be cooked on the hot plate stove. They had heard about "hot plate cooking" but never experienced it. Like Basil, each had her private rickshaw, and their runners waited for them in the paved court under the windows of my room, drawing the rickshaws together facing each other with shafts

overlapping and eating a supper out of little packets they produced from somewhere in the rickshaws. Afterwards they curled up on the carpeted footboards and dozed.

Mr. Ho had packaged spaghetti, spaghetti sauce and canned meat balls, all from San Francisco. Since one never ate raw fruit in Shanghai, dessert was not so simple. The kitchenette had no refrigerator and I mistrusted the cockroaches with any food prepared ahead of time, for they could squeeze through the smallest crack and such things as plastic wrapping was not known then, at least to us. However, Mr. Ho had canned pears from Canada, and Jim added exciting little cakes from Kiesling's.

Stops and Ayrton approved the apartment, which they freshened with a sweet bouquet of white and lemon yellow stocks. They said they thought I should have a servant to help with the cleaning and the battle with the cockroaches. After lively discussion it was agreed that I could try to find an amah and train her as a 'home-side maid' but none of my three guests could guarantee that I would succeed: Chinese servants had a very strict class system and nothing was so awful for them as to "lose face" by losing caste. A baby amah would lose face if made to do laundry for anyone other than a baby, and a wash amah, who washed clothes, would never consent to wash dishes.

The amah would have to be found through an advertisement in the daily English paper, and what should such an advertisement say? We finally agreed on a simple statement of fact: "Amah wanted to help young Canadian woman with housework. Please apply after 6 P.M." My address followed.

The only applicant to answer appeared two evenings later, a sad-faced Chinese woman with thin black hair cut shoulder length. She wore a black cotton jacket and pants and had a note written in English saying that the amah was a good lady's maid. For a reference I was to phone the given number.

I phoned the number as the amah sat meekly on the very edge of one of my three wooden chairs. An English voice assured me the amah was clean and honest and very clever at mending runs in stockings. "I've employed her for odd jobs of sewing but now we're going home on leave and I think she needs work." No, she did not speak much English.

I explained to the amah that I wanted her to sweep (showing her the broom), keep clean (gesturing around the room), maybe fix kitchen. Jim added a few sentences in Chinese. She nodded impassively and added,

"Please Missy I no savee cook. Can make tea."

"Oh, that's splendid if you can make tea!" We agreed that she would come next morning at 7:30 and stay until I returned from the office.

"She may not show up at all," Jim commented. "One thing I noticed, though—she has bound feet. That is rather unusual. It means she's not coolie class."

Amah came early next morning, bringing me tea in bed soon after seven. As I scrambled awake I asked her how she had got in. She replied, "Have askee this look-see man." That is how I learned that Mr. Perkins Yue employed a night watchman.

What Amah did all day I did not ask, neither of us having the vocabulary, but when I got home the apartment gleamed—even the windows sparkled—and my personal laundry had been washed and ironed. Perhaps she washed her own white jacket at the same time: it always looked spotless.

Every morning she woke me with tea, and she was never in a hurry to leave at night. In fact, I suspected that she hung around out of curiosity, intrigued by Jim's daily arrival and our plans for dinner. She told Jim in Chinese that if we left the dinner dishes she would wash them in the morning but we said no to that because of the cockroaches. Dishes had to be washed our way, in very hot water and put away in the high cupboards.

There was one task I left for her. Jim stepped on any cockroaches that came his way with a crunch that made me shiver. Amah caught and dispatched them somehow with her fingers and a satisfied grunt, "Have got!" I could not do either. I just imprisoned the cockroaches in upturned glasses, leaving them for Amah to look after in the morning.

One evening Jim arrived wearing a silly expression and carrying a paper bag containing a large live crayfish or "Pacific lobster".

"Jim! What are you going to do with that?"

"Cook it. And eat it."

"Look, I can't cook live lobster."

"Amah and I will cook it." A word or two in Chinese. A nod. Amah produced the largest saucepan, filled it with water and set it on the hot plate to boil. Jim poured himself and me a drink. A little later there was activity in the kitchenette and loud cries from Amah of "Oy!" and "Yi!" and from Jim, "Watch out!" Presently he joined me rather sheepishly.

"He's quite a lively fellow. Amah says she can do better alone. I might add she is welcome."

"Oy!" "Yi!" "Oy!" "Oy yi!" Silence.

Amah appeared in front of us. "Please Missy, this fishee have go walkee-walkee."

"Have catch?" demanded Jim.

"No can catch."

We all went into the kitchen. Behind the table leg on the floor was the lobster, peering at us and waving a large nipper threateningly. We all went into action.

One of us poked him with the broom handle from one direction. Another thrust the dust mop at his claw and tugged smartly when he fastened on to it. A third had brought a large towel from the bathroom and threw it over him. Between the three of us we got him into the pot.

Amah waited and shelled him for us and we gave her one large nipper to take home with her.

We never tried to cook another lobster.

9

WHO
CAN ENJOY
ALONE?

-English

"THE CHINESE HAVE a saying," said Jim, flicking his dish-towel. " 'There is Heaven above and Hangchow below.' They mean Hangchow is so beautiful. It's been a holy city for centuries and is full of temples and ancient tombs, so I'm told. Marco Polo mentions it in his writings of China."

"It must be interesting." I was scrubbing the potato pot.

"I know you'll like it," said Jim, "so I've engaged a room for three weeks from next Saturday."

I froze. "You've what?"

"It's more than three months—three months and a week to be exact. I thought if we got married on Saturday and each asked for Monday off we could have a short honeymoon in Hangchow now, and then go to Japan later on, in the summer when I get my annual three weeks."

"*Get married!*"

"We can't be married in less than three weeks," he said reasonably, "because here in Shanghai for Britishers the civil ceremony at the consulate is mandatory—you can have a service in the church too, if you want one. But at the Consulate banns have to be posted for three weeks and I posted them this morning."

The potato pot was forgotten. "You posted banns! You might have asked me!"

"Why?" He was still being reasonable. "I know everything about you the Consul wanted to know. Anyway you can go and read them in the morning and change anything that's wrong. They're on the bulletin board in the main corridor by the entrance."

"But I *can't* be married in three weeks, Jim. I haven't a dress and my trunk hasn't come from home—and what'll I tell them at the office? I have a contract."

As I said it I knew the contract was covered. "No children for six months." Safe enough.

"The Chinese tailor will make you any dress you want. Just show him a picture or draw a sketch, that's all. You don't need your trunk. I'll just move in here the way it is—we'll get a bigger bed. And you don't have to tell the office anything. They'll hear soon enough."

I stared at him. The thought of marriage had been in the back of my mind, but certainly not as anything immediate.

"I think I've been very good." He was not so reasonable now. "That's only because we're going to be married. We *are* going to be married, aren't we?"

I tried to think of another prospect. Suppose we didn't get married....

"Oh, yes, Jim. Yes! The answer is yes!"

"At last," he said as his arms went around me, and that was very nice, too.

He was right about everything. The tailor made a dress from a simple design I sketched. We didn't need the trunk. We bought a bigger bed. And the bald man, Morse Friedman, popped into my office very soon after I arrived at work on Monday morning.

"So you're going to get married."

"How do you know?"

He nodded backwards. "The Big One downstairs. She checks at the Consulate every morning on her way to work to keep up with the banns. It's good, I'm glad—everybody should get married. But Fred won't like it. He won't want to lose you."

"He won't lose me. Lots of married women work. Look at Mrs. Chandler."

He wiggled those heavy black eyebrows up and down,

The author and her husband.

up and down. "True," he said. "So true." And out he popped.

I expected a summons from Mr. Baker, but none came —perhaps Morse Friedman had spoken to him. The day passed and no one else said anything at all.

Phyllis and Louie said they had known all along. They would be in Peking in three weeks time, but they arrived one evening before they left with wedding gifts and good wishes.

Amah would have to be told. She might not want to look after two people in my small apartment. I waited until a week before Hangchow Saturday, and then told her, using a pidgin English phrase Jim had suggested.

"Amah, next Saturday, I catchee marry."

Her usually gloomy face turned up at the corners. She asked, "This leddee Master?" (Jim had red hair).

"Yes, Amah. You like?"

"I likee." She went back to the kitchen but reappeared

in the doorway a minute later.

"Please Missy. I likee you."

"Oh, Amah, I'm so glad. I likee you. I don't want you to leave me. Next week you must bring two cups of tea, maybe."

"I no leave you, Missy. Two cups can catch."

It sounded like a marriage benediction.

There were so many ways to be married in Shanghai. Most foreigners followed the consular ceremony with a church wedding. There were twenty-four churches listed in the telephone book, not counting synagogues and mosques. Some were Anglican, some American Episcopalian, while others followed the United Church form of service. Perhaps ten were Roman Catholic, one Christian Science, two Russian Orthodox.

Orville was the most married man we knew. After the civil ceremony, each of his seven Russian wives had insisted on a lavish and picturesque event in their own Russian church, which Orville attended in tail coat, peppered trousers and white gloves.

This was followed a week later by still a third wedding at his own American church. Nevertheless, in one or two years came the inevitable divorce and Orville would pick another bride from Del Monte's line-up of eligible ladies. He was always well-received and it was generally accepted that his ousted ladies received generous settlements. Now, after being married twenty-four times he had a son by Katie, and everyone felt both were settled for life.

Traditional Chinese weddings lasted three days and cost a great deal of money. Those who knew the Chinese customs well claimed that men of moderate income spent all their lives paying for their weddings and their funerals.

On the first and second wedding days many gifts were exchanged by the participating families. We often saw the chanting processions threading through the Settlement's crowded streets. Men in red costumes bore shoulder yokes swinging trays and baskets piled with fabrics, blankets, crates of geese or chickens, large enamelled kongs or vases, bowls of gold fish, some of them eight and ten inches long, even shrubs and flowers.

Friends and relatives of both families spent all three days feasting on expensive foods and watching hired entertainers who kept up a round of music, juggling, acrobatics, pantomime, puppet shows, dancing and acting—all at the groom's expense.

On the third day a red heavily curtained sedan chair brought the bride from her parents' home where she had been waiting. She was dressed in richly embroidered red silk or satin, a costume handed down from generation to generation. With eyes downcast below her high red head-dress and hands folded in the sleeves of her marriage coat, she was led on little red-slippered feet by her bridesmaid from table to table to meet the guests. We attended several such weddings and noticed that the bridesmaid did all the talking, the bride only smiling and bowing ceremoniously. Then the bride was led away to the interior of her new home and the feasting and merry-making by groom and guests continued late into the night.

A popular portrait of Sun Yat Sen - father of the Revolution

In their reform program Chiang Kai Shek and his wife tried to introduce less expensive wedding customs. Madame Chiang was recognized as a leader of fashion and she advocated simple white wedding dresses and veils, a difficult innovation since white was traditionally the colour of mourning. Throughout China mass marriages were organized at which as many as fifty couples were wed in a joint ceremony. The brides all wore the white gowns, often paid for by the government, and the grooms dressed in navy blue business suits. A large portrait of the Father of the Revolution, Sun Yat Sen, Madame Chiang's brother-in-law, replaced the ancestral tablets used at traditional weddings. At the high point of old-style marriages, bride and groom use to bow to the ancestral tablets: in the mass weddings each couple came forward and bowed three times to Sun Yat Sen's portrait.

Afterwards the fifty families shared a reception at the City Hall or other administrative office which lasted for two or three hours only, with a liberal donation towards expenses made by the Central Government.

We decided to have only the simple Consular cere-

Pagoda of Six
Harmonies,
or Liu Ho Ta, at
Hangchow

mony at the British Consulate on the Bund opposite the Public Gardens. With Stops and Ayrton away there was no one I felt I should invite but Jim's friend Peter and another close associate, a Scotsman named Big Doogie, were witnesses. However Jim had many friends, both white and Chinese, and a sort of open house reception was arranged to start at noon at the home of one of the Council's senior staff. There was a long table of refreshments and many gifts including an enormous basket of flowers from the Baker agency and two bottles of champagne from Ho Li Moses.

We left for Hangchow at two in the afternoon but the partying continued 'til past midnight. Host and hostess, we heard later, were not too pleased about this, but their daughter caught my wedding bouquet and she and her mother talked until the last bottle was broached and the last guest hilariously departed. Within weeks the daughter married the man they had talked about that night and went home with him to Australia.

In Hangchow the taxi eased through city streets too close and crowded to be seen. We were pressed in by walls, glimpsed the open apertures of marble tombs, came out to open sky above water dotted with green islands spindled with slender pagodas.

It made a difference, being married. The stiff defences of independence were gone. I could sit close to Jim, hold his hand, absorb his strength and calm.

Since Hangchow was 100 miles from Shanghai, he explained, the dialects were different, and it would not be so easy to talk to the local Chinese. They might not understand him, nor he them.

We had come the 100 miles by train, a short string of rumbling, compartmented coaches, and travelling slowly past muddy creeks, rice paddies and groves of mulberry bushes where silkworms browsed on leaves. Tea had been served by the train crew, pale amber liquid in covered cups. Interest had centred on an elderly Chinese who sat in one corner of the compartment. His round black silk cap had a red button on the top, and several young Chinese university students from other parts of the train crowded our compartment to talk to him with respect and reverence.

They told us in English that the red button signified that he was more than 70 years old and of high academic standing. This was the reason for their reverence. They said he was a fur merchant from Peking, and at one time he leaned from his seat and fingered the short fur jacket I was wearing.

Jim barked, "Haw va haw?" which even I understood: "good, not good?" The old man sat back, saying a brief "haw," the jacket was not really all that good. Jim asked in English, "How about Missy?" Laughing, the students translated.

The gateway to West Lake at Hangchow, which was praised by Marco Polo

The old man looked deeply into my eyes and I let him look. He could see nothing there that I didn't want him to see, I felt. Then the old man smiled and held up his hand with thumb erect. "Ting haw," he said, and the students were delighted. Jim translated for me. "Number One cargo, top grade."

It was an exquisite wedding gift.

Our hotel stood on a hill slope. Bordering the steep approach, japonica, forsythia and other flowering shrubs were bursting into bloom. Several pagodas thrust from the trees on surrounding slopes. Some were obviously old enough to have been there when Marco Polo travelled through Hangchow in the 13th Century, but the one nearest to the hotel was very new.

As Jim registered—"Mr. and Mrs."—he asked about the new pagoda, and the hotel clerk replied in English that it had been erected recently by a rich man in memory of his faithful wife.

Every half hour, gongs summoned to prayer monks from the temples in the surrounding hills; faraway gongs echoing softly from the valley mists, gongs nearby breaking into deep imperative voice, treble gongs sounding with staccato repetitions.

The hotel had a pamphlet containing the names of all the temples around Hangchow. Before dinner we walked down to the lake, where a boatman with a flat-bottomed boat poled us among the islands. Each had its temple, the curved roof poking from bamboo fresh with green leaves and hung with blossoms. The air was fragrant with in-

cence. A priest on a small wooden dock was drawing bamboo buckets full of water from the lake. With some help from the boatman, Jim asked him the name of the island temple but could not understand the answer. The priest tried sign language. He made circles in the air, pointing up, pointing down, almost patting the lake surface, holding up three fingers.

Jim was mystified. "He keeps on saying, 'Here light.'"

The boatman poled us up a creek and took us to a villa owned, he made us understand, by a rich man in Canton. The family was away, but the boatman produced keys and took us into the extensive gardens. We passed through round moon gates to fruit gardens, to rock gardens where shrubs were opening coloured buds, and to gardens created around lotus ponds in which floated only last summer's dead brown stalks.

We were shown the main wing of the building, the special court fronting the rooms of the Number One wife and the larger well-screened court of the concubines. At last I felt myself to be in China, the China one read about—mysterious, cultured, beautiful, but perhaps a China of the past. The villa gave the feeling that it had not been used for a long time.

As we walked back to the hotel in the glow of the sunset that was just like those we knew at home, we came to a group of boys sitting on a fence. One of them jumped down, scooped up a handful of mud, shaped it into a ball and proffered it to Jim. Jim asked, in English, "How much?"

The boy answered "One doll-o," and his companions on the fence echoed in chorus, "One doll-o. One doll-o."

Jim said, in English, "Too much." The boy emphatically denied this and his companions shrilly backed him up. "Joss," they said. "Haw, haw," nodding their heads. "Joss." Jim looked as though he took them seriously, and the boys fell into an eager silence. Then Jim said suddenly, in Chinese slang, "Put it in your eye," and he walked on. The boys understood and broke into ecstasies of merriment. Some laughed so hard they fell off the fence backwards.

Back at the hotel we checked the pamphlet of Temple names and quickly found what the priest had been trying to tell us: the name of the temple was Three Pools of the Moon's Reflection.

All the temples had lovely names. Next morning we decided to walk among the hills and find the Temple of the Golden Dragon, which the hotel clerk said was in a cave.

I had learned something about dragons from Mr. Choy. He had told me that unlike Japanese art, which was based on realism, Chinese art was symbolic. Everything in Chinese art—the peach, the lotus, the chrysanthemum, the bat—was a symbol with a literary meaning. The dragon was the symbol for Man and was often shown pursuing the ball of perfection. Only a dragon representing the Emperor could ever be depicted as holding the ball of perfection in its claws. A wealthy Chinese living in the French Concession had recently found himself in trouble when, in 1933, he surrounded his villa with a high wall topped by two dragons holding balls in their claws. Even though the Emperors had been deposed in 1911 the Central Government made the wealthy Chinese remove his dragons.

We walked a long way up the mountain road, which was actually a trail beaten smooth by many feet. At last, in careful Chinese, Jim asked a group of adults standing

A temple at Hangchow

before a red and gold gate at the roadside how much further we had to go. A smiling woman stepped forward and replied in the Shanghai dialect. The Golden Dragon was far, much too far. Why not come in here, where they were going, to the cave and temple of the Purple Cloud?

"There is much fun here," she said, so we went in.

We soon lost our new friends among many small ornate buildings cupped in a fold of the hills. We passed through a small shrine with a large, grim image of Buddha, and followed a narrow path into a mammoth cave. The path skirted the dark abyss, up and down, around corners, through a maze of connecting galleries and small caverns. All were dimly lit by bare electric light bulbs dangling from single threads of wire. Often water trickled down the rock walls and the path was slippery. Many niches large and small were splashed with red and gold paint and enshrined figures of gods. Water collected in shallow basins in front of them and passing Chinese threw copper or silver coins into the water. So did we.

At last the path ended in a small rounded area with a deep cleft extending along the furthest wall. The cleft was three to four feet wide and went straight down, but we were protected from falling in by a low stone wall. The Chinese were making a sibilant sound which Jim said meant water. One young man motioned to us, picked up a stone and dropped it over the wall. We listened with him and what seemed like many seconds later heard the splosh of the stone entering water far below.

The Chinese had a piece of paper in his hand and threw it after the stone. I tore some scraps from an envelope in my purse and Jim and I followed suit. We did not know what we were doing until I asked Mr. Choy. He told me that the people's god of water was also the god of literature—we were glad that we had done the right thing.

Near our hotel, on the valley floor, was the Temple of the Dancing Fish, and we stopped there on our way back. This was no cave. The first walled compound was filled with blossoming plum trees. A moon gate admitted us to a court around a pond where the monks offered us, in exchange for coppers, cabbage leaves with which to feed the fish. They were carp, some gold, some white, some black, and they came lazily to take our cabbage, for they were very fat. All the same they pushed themselves over the backs of their fellows to take the greens and Jim understood the monks' explanation that this was dancing.

For a few more coppers we were allowed to swing a heavy beam that struck a hollow log shaped and painted like a fish and hung on chains. This was the main temple gong, and its deep boom seemed to come out of the fish's mouth.

Before we left, the monks broke off branches of plum blossom and piled them into our arms. The hotel clerk assured us this signified much happiness, but Mr. Choy said no, they wished us many children.

10

THE WILL TO DO
THE SOUL TO DARE

-English

No census had been taken in Shanghai since 1900, I was told, but the population in 1933 was estimated in excess of 3,000,000, about 35,000 being non-Chinese. The figures did not attempt to include the swarming, constantly moving river residents, who were all Chinese, nor the very old city of Nantao on the south, from which the foreign communities had sprung.

Among the foreigners it was customary for offices to close at 5:30 and dinner to be served at 8:00. Movies and theatre started at 9:30. The interval between office and dinner was called the Cocktail hour, and people went to their canteens or clubs for a relaxing drink or two and perhaps a game of cards with wives who had often been at the club all afternoon.

Jim and I preferred to spend the Cocktail Hour exploring this unusual city which was to us like a vast pomegranate containing many little pockets of different flavours.

Four governments existed side by side. Nantao and the countryside all around Shanghai were under the jurisdiction of the province of Kiangsu which, until the coming of Chiang Kai Shek a few years before, had been its own kingdom ruled by a War Lord.

The French Concession was controlled by a Council appointed by the French Consul, who was in turn appointed by France. Most regulations in the Concession came from Paris.

Two Chinese sections of the city, Pootung across the Whangpoo River and Chapei north of the Settlement, had a special municipal government headed by a Mayor responsible to Chiang's Kuo Min Tang, centred in Nanking.

The International Settlement, which was the heart of the city, was administered by the Municipal Council, whose powers were laid down in the Land Regulations passed by the Peking Government in 1854. Changes in the Land Regulations had to be approved by the Kuo Min Tang which had replaced the Peking government and was, in 1933, firmly established in Nanking. Reforms were hard to come by, for Chiang and his wife and members of their government were fiercely nationalistic and determined not to extend in any way the jurisdiction of the foreign powers.

In 1930 the Central Government had changed the Land Regulations, increasing the number of Chinese councillors to five. There were also five Britons, two Americans, and two Japanese. Councillors were elected by the Settlement ratepayers of their own nationality.

There was conflict between governments on the Outside Roads. On paper, Settlement boundaries were clearly defined, but dozens of well-to-do and influential foreigners lived beyond them. Chiang Kai Shek's modernizing government had built an airfield three miles outside the Settlement and sold the foreign Council a strip of land thirty feet wide and three miles long on which to build an international highway to the airport.

The project was expensive, for besides the money paid to the Government for the land, Chinese families demanded heavy compensation when the bones of ancestors who were buried there were removed to other locations. There was no road building equipment in Shanghai—everything was done with shovels and wheel barrows and coolie labour. We once saw a strip of Settlement road under repair being flattened by a roller pulled by perhaps twenty chanting coolies hauling on ropes.

Hungjao Road was, however, triumphantly opened and became a popular "country drive" for all nationalities. One could drive its three mile length without a Chinese license, but right where the asphalt ended Chinese

The Control Tower at Shanghai Airport.

territory began. Under treaty, exception was made for the driveways and houses of the rich who built out there —these were still under Settlement control. You could drive to Fred Baker's front door, for instance, without a Chinese license, but park you car off his driveway and you could be in trouble with provincial police, even though you were in Fred's garden.

The provincial police were not kind, for the province was contesting Chiang's right to sell the Outside Roads, and maintained that the money he received should have gone to Kiangse. Yu Yuan Road, leading to lovely Jessfield Park, also bought, cleared and landscape by the Settlement, and Edinburgh Road which branched off it, were quickly built up with houses owned by foreigners and Chinese and these were left alone. Others were blocked with deep ditches and barricades so they could not be used by foreign cars. Pedestrians on these roads were easy prey for armed Chinese bandits.

Even on Hungjao there was friction. An American family out for a drive stopped to watch Chinese children playing in one of the small villages that clustered along Hungjao. A Provincial Chinese policeman jumped on the running board and in voluble Chinese with authoritative gestures seemed to be demanding that the car be driven to a building on a side road. The American was

a newcomer and wishing to avoid trouble with his family in the car, he started to comply. As soon as his car left the pavement he was stopped again and informed in clear Pidgin English that he was in Chinese territory without a proper license and must pay a fine of $250. He found no sympathy in the courts—the facts were indisputable.

Another episode had shocking impact. A Chinese bus en route to the airport in a hurry swerved too far to the side of the road and knocked down a country man who was walking on the shoulder. The man was pinned under a wheel, which, of course, was off the pavement. Provincial police arrived instantly and at pistol point refused to have the man or bus moved until they had sent back to their headquarters for instructions. Cars and spectators accumulated, a Settlement ambulance arrived, but for forty-five minutes they all had to stand by listening to the victim's diminishing moans. When the instructions finally arrived he was dead.

Jim told me never to become involved in an argument with any Chinese, even a Settlement policeman. "In case of trouble insist on going straight to the nearest police station. There will always be a white sergeant on duty there." He showed me the police stations in those areas of the city where I operated alone.

Early one morning as I drove to Seymour Road Market to buy supplies, a pedlar with bottles of milk in baskets slung from a shoulder pole swayed one basket against the side of the car. Milk splattered the cobbles. Dutifully I drove to nearby Bubbling Well police station, a major police centre frequently involved with armed robberies, riots and murders. In a large hall in a large building a sergeant perched on a stool behind an enormous open Doomsday Book. I stood meekly in front of him.

"I have to report an accident."

He adjusted his glasses, picked up his pen, dipped it in a jar of ink and wrote with great care.

Name? Address? Husband's occupation? Time of accident? Exactly where? What happened? Anyone injured? Property damage?

I said, "I think two bottles of milk were broken."

He stopped writing. His pen hung above the Doomsday Book like a hovering eagle as he stared at his detailed and meticulous notes. He opened his fingers and the pen dropped, rolled down the page and off the book onto the desk. He said with terrifying gentleness, "You may go."

It seemed a long way to the door. I was about six inches high and felt his eyes scorching after me. At any minute I expected a giant foot in a policeman's boot to descend on me, *crunch,* the way Jim stepped on offending cockroaches. With vast relief I scurried over the lintel, regained my normal size, climbed into the safety of the car and drove home.

When the white traders first came up the Whangpoo River the city of Nantao had a wall around it. Most of the wall had since disappeared but there were still parts of it standing, for a short distance between the old city and the French Concession, and along the Whangpoo, where you could still see the water gates.

The car license under which Jim drove in the Settlement and Concession was not recognized by the two Chinese governments, Central and provincial, who issued their own licenses. Streets in the Chinese cities were too narrow for cars and there were no motor roads in the country, so very few foreigners bothered with Chinese licenses. When we went to Nantao we parked the car on Avenue des Deux Republiques and went sightseeing on foot.

This was the city which the tourists loved, and the city played up to them. Mediaeval balconies like those in Europe in the 1500's jutted over cobbled streets only wide enough to allow two rickshaws to pass at the same time. Shopkeepers lived above their shops, and waste water was thrown from the balconies to trickle away between the rounded cobbles. This made it prudent to walk well under the balconies and close to the open fronts of the stores, which were exotic bazaars to tempt the tourist dollars.

Mediaeval guild stores which sold similar merchandise were all grouped together in the same street. The twenty little shops in the Street of Silks were a warehouse of colour and texture. Turning the corner, you found yourself among the skilled embroiderers where men,

women, boys and girls added emphasized delicate nose-gays and bird designs on rich brocades and silks.

Clay cooking saucepans of many sizes lined the Street of Pots. The Street of Joss was festooned with strings of silver "joss money," and fragile paper and bamboo offerings to be burned at funerals or the graves of ancestors. Along the Street of Carvings bone and ivory ornaments, wooden chests, tables and wall plaques were filigreed with expert art by small boys or men using primitive drills spun on a piece of string between the palm of the hands.

Scrolls and panels hung like banners on the Street of Paintings, where artists worked with brush and stylus, sitting cross-legged or on their heels on the floor in front of small raised tables. Few visitors left this street

Artist at work, painting flowering fruit sprays.

without four scrolls depicting the four seasons of the year. Designs and colours differed, but the symbols were always the same: flowering fruit sprays for spring, peonies or lotus for summer, chrysanthemums for autumn, evergreen and white narcissus for the winter months. These four panels were said to bring good joss to the homes where they hung, one at a time, in the appropriate season.

The most popular avenue in Nantao was the Street of Birds, crammed with people and cages and shrill with the piping of finches and canaries, the crowing of roosters, the hoarse shouts of parakeets and the wicked laugh of the mynah birds. Crickets and birds were popular pets among the Chinese and respectable Chinese gentlemen all over Shanghai took them out for an airing every evening. One of the stories Louie Stops told with graphic enjoyment concerned the time they decided to have their chesterfield re-covered. Having picked upholsterer and fabric they left the matter of transportation

to their Chinese Boy. He elected to use a wheelbarrow and muscled barefoot coolie. The Boy asked Stops and Ayrton if a friend of his might go along and take his pet bird for the ride. Permission was given and away went the wheelbarrow, two side shelves flanking a centre wheel. The chesterfield was loaded on one side and the smiling friend in long silk gown sat among the cushions, his caged bird on his knee. Weaving through the traffic the sweating coolie between the handles performed a miracle of balance.

Behind a section of the old city wall edging the Rue des Deux Republiques was the oldest British cemetery in Shanghai. It had no headstones. Gravel walks wove under half a dozen trees around a few large low mounds covered with thick English ivy. Along the wall of warehouses on the Nantao side of the small area were less than a dozen plaques: To the Memory of all those who died in the Smallpox Epidemic, 1858.... To the Memory of twenty-eight British Soldiers killed in the Boxer Rebellion.... To the Memory of men, women and children who died in the 19th century of typhoid, or dysentery, or measles, tuberculosis or childbirth.

After walking in the cemetery beside Nantao's ancient wall, the teeming streets of the Chinese city where these people had suffered and died lost some of their glamour for me.

In the middle of a mud-coloured pond near the Whangpoo the famous Willow Pattern Tea House stood on stilts. This was another tourist favourite. Postcards of the tea house could be bought in all stores that sold such things, or one could have one's picture snapped with the teahouse in the background. The pavilion was full of small tables, the patrons nearly all Chinese. It was approached by angled bridges across the water, the angles designed to keep away the devils who could only fly in straight lines. In this again, perhaps, they were similar to the light-eyed foreigners who were easily bamboozled by the sly tricks of Oriental traders—the eager tourists paid four and five times as much money as their souvenirs were actually worth without question or bargaining. Postcards and snapshots did not show the beggars

who populated the angles of the bridges; Chinese suffering from running blindness, elephantiasis, twisted limbs or idiocy. They sat or lay in every corner whining for coppers.

Near Hongkew Market behind the Astor House stood a large Roman Catholic church with a congregation almost entirely Chinese and Japanese. At that time it was attended by a priest named Father Jacquinot, who was greatly loved by his people. He had only one hand, having lost the other, it was said, in the explosion of a Chinese firecracker.

The big Roman Catholic Cathedral was, of course, in the French Concession; the other churches were spread throughout Shanghai. Outside the city, in provincial territory, was Ziccawei Church and Mission, where the Jesuit Fathers maintained the big Observatory whose weather forecasts guided all coastal shipping. The Jesuits had been in China for a long time and were deeply respected. It was they who were credited with designing the high, rounded bridges, like moon gates over the creeks, which allowed junks to sail under them.

We drove to Ziccawei on a rain-washed afternoon when the streets shone wet and Avenue Haig uncoiled like a sleek steel serpent between pigmy trees on the boulevards. Abruptly the houses on either side became

small crowded stores spilling people out onto a cobbled street. This change signalled Chinese territory, so Jim parked the car on Avenue Haig and we prepared to walk.

There was a creek crowded with river craft, and a bridge. Just beyond the bridge the water went underground into a culvert which conducted it to the river. We crossed the bridge and were once again in another world.

We could easily have been in France. The twin-spired Cathedral, fronting a green village square, was built of imported brick. Behind a high stone wall was the dome of the Observatory. Wide gates opened onto a driveway curving between beds of bluebells and pink and white English daisies underneath short palms.

Soon after founding Ziccawei, many years before, the Fathers had begun to adopt orphan babies. These had now grown up and married, and other Christianized Chinese had moved into the vicinity. They lived in neat terraced houses walled in white. We saw two crocodiles of laughing school children on their way back from some game, the girls wearing black skirts instead of the usual Chinese pants. Every now and then thin chimes sounded from the tapering twin towers.

Two Japanese students walked in the green and quiet square.

"That says a lot about Ziccawei," said Jim. "They couldn't walk anywhere else in Chinese territory without a row beginning. The Japanese are China's traditional enemies—the Hai Dau, the Sea Robbers."

The chimes sang overhead, and I said, "I think I'll be a nun."

He put his strong arm through mine and laughed, "Not yet."

11

HAPPY IS HE
WHO OWES
NOTHING

-Greek

THE JAPANESE WERE THE LARGEST group of foreigners in the Settlement, outnumbering the British two to one. It was claimed by Municipal offices that the Japanese population at that time exceeded 15,000.

A great many Japanese-owned silk factories sprawled over Yangtsepoo. Municipal police there and in Hongkew were nearly all Japanese. From Hongkew Market to the northern limits of the Settlement, along Minghong, Woosung, Range and other roads, stores and houses were built in Japanese style. Even the smell in these streets was Japanese. Merchants from Tokyo, Kobe and other cities in Nippon sold Japanese foods, Asahi beer, Japanese manufactured goods, fine china, silks, cotton kimonos. The Chinese could never pronounce the letter "r", substituting usually the letter "l". With the Japanese it was exactly the opposite. A fish shop opposite the Hongkew Market had a large permanent sign beside the door, FRESH RAW ROBSTER. If you said to Japanese, "It's a lovely day!" he was likely to reply, "Yes, rovery."

In Hongkew, of course, were the suki yaki houses where groups of foreigners gathered for "skiaki parties." At the suki yaki houses one took off one's shoes in the cobble-stoned entrance hall and put on cretonne slippers provided by the House. A smiling, bowing Japanese woman, in kimono and bright sash, ushered one up shallow stairs, past the kitchen where appetizing aromas drifted with the steam above copper cooking pots, to a narrow covered deck surrounding a garden where a pool, rock and twisted shrubs opened to the sky. The dining rooms off this deck were divided into large or small areas by sliding panels of wood, straw and paper. There was no music, but the voices of other diners provided sufficient babble, coming from all sides in Russian, German, English, Italian, French, perhaps raised and thickened with beer which foreign tradition elected to mix with suki yaki.

It would have been useful if we could have left our legs from the knee down with our shoes in the lobby. No concession was made in the dining rooms to the stiff knees of the Caucasians. One sat on the floor without back support around tables which allowed no space for legs, while the attendant carried in a brazier of glowing coals and, sitting comfortably on her heels, cooked supper. The mixture of greens, soy sauce and shaved beef or chicken was worth it. One of several small side dishes placed in front of us contained a raw egg which we beat with short disposable Japanese chopsticks. A morsel garnered from the steaming central dish was dipped first in the egg and was then just the right temperature for popping into the mouth.

Some Japanese residents of Shanghai were skilled in massage, and many British and American men and women engaged Japanese masseuses to come regularly to their homes for this service. Japanese hairdressers and manicurists offered a similar home service. Two big Japanese shipping lines had ships calling frequently, docking in Yangtsepoo, and the 22,000-ton ferries, Shanghai Maru and Nagasaki Maru, left every other day for Nagasaki.

There was, however, little social intermingling between the Japanese and the other foreigners. We knew one man who had a Japanese wife. This was a tall Dutchman nicknamed Van, proprietor of the Village Inn on Love Lane off Bubbling Well Road. It was our favourite place for dining out, small and intimate with a merry three-piece orchestra who played songs one could sing along with if one wished. Van kept a watchful eye on patrons and staff from a square enclosure in the middle of the room, and his Japanese wife was always beside him, peeping shyly round him in soft-coloured kimono, giving the impression that she was a pansy in his button-hole. Wherever he went she went too, but once he left her behind in the square enclosure. This was when a celebrating Dutchman, flushed with drink, climbed up on his small round table and began to dance. Van appeared at the table side without his button-hole, saying nothing but alert and watchful. Luckily the dance turned out to be only a few clumsy steps until the man's friends coaxed him to the floor again.

The Japanese of Shanghai took themselves very seriously. Two young Japanese men brought before the management of Hongkew Market for some small breach of the rules, like sleeping on a table in off hours, beat their breasts when accused and exclaimed in defence, "But we are Japanese!"

The pomposity of Japanese naval officers was a current joke. They were short by Western standards, their uniforms plastered with heavy gold braid and epaulets, long swords tangling with their feet.

A friend in the Customs service repeated a story told him by the Scottish captain of a river boat who had come on a Japanese gunboat hard aground on a mud-and-sand spit up the Yangtse Kiang. It was during one of the recurring periods of war between the Chinese and the Japanese, and the gunboat was in danger of being captured by armed bandits from the shore. The Scottish captain put a line aboard and pulled the vessel free. In time he received an effusive letter of thanks in the name of His Imperial Majesty, the Son of Heaven, and an invitation to attend an official presentation on one of the Japanese cruisers anchored in the line-up of warships in the Whangpoo River.

With visions of silver trays or tea sets dancing in his head, the captain had his buttons polished with special care. On the appointed day a pinnace from the cruiser called for him. Officers in much gold braid received him, the cruiser crew was paraded for him and he was handed a fair-sized box, elaborately wrapped. Everyone bowed several times.

Back on his own ship, members of the Captain's crew who had participated in the rescue of His Imperial Majesty's gunboat were summoned to watch the opening of His Imperial Majesty's gift of thanks.

The box contained six small bottles of Japanese beer.

When a Crown Prince was born to the Son of Heaven the Japanese in the Settlement were told to celebrate. They did so with their usual solemn intensity and many of them appeared in couples on the foreign dance floors. It happened to coincide with the Western New Year and happy Scotsmen were raising the roof to Hogmanay.

Watching from the sidelines as kilted Gaels pranced and shouted, Jim remarked, "In Canada our Mounties watch our Indians when they do this."

We were laughing, but the Japanese dancing past us looked at us with solemn reproach. The birth of a Crown Prince was a reason for celebration, but not for laughter.

Anti-Japanese feeling was particularly acute in the countryside of the Chinese district of Chapei between Shanghai and the great Yangtse River. At one time Japanese pirates had occupied an island in the Yangtse opposite the mouth of the Whangpoo River and taken their toll of river shipping and the delta farmlands. Chinese forts, to aid in fighting off these unwanted guests were erected at Woosung where the two rivers met.

The flat, fertile fields of the Delta were capable of yielding three crops a year: rice, followed by cotton, followed through the winter by soya beans. In times of trouble the Japanese landed their naval parties on these riverside farmlands and crops were destroyed. This happened in 1924 when two Chinese provincial armies were fighting in the area and naval forces from British, American, Japanese and Italian warships came ashore to protect the Settlement, with the Japanese in Chapei. Again in 1927, when Chiang Kai Shek's armies advanced down the Yangtse from Hangkow, naval forces rallied to protect the Settlement. Chiang, however, had an easy victory: the area was won over easily by his 'honeyed phrases.' In 1932, one year before my arrival, there were anti-Japanese boycotts and disorders in the Hongkew district of the Settlement following Japan's annexation

of Manchuria. Japanese guns flattened the forts at Woo-sung and fired on the Chinese 19th Route Army camped in Chapei, and there was furious fighting in the streets adjacent to the Settlement.

Soon after our wedding in 1934 Big Doogie, a friend of Jim's who had witnessed our wedding, and his Russian wife invited us to accompany them on an overnight cruise on a houseboat through the recurrent battle ground.

The houseboat was berthed at a wharf in Yangtsepoo and looked like a brown cocoon. We had to step across the boats of several river families to reach it. From a narrow deck we descended to an open well, but the living quarters had been fitted up for European use and were not Chinese. There was a living room, with settees that pulled out to make a bed, a bedroom with double bunks, a dressing room with bathroom. Tucked into the prow was a tiny triangular galley. The white-coated cook proved also to be the Lao-dah, captain of the three man crew. They poled us into mid-stream, then two men handled a yuloh, the large curving rear oar pivoting on a metal pin.

From a trough in the deck a mast sprang upward and a square brown sail unfolded to the top. We tacked down-stream among the bobbing sampans, high-prowed junks, smooth naval vessels, stinking pig boats, disdain-ful ocean liners. From their sterns flew flags of many countries—we watched eagerly, but on that day unsuc-cessfully, for our own red ensign.

We were served drinks and dinner by our captain-cook as though we were on shore. Coffee was served in the open well, the river gleaming satin under the chiffon darkness. The great patched sail, battened with strips of bamboo, hung between us and the stars, which were the same stars that lit the skies at home.

Well down the Whangpoo towards the Woosung Forts we turned into one of the many creeks that cut the alluvial plain. Now the sail came down, foot by foot, but the houseboat kept moving, propelled by the men on the yuloh. We had a curious gait, jerk, bob and swing, like a crippled duck.

Perhaps an hour later we tied up to the bank where we

The houseboat lying in one of the side-creeks. The structures in the background are round with straw roofs. They contain ice from the creek which is used in summer

were to spend the night. As we stood in the well, a huge shape towered above us, a wild white eye glared down on us, great fangs slobbered in a gaping mouth. It was a sea-going junk with a dragon head prow coming up on the incoming tide to spend the night in the creek. It swung silently past us to the rhythm of its giant yuloh and tied up just ahead of us.

Jim and I woke early with an urge to explore. The tide had turned some time before and with it had gone the wild-eyed junk. The creek bank was a long way off, above a stretch of oozy mud at the end of a long, steeply sloping plank. I went up it on hands and knees.

We followed narrow paths between rice paddies. A country man was spread-eagled on a six foot water wheel. His face looked half asleep but his feet rose regularly from paddle to paddle, lifting water from a ditch to the flooded rice field. A little further on the same task was carried out by a water buffalo walking in a circle, on its head a small, impassive child with a short switch.

The water buffalo was the only domestic animal in this part of China, Jim said, and very few farmers could afford to own one—five or six farmers would share one.

He quoted a Chinese proverb used to describe and excuse old people: *"lao nyui kang dien"*—the old buffalo pulls the plow slowly.

There were cats and dogs around the villages, but

Farmer and Water Buffalo cultivating rice

they lived their own lives, the dogs as scavengers, the cats warring on the rats.

Not far off, the black roofs of a village rose above an encircling wall of woven split-bamboo strips. Other villages dotted the wide landscape. On the right was a larger walled town hugging the lip of the Yangtse Kiang. This was Pao Shan.

We entered the nearest village through an opening in the woven bamboo wall. The path led through clusters of one and two-room houses grouped around common open areas, the houses built of woven bamboo plastered with mud, white-washed and roofed with tiles of black-stained bamboo. Three white geese ran at us hissing, big wings spread, the village watchdogs. From one of the houses came a pink-cheeked happy looking Chinese woman, dressed in blue jacket and shin-short pants, a thick black pigtail hanging down her back almost to her knees. She spoke to the geese and they subsided, pecking the ground for food. The woman called something, smiling, and several plump young children ran around a corner of the house and then stood, grinning at us. Jim greeted them in Chinese and we went our way. As we walked out of the rice and cotton fields again through another opening in the bamboo wall Jim told me that when she called the children the woman had said, "Come see the funny-looking foreign lady!"

"So what did you say in reply?"

Author and husband with water buffalo on the shore of Yangtze Kiang

"I told her she had pretty children."

Grave mounds appeared on higher ground, and we walked towards the biggest. Three wispy trees postured on the slope of it, and a tethered, bearded goat chewed on a meagre cud. As we walked through the tall grass my foot knocked loose a long bleached bone. Cow, I thought, or horse. Then I remembered there were no cows or horses, and I stumbled on a human skull along with other scattered bones that unmistakably belonged to it.

"It was a person."

"Poor fellow," Jim said. "Some poor beggar who couldn't afford a funeral or, more probably, a Japanese or Chinese soldier left over from the last war. After all, it was only three years ago."

We turned back to the houseboat. Seen from above, the long plank looked impossibly slender and the mud evil and hungry. I froze in dismay until the captain-cook appeared smiling with a long pole. Clutching it I teetered to the safety of the afterwell.

We spent all day on the Whangpoo, flitting like a brown water bird, nosing in and out of creeks, mooring for lunch at the wharf of a hotel painted pink. Jim and his friend reminisced of bachelor hunting parties in houseboats in interior pheasant country and friendly farmers who exchanged a hundred hen's eggs for one empty, clear-glass gin bottle.

"Sometimes they used them to store oil, more often

built them into the gates and walls of houses to trap wandering devils. Since the devils only fly in straight lines they can't get out again." Just like some confused wandering foreign devils.

By moonlight we came again to the wharf in Yangtse-poo and picked our steps carefully over the river boats in which the families of the river men were sleeping.

Miles away, across city and creek, cotton field and rice paddy, the bones of the unknown man lay white in the long grass, dampened once again by the dew.

12

GIE YOUR TONGUE
MAIR HOLIDAY THAN
YOUR HEID

-Scottish

THE TIME WAS CHING MING, known to us as the time of clear green light.

The weather priests at Ziccawei reported the rising temperature and said that the humidity was at saturation point. The air held so much water it could hold no more. Tiny droplets of moisture were suspended all around us. Reflecting the new green of grass and budding leaves, they gave the effect of pale very clear green light.

When I followed a short path off Hungjao Road and found violets growing on a creek bank, I could have been walking in a green glass bowl.

Ching Ming was also known as Tomb Sweeping Day and all over the countryside small groups of Chinese gathered at hundreds of grave mounds, planting banners, leaving packages containing food and burning strings of joss money. It is difficult to explain the meaning of "joss". It had a mystical meaning that was more than just luck. The "joss money" decorating grave sites was silver paper imitation money. It seemed to me the average Chinese approach to joss had something of the same reverence with which Occidentals regarded their horoscopes—a reaching for superior occult influence that was not connected with religion.

They believed that the spirits of those who died were not quickly divorced from earthly pleasures by death. They stayed around the graveside for years, gratefully accepting the offerings made by sons, grandsons and even great grandsons at the time of clear green light.

This annual ceremony was the reason it was so important for a man to have a son to survive him, and since infant mortality was high three sons was the safe number. If a poor man's wife gave him so many daughters that there was not enough food to raise three robust sons, some of the girls must be given away. If a rich man's wife had not borne enough sons by middle age she might give him a compatible concubine as a present on his forty-fifth birthday. The comfort and well-being of a man's spirit, and also of the spirits of his father and grandfathers, depended on his sons.

I spoke to Amah about Ching Ming and she said shyly, "English no do this fashion." No, I admitted, they did not. "No pay chow," continued Amah. "English pay flowers." Startled, I realized she referred to Easter, when the foreign cemeteries were thronged with families leaving flowers at the graves of their dead.

About this time Amah asked for three or four days leave to go to her home in a village near Hangchow. She said she would go by rickshaw and it would take one day each way.

Since she had only been with us a comparatively short time Jim asked her why she wished to go. She replied, "Must puttee mother floorside."

This so obviously meant a funeral that I was ready to be concerned, but Jim interposed quickly, "Your mother what time die, Amah?"

"Please Master. Twenty year have makee die."

"What side puttee this twenty year?"

"My homeside kitchen have puttee."

For twenty years the coffin had been kept in the kitchen until the soothsayers allowed a lucky day to carry it out to the fields.

We gave permission, and Jim suggested to me that part of her motive in wishing to go was to tell her relatives about her job with us and our funny foreign wedding.

We shared Russian Easter with a Londoner named George Bloomfield and his Russian wife Onya.

During the First War Bloomie, a youngest son, enlisted with the Coldstream Guards, who were leaving almost immediately to fight in France. He went home on leave to tell his parents of his enlistment and imminent departure, and said his mother sobbed, "Oh, my poor boy."

But his father shook his hand, said, "Do you good," and gave him half a crown.

They were special friends of ours. Onya was the only Russian we knew who said her family was not affected by the Revolution. "We were not important enough."

On Russian Easter we went with them to the onion-topped Russian church, going first to the grounds at the back to view rows of high round Easter cakes given to the church as offerings to the priests and the poor. Then we went inside where the air was heavy with the smoke of incense. There were no pews, no organ. People stood on the slightly sloping floor of the rounded building and sang the service a capella. There were many men in the congregation and the sound of their voices was deep and beautiful. When it was over we all went outside to the cakes again and everybody started kissing each other, saying, "Kristus voskrist!"—The Risen Christ! They kissed the priest. Women kissed men and other women. Men kissed women and other men.

"Let's get out of here!" said Bloomie.

So we went to their home and ate the high round currant cake which Onya had made for us.

Then it was the Dragon Boat Festival. This ancient festival on the lunar calendar was linked with the planting of crops and was second in importance after Chinese New Year. The Chiang Kai Shek government anxious to bring China in line with the the rest of the world, had imposed the solar calendar and outlawed the lunar program, including the Feast of Lanterns. Through one of the Chinese cadets on Jim's staff we learned that the Dragon Races associated with the Feast were to be held secretly in Chinese territory. The cadets were university students apprenticed to the Council to learn the basics of running the Settlement. The cadet confided to Jim the name of the park where the outlawed rituals were to be held. We parked our car at the edge of the French Concession and hired a Chinese taxi to take us the rest of the way.

We saw the driver studying us uncertainly in his rear-view mirror. He tried to drop us at a theatre, then at a restaurant, but Jim was able to convince him that we meant no harm and finally he took us to the park. We entered through a gate in a high wall, paid the admission and passed through moon gates into a series of small courts and gardens. These were made picturesque with rock sculptures built up into small hills and landscapes. In one court the materials used included "clinkers." Before the days of oil furnaces, these used to foi m on coal grates and cause a lot of trouble. The furnaces had to be extinguished before the larger "clinkers" could be removed, but here they were used as an art medium.

We came to a plaza of small stores and found in one a Pekinese artist displaying his paintings. He did not speak the Shanghai dialect and Jim had very little knowledge of Mandarin, the dialect of Peking in those days, but a Chinese student looking at the paintings served as an interpreter. Between the three of them I had an impromptu lesson in Oriental art.

The artist repeated what Mr. Choy had already said, that Chinese art is fundamentally symbolic and never without a poetic meaning. No picture was complete, he said, without an accompanying poem. He spoke to the student who translated for Jim who translated for me. If I had a question, it went back to the artist by the same route.

I was attracted to a five-foot panel, done in red on creamy paper, depicting in a minimum of brush strokes a monkey looking over a cliff. Three or four strokes at the top and maybe five at the bottom were all the cliff needed, and I thought the cautious interest of the monkey as he peered over the rim gorgeous. The artist, who wore a scholar's cap, said it was not a picture of a monkey looking over a cliff but a reminder that nothing is done in secret from the gods, who were symbolized by the monkey. We asked the price of the monkey, but it was far too expensive for us.

We left him at last to find the Dragon Boats. There were two of them on a large pond surrounded by gently

sloping grassy ground. Hundreds of Chinese spectators stood on the slopes, but we seemed to be the only foreigners and the Chinese moved away from us if we approached them—so conversation was impossible.

The two boats were about thirty or forty feet long, almost smothered in paper flowers. Each had an ornate dragon's head rearing at the prow, and one bore a flower-framed portrait of Dr. Sun Yat Sen. On each side of each boat twelve to fifteen men handled paddles, and other men moved about on the decks.

The two boats started side by side from one end of the pond, moved furiously to the other end, turned and started back, stopped dead together in the middle, swung around and paddled leisurely away in opposite directions. The spectators were vastly pleased. There seemed to be nothing competitive in the race. One by one, crew men left their paddles and jumped into the water. The crowds shouted excitedly. The paddlers put something in their mouths before going overboard. Jim surprised one onlooker and asked what it was the men put in their mouths.

"Eggs," was the answer. Eggs for the dragon who lived in the pond.

"Do they eat the eggs or leave them in the water?"

The man shrugged and turned away. It was all we could learn about the Dragon Boat Race and I felt I

115

should not speak of it to Mr. Choy.

Years later a scholar of Chinese culture told us the story of a popular poet who, in melancholy mood, attempted suicide by drowning. In his day, the whole local populace joined in an effort to save him. The Dragon Boat rites re-enacted the tragedy and were a significant tribute to the Chinese regard for knowledge and creativity as expressed in the arts.

On the Fourth of July the Americans held a hot-dog picnic in Jessfield Park and in all the streets of the Settlement all day long Chinese popped firecrackers. There was also a football game between a team from the British navy and a team from the U.S. Marines. It was played at the Canidrome and all business offices in Settlement and French Concession were closed as the entire white population turned out to watch the contest.

English residents of the Settlement firmly maintained that it was a Welsh regiment sent from Hong Kong in 1927 in case of trouble arising from Chiang Kai Shek's advance on the city who taught the Marines to play football. Apt pupils, the Marines soon won all games, until the British navy sent a call to the main Pacific fleet stationed at Wei Hai Wei for their best rugby players. On this challenging team was a very young man who, in British navy style, had grown a very full beard. "Look!" jeered the Marines before the game, "They have sent their grand-daddies to play us!"

Ironically, Grand-daddy Hamm scored the first point in the game, which ended that year in a tie.

Ten days after the Glorious Fourth everyone was celebrating again as Juillet Quatorze commemorated the taking of the Bastille. Festivities centred in the French Park, which, like the British Public Gardens, was normally closed to the Chinese who so greatly outnumbered the foreigners. It was thrown open to all in honour of Bastille Day and the Chinese population invaded it like ants.

All day long, crowds in gay summer clothing swarmed the streets of the French Concession, converging on the Park where bands played in small pavilions and strings of paper lanterns hung among the trees and festooned the winding paths. Soon after we arrived in the late afternoon French police moved through the crowds and section by section the lanterns came alight. On a big pond where pink and creamy yellow water lilies bloomed around a tea house pale green lanterns were attached to small wooden rafts and set adrift among the lily pads.

There were too many people. There wasn't room for them on the paths and grassy places and benches were so hidden by their crowded occupants as to seem nonexistent. The visitors sat on the flower beds and sprawled along the borders; shrubs were flattened and blanketed by bodies. Discarded candy wrappers, cigarette boxes, empty lunch bags and other litter made a carpet underfoot.

Six French sailors filled with patriotic fervour, wearing white bell-bottomed uniforms and wide white tam-o-shanters topped with blue pom-poms, decided to rid their park of the destructive hordes. Shoulder to shoulder they charged and the crowds scrambled and ran before them, then came surging back as the sailors charged in another direction.

Foot-weary, with no place to sit, we stood on a slight elevation near a bed of trampled heliotrope and watched the heave and pulsing of the vast throngs as the six valiant Frenchmen rushed to and fro.

As a people the Chinese were not obviously athletic. Apart from professional wrestling there seemed to be little philosophy of sport in the Chinese culture practised in Shanghai. The "line of beauty," I was told, was the weeping willow, not the human body. The "perfect form" must show no bone or muscle bulges.

Pieces of smooth jade, red, white or yellow, the size of pigeon's eggs were carried in the pockets of gentlemen's sleeves and constantly rolled between the fingers to develop a flexibility that Western violinists envied. Taking his bird for a walk in its wicker cage in the the evening was a Chinese gentleman's sufficient exercise.

This kind of aesthetic inactivity did not suit the white communities. Soon after they were granted their swampy concession of land, the British organized for sport. Cricket pitches and soccer fields were set aside and some doughty sailor types dared the treacherous Whangpoo in small sailing dinghies from a wharf in Hongkew magnificently named the Ming Hong Yacht Club. The mainstay of well-being was the Race Course, developed by private members almost in the centre of Central District. The land was bought, the graves paid for and moved to new locations, the land levelled and surfaced by Race Club members. They built the Grand-stand and the stables across the street, where tough little Mongolian ponies were housed and trained for the Annual Races.

There were only a few real horses in Shanghai. If Jim and I saw one—whether we were on foot or in the car—we would follow it for blocks. These glossy, well-trained mounts usually belonged to British Army officers or turbanned Sikhs, of the Municipal Mounted Police. The Races were contested only by Mongolian ponies impor-ted from northern China by Riding Members of the Race Club. Long-tailed, short-legged, shaggy-coated, they were groomed, domesticated and trained, often owner-ridden in the Races. The Race Club proudly boas-ted "the only honest races anywhere."

The central green of the Race Course oval and the cor-ners around it were designated for other sports—polo, cricket, soccer, tennis, bowling, grass hockey. These went on all year round. On Sunday evenings in the summer, bands played and the British troops in garrison staged the Sundown Retreat. You could sit on the grass in the Race Course, or graze a knee or skin an elbow, without fear of infection. The grounds were strictly maintained on foreign standards and the catarrhal, basic-minded Chinese were not allowed to enter.

Then, on three days set aside in the autumn as Race Days, all offices in the Settlement were closed and all na-tional flags flared against the wide skies from the roof tops. All kinds of international costumes and skin co-lours rubbed shoulders inside the Race Course enclo-sure, and outside, paternally watched by Police Riot Squads, mobs of Chinese joyously chased each other in adjacent streets, let off firecrackers and relaxed accord-ing to their own ancestral customs.

A street vendor selling paper flowers for the New Year's celebration.

Christmas among those nations who celebrated it was an intimate festival shared by family and close friends. About three weeks after Hogmanay came the Chinese New Year.

It was the biggest date on the Chinese calendar. Weeks before were spent in preparation. Chinese homes were thoroughly cleaned. Every effort was made to pay up all outstanding debts. The night itself was one continuous wave of popping firecrackers. What interested us most was the ritual surrounding the benign Kitchen God.

He was not one of the major deities and I have never

恭喜發財

read about him in any books nor found a Chinese or student of Chinese culture familiar with him. For two weeks before the Chinese New Year rough sketches of him on rather cheap red paper literally littered the windows of Chinese food stores fronted by packages of sticky-looking candies. On other Chinese special days one could see through the front windows of Chinese homes the front-room joss pieces, statues of the major gods or incense-burners arranged on little tables covered with embroidered cloths and set with lighted candles and dishes of sacrificial food. Not so the Kitchen God. He did not live in the red and gilt niches in the front rooms observing the family on its best behaviour. He was pinned on kitchen walls and knew the secrets of family living, petty squabbles, ill tempers and other regrettable lapses in behaviour.

On New Year's Day he departed via the kitchen stove for the spirit world to make his off-the-cuff report on the facts. A bad situation—were it not for the sticky candies. For a full week before New Years Day they were offered on a narrow shelf in front of the god's portrait. The hope was that his lips would be sealed by the stickiness long enough to get a new Kitchen God pinned in his place who would protect the family from the wrath it might deserve.

I asked the Amah to buy me two Kitchen Gods. He was a lovable being with high head-dress, long white moustaches and lightly sketched children's faces peeping from the folds of his robe and sleeves. One of him was pinned in the kitchen to follow the usual routine. The other was framed by me and hung on our dining room walls, near kitchen doors, for many many years both in China and in Canada.

13

THE GREAT AND LITTLE
HAVE NEED OF
ONE ANOTHER

-American

O N ITS WAY TO THE downtown area Wei Hai Wei Road curved around one end of the Race Course as Bubbling Well Road curved around the other.

On Wei Hai Wei across the busy street from the Race Course a small wooden panel was set in a high brick wall. The Chinese characters painted on the panel translated into English as "Place the Baby Here." The panel was the front of a stout wooden drawer, the brick wall enclosed a Foundling Home supported by wealthy Chinese.

All such large premises in the Settlement had Indian watchmen, and the watchmen at the Foundling Home had the special duty of picking up any baby left in the drawer and carrying it indoors. There it was raised by Chinese amahs under the supervision of Roman Catholic nuns. The babies' origins were never known. Nearly all were girls, Chinese or part-Chinese, born to the very poor in the alleys of the industrial districts or in the river boats that crowded the mud-banked streams.

The Home named them, reared them, taught them, launched them with jobs and spouses. There were no windows facing the curving street where curious eyes might see who placed the baby in the wooden drawer— nobody cared. As far as I could learn, half a dozen foundling boys were brought up by the home, and only one child apparently had all-white parentage.

Poverty was difficult to combat under the Land Regulations, signed in 1854 by the Chinese Government and

121

the foreign powers, and virtually unchanged in the next 90 years. Under this agreement each nation looked after its own people in the Settlement. Few Chinese lived in the Settlement and there was little industrial development in 1854. Any changes or additions to the Land Regulations had to be approved by the Central Chinese Government. This virtually meant that there were no changes authorized, since the Chinese were determined to restrict the expansion of foreign authority.

Population in and around the Settlement doubled and redoubled, tripled and tripled again. Sprawling mills of the lightest possible construction multiplied under Chinese, Japanese and Western ownership. Settlement authorities found themselves faced with a corpulent giant and no means of controlling it.

A municipal building inspector described to us over dinner one evening some of the problems of his department. The average Chinese house, he said, was one of a terraced row fronting on an alley and containing downstairs a living room and kitchen and upstairs two bedrooms. Such a house would be leased by a Chinese tenant from the Chinese landlord or owner, who probably owned the entire row or street of houses and lived in another part of Shanghai or even another city.

The tenant would then run up a partition separating the open stairs from the living room, which was then occupied by himself and his family, including perhaps one or two married sons. The other rooms, including the kitchen and the hall, normally ten or twelve feet high,

would be divided horizontally into two storeys, making a honeycomb of rooms and lofts, some without windows, each section occupied by an entire family.

One municipal survey showed the average capacity in a district to be seven people to a unit, several units to a house. They cooked on small open braziers, bought their water by the cup or can-full from the nearby water shop and set out their family buckets on the street at night for the sanitation wagons to empty.

Since structural alterations were all made inside the houses where foreign jurisdiction did not extend, inspectors were denied the right to enter the houses and detection of such living conditions was difficult. If he found the house overcrowded, the inspector's only remedy lay in argument and persuasion.

Babies not surrendered to the Drawer on Wei Hai Wei

road might be brought up in these surroundings. If they died, their bodies were wrapped in faded blue cotton and left for the Chinese Benevolent Society's van to gather up in the pre-dawn on its daily rounds for just this purpose; or the small corpses would be left in some vacant lot for wandering dogs to scavenge.

There was another small section of the Settlement reserved especially as a sanctuary for babies. Mrs. Fairfax, wife of the lean printer in the advertising agency, took me there.

The visit seemed important to her and because we liked her and her husband very much I went with her.

It was in Bubbling Well Cemetery, a narrow strip under a sunny wall where roses and other flowers were carefully cultivated. The tombstones were small and close together, each engraved only with one Christian name, and Mrs. Fairfax knew them all as if they were neighbours—her own small son lay in one of the graves. She introduced them lovingly.

"Baby Stephen was stillborn, and little Harry here was dropped by his amah into scalding bath water. Susie was two—she was scratched by a cat that turned out to have rabies. That was a dreadful thing, such a small scratch. Doctors thought the cat must have been licking its paws and that was how the infected saliva got into the bloodstream. Mark had dysentery, and Michael and Penny— that's the worst hazard here for children. It takes so many of them. Some people call this part of the Cemetery Dysentery Street, but it has another name that I prefer—Baby Row. This grave is bigger. Billy was six, nearly ready to go home to school—really past the dangerous years. But he contracted measles, a virulent strain, and died of it. He was an only child."

"What happened to your own baby?" She was pulling grass from a grave and nipping off the faded nasturtium blooms.

"Dysentery. And do you know, I saw the fly that killed him. We were having tea in a friend's garden. The cover over the sandwiches was left turned back for a few seconds only and a fly lit on one. It was shooed away quickly but before we could stop him little Donny took that very sandwich and ate it. It was the small tea kind, you

know? No crust." She added, "He was an only, too.
There was an accident when he was born. I can never
have another."

"Just from a fly!"

"Just from a fly."

There were kindergartens and primary schools which
took the children of non-Orientals through their early
education. By the time the children were nine years old
it was generally considered wise to send them to boarding school to learn home-style customs and discipline
away from the constant attention of devoted amahs and
obedient House Boys.

One trusted boarding school, not so far away as England or the States, was in northern China on the island
of Wei Hai Wei, where the British maintained a strong
naval outpost. Every year, early in September, when
mists began to veil the inlets of the south China coast, a
chartered steamer conveyed nine to fourteen-year-olds,
numbering about three hundred, from Shanghai to the
wharf of the boarding school. Because of the "pirates"
who infested the south China seas, this children's steamer, like all other passenger vessels between Nagasaki
and Hong Kong, carried four or five armed Russian
guards.

The pirates were not essentially vicious. Many of
them had been small farmers who had lost their land because they were unable to meet the tax demands of the
local War Lords. Chiang Kai Shek was the first leader
since the revolution who was able to unite the majority
of the provinces of China and break the power of the
War Lords. The War Lords had been empowered by previous dynasties to collect taxes from the people and to
invent what taxes they collected. A survey quoted by O.
Edmund Clubb in his book, *Twentieth Century China*,
speaks of "a contemporary listing of forty-four taxes" to
which the people of Kansu Province were subjected. Beside the land tax, these included an acreage tax, purifica-
tion of the countryside tax, skin overcoat tax, stocking
tax, kettle tax, kindling wood tax, house tax, bedding tax,
miscellaneous expenses tax, hog tax, extraordinary tax,
additional goods tax, and many others equally vague.

Not content with collecting for the current year, some War Lords collected in advance, and the North China Daily News carried a story of hardsh p in Fukien Province, south of Shanghai, where taxes were being collected ninety-nine years in advance.

Peasants who could not pay their taxes were dispossessed and had no other means of support but banditry on land and piracy at sea.

During my first year in Shanghai, when the chartered children's ship had set out from Shanghai for Wei Hai Wei, word was flashed to the Settlement that as she emerged from the Yangtse Kiang, the steamer had been captured by three strongly armed Chinese private junks and taken away into the morning mists.

Near panic hit the parents of the Settlement. How? Why? Who? Where would the children be taken? What would happen to them? Even those of us who had no children were shocked and terrified.

Authorities quickly tried to reassure us. A ship loaded with silver bullion bricks to be taken to the banks in Hong Kong had been scheduled to leave Shanghai about the same time as the children's transport and surely had been the prize the pirates were after. Sailing orders on the silver ship had been changed at the last moment and the surprise and chagrin of the pirates could easily be imagined when, instead of millions of dollars in silver brick, they found themselves confronted by the frightened faces of three hundred young children.

No doubt they would fear "losing face" if they admitted making a mistake and released the children. Perhaps they would hold them for ransom; if so, under what conditions would they be held? How fed? By whom consoled? How reliable were the Russian guards?

Not to worry, said the authorities. The Chinese were universally known to be fond of children. Moreover, the British Navy had taken over. The British Navy would find the captured ship. The British Navy was rumoured to be already in touch with the pirates via the Bamboo Wireless.

Three days later the ship was located in a southern bay which was the stronghold of a tough band whose leader was a woman. The concern of the Navy was to effect recapture without gunfire, which might frighten if not injure the little prisoners.

We spectators never knew the details. We thought money had changed hands. The pirates put up some resistance and one Russian guard, supporting the Navy, was killed. The children were basically unharmed. They had been kept day and night in the ship's dining room and "fed a lot of oranges," they said (the orange crop was ripening just then in southern China). By the end of the week the pupils were all safely back at school near the British Naval Base, learning their tables and dates.

That summer the weather priests at Ziccawei reported temperature records broken. To me, the heat was unbelievable. It was too hot to wear anything made of silk—everyone wore cotton and as little of that as possible. Foreign men carried small towels to mop the perspiration that flowed from them. In spite of my own bewildering discomfort, I found it amusing to see Chinese businessmen of dignified mien and portly proportions discussing affairs with their fellows on street corners wearing only white cotton under-drawers, and straw sandals, carrying flowered paper parasols and expertly fluttering fans.

Our one-room flat became an airless oven and Perkins Yue miraculously conceded two larger rooms upstairs at the end of the building so that windows faced in two directions. Walls were repainted for us and floors refinished with the famous Ningpo Varnish, hard, glossy, and rich in colour.

I was prostrated with heat stroke. We moved, but I got worse. The doctor prescribed frequent luke-warm baths, but one morning, en route from bath to bed, I fainted on the shiny varnished floor. When I came to, Amah was crouched beside me moaning, "How fashion Missy fall down? How fashion?"

Almost blinded with searing head pain I could only say, "Call Master," and crawled to the bed. Amah kept cool cloths on my forehead and tucked under my pillow an embroidered handkerchief gently fragrant with a special perfume of her own. We did not know then that she had never used a telephone and was terrified of the white man's devil which she thought lived in the wires—

anything electrical was a devil to Amah.

The telephone rang on Jim's office desk. He answered and heard nothing. Irritated, he was about to hang up when a very small voice far in the distance whispered, "Master!"

"Amah? Is that you? How is Missy?"

The voice became stronger, quavered, "Please Master, Missy face no velee goodee."

"Stay with her, Amah! I come now."

He brought the doctor with him. When the pain was somewhat subdued I asked the doctor, "Is it true that Ningpo Varnish is made with pig's blood and the sap of a plant that's a cousin to poison ivy?"

"Why do you ask that?"

"Because if I were at home I'd think these blisters were poison ivy rash."

"Any Ningpo Varnish around here?"

"All over the floor."

For a week in hospital I was rolled every two hours in sheets freshly wrung out of potassium permanganate solution, which died me purple from head to toe. The room was large and cool with seven empty beds beside my own.

I said to the matron, "I know the hospital is very crowded. I don't mind if you put someone else in here."

She replied, "We don't dare. One glimpse of you and they'd die of fright."

At the end of the week, the burning pain subdued, a little Australian nurse sat beside my cot on the shaded balcony and sponged away the purple dye with swabs of cotton.

The doctor recommended two or three weeks right out of southern China. Jim's short leave was due so we went to Japan. When we came back my contract at the office had expired—but being pregnant, I continued to work without renewing it.

The pregnancy proved difficult. At last when the final red mist of pain had dissipated, Jim sat beside my hospital bed. Certain that no baby life could have survived those last hours of tortuous agony, I asked him fearfully, "Do we have a baby?"

He said, "We have two babies."

"Boys or girls?"

"One of each."

I began to laugh and closed my eyes, then opened them again. "Never any more. Never never never."

"Agreed." He shook my hands and I floated back into oblivion.

14

WHEN A ROGUE KISSES YOU, COUNT YOUR TEETH

-Hebrew

IT HAD NOT SEEMED that having a baby need change our life too much; having two disrupted everything.

The twins were the first born in the white community in fifteen years and the papers connected their arrival with the birth of the world-famous Dionne Quintuplets one year before. These multiple births were presented as a remarkable new achievement of the Canadian people and the readers loved it. Masses of flowers tributes came from perfect strangers and two or three times a day members of the hospital's Chinese staff poked their heads into my room asking, "How two-piecee baby?"

We didn't have enough baby clothes and Jim ventured into The Baby Corner of Wing On's big department store to fill in the gaps. I had given him a list but as soon as he approached the counter he forgot about it. The word "twins" flashed like magic into adjoining aisles and Jim found himself surrounded by three eager Chinese salesgirls and a dozen or more experienced customers arguing with each other in a babble of languages as to what was necessary to buy and what was not. Finally, he said, he just tried to picture to himself what a dressed baby looked like and then bought two of everything to show no favouritism. Some basic unseens were missing but somehow the nurses at the beautiful Country Hospital, foreign-run, provided them.

They had to have names within ten days to be registered with the Consulate as Canadians. Pat was easy.

On the coil of rope on the *Empress* Jim had remarked that he had always thought that it would be nice to have "a dark little daughter called Pat": here she was. The son was more difficult; Jim wanted something virile (he said) like Henghis or Hercules. In the end we named him for his dad.

Jim was Jim so I called the baby "J". Later Patty picked this up as Dei or Dei-dei which enchanted Amah because Dei meant brother. I often called the little sister Si'au Papei, a popular Chinese nickname meaning Small Precious. Dei-dei echoed the Papei, easier to say than Patty, and so the twins were named.

Of course I had to resign my job.

The twins were very small. The doctors and nurses in the hospital didn't want us to take them home until they each weighed five pounds—which neither did even after eighteen days. Then a flu epidemic struck the hospital and it was felt safest to let us come home with detailed instructions and directions to telephone the hospital any time, day or night. They had to be fed around the clock every three hours, and I was determined to do this myself. Amah took over the laundry, I washed and sterilized the bottles and prepared the formula. Every three hours I accomplished the double feeding—I held one baby to my breast with one arm, and propping the other in the crook of my knee, fed it from the bottle. It wasn't easy.

During the day Amah always managed to be free at feeding and brought the kitchen stool and sat wistfully watching. She told me several times that her former English Missy, the one who had recommended her as a lady's maid, had allowed her to "do baby busy." Every evening she left at seven. Jim was on night inspection work and left at eleven. I faced the dark hours alone with the two infants, and sometimes we all three howled together. When they had passed the five-pound target and sometimes slept through the late feeding, I allowed Amah to sit beside me during the day and feed the bottle-fed baby. Her bliss was beyond description.

Our two-room flat soon proved much too small, and there was no space at all for drying the babies' laundry.

Automatic washers and dryers were as yet unknown.

Jim asked everyone he knew about possible larger living quarters. He won a new nickname, "The Twinny Man." One morning his work took him to the Superintendent's Office of a large Chinese Hospital and the Superintendent, a big vociferous German, greeted him in full voice.

"Ha! The Twinny Man! Himself! How is it with the little babies?"

When Jim mentioned our space problem the bachelor Superintendent, who had his own quarters in the hospital, clapped him on the shoulder with an enthusiasm which Jim said almost drove his spine down between his knees. He said he had the very place, just completed, a jewel he had planned for himself as a nice cool place to drink beer. The Kindchen must have it, he would not take no for an answer: I must be taken that very day to see it.

The Jewel was the top floor of a large house which stood in a walled garden on one of the Outside Roads. Being on the third floor, it was above the malaria level since the anopheles mosquito which spread the malaria organism normally did not fly so high. The apartment was also double-screened throughout.

A sort of penthouse, the Jewel was smaller than the two floors below, which each now contained a full size apartment. The surrounding roof space on the third floor Mr. Ahrens had turned into three balconies. One small one facing south was ideal for drying laundry. A second outside the kitchen door was like a small back yard, Amah's own. The third balcony, roofed, fully sixteen by twelve feet in size, on tree top level and equipped with flower boxes, became our outdoor living quarters.

In front of the house was a small paved court shut off by heavy iron gates from a square fronted by other houses on two sides. A third side was walled by a row of garages and the fourth was open to busy Outside Road leading to a Chinese village called Jessfield which was, of course, under Chinese jurisdiction.

Our landlord was a native of Alsace-Lorraine which was convenient he told us, because France and Germany were at the time disputing possession of the territory.

Mr. Ahrens had two passports, one French, one German. "If I am in trouble with the French, then I am a German, if in trouble with the Germans, then I am French. But you will find I am a good man." His eyes twinkled merrily.

Amah and Jim's senior foreman Chang hired a dozen carrier coolies and our belongings were moved, with music, from Wei Hai Wei to the new apartment. The house provided servants' quarters and Amah happily moved in her immaculate steel bed, red blankets, dresser and small shrine. Our staff was increased to three.

We allowed Amah to hire the new servants, stressing three things: must be clean, must do busy proper and there must be no fightee-fightee in the kitchen. Soon, a plump cousin from the Hangchow village, Ah Zee, was helping Amah with the laundry and the housework. Ah Zee spoke no English and was nicknamed by Jim the Hangchow Hen.

Amah next introduced a boy of about thirteen or fourteen, a smiling round-head who carried coal and ashes, washed floors and ran errands. He had a name but we never even tried to pronounce it. Amah said he was a makee-learn-pidgin (pidgin meaning business), and hoped one day to be a House-Boy for a foreign family. To us he became The Pidgin. Stops and Ayrton always called him the Smiling Butler.

Twin prams were not stocked anywhere in Shanghai and the English Department Store, Whiteaway Laidlaws, said that to import one would cost me $800, with of course no re-sale value. We had two baskets specially made at a Chinese basket-store. They were small and light enough to be carried under one arm, but large enough for the babies to sleep and play in them by day. They had their cribs at night.

Our landlord came often to see us. He brought presents for the babies and had tea, balancing the tea cup in his big hands, with knees pressed uncomfortably together.

If anything was needed we had only to tell him. "It shall be! You will find I am a good man."

As winter drew near I grew worried that there was no sunny window where a flowering plant or bulb might grow. It seemed to me that rooms where no flower could grow would not be healthy for the babies. "Show me where! Show me where!" I picked the spot and the very next day the carpenters were cutting through the wall.

One day Fred Baker telephoned. I had expected that he would never speak to me again since I had left the office so suddenly, but he said his new wife had never seen twins. Would I mind very much if he brought her to visit? Delivered in their chauffeur-driven car to our iron gate, he and Fran walked up the double flight of stairs to the Jewel. It was one of those instant affinities. Before she left we were close friends. She had a baby girl about the same age as the twins and we had an endless list of things to talk about. After that first visit we phoned each other at least once every day and sometimes two or three times. Frequently the Baker car purred to our iron gate to bring Fran to the Jewel or take me to the Baker home on Hungjao Road.

It was true that Fred found her on a London street— she was in a queue waiting for a bus. He fell head over heels in love, managed to board the same bus, followed her home and two or three minutes later rang the doorbell and asked her parents' permission to call. The talents which had built him his successful Agency sold him as a husband. He adored her and she him.

As the children grew bigger they were included in the daytime visits and one afternoon when the twins were about 18 months old Twin Sister disappeared at the

Baker home. First the amahs, then the entire Baker staff were organized in the search. She was not in the house and not in the garden.

I said, "She loves bathrooms" but there was no child in any of the Bakers' three bathrooms.

Panic began to mount. Perhaps she had squeezed under the driveway gate and wandered off in the Chinese countryside. Perhaps she had been stolen away. We telephoned Jim to see if the Municipal Council could arrange to have a nearby pond dragged. For a short time the Settlement seemed on the verge of emergency mobilization, then somebody remembered a new guest room was being added to the Baker home and the ensuite bathroom was completed. We checked this fourth bathroom and there she was, happily playing with the shining new faucets, well soaked from adventures with the shower, filling and refilling every available utensil and arranging them with housewifely care in various corners.

A few months later our bathroom sparked more excitement. A tap was leaking and I telephoned Mr. Ahren's office but he was out, his Boy did not know when he would be back. A second call received the same answer as did a third. When Jim came home that evening he said it was strange the Boy knew so little. Perhaps we should telephone the German couple who occupied the ground floor apartment and who were friends of Mr. Ahrens.

When I told the man who answered the call about our problem, he replied, "He has disappeared?"

I said, "No, I didn't say that. It is just that the bathroom tap is leaking and it is the hot water tap——"

"He has disappeared!" exclaimed the man again and the phone went dead.

Later that evening Jim and I went down to see the Germans but they were busy packing and had no time to talk to us. In the morning the ground-floor apartment was empty and no one answered Mr. Ahren's phone.

The mystery was unresolved for several days. Then the morning papers carried an important story about the Police finding our kindly landlord in a vacant lot near the hospital, lying in a patch of weeds and dying of poison. The paper said the police did not know whether the poison was self-inflicted or had been given Mr. Ahrens by somebody else. The only thing the Superintendent had said before he died was "I am a good man."

The papers carried the story for several days. Mr. Ahrens' death was linked with the breaking of a round-the-world drug ring, the shooting death of a man in Buenos Aires, a suicide in Vienna and the arrest in San Francisco of a pretty Chinese girl, daughter of a wealthy Shanghai family, who had been found in possession of a suitcase full of drugs. It was said that our landlord-friend was a source of supply, for he was also the buying agent for the big hospital where he was Superintendent and had ready access to the drugs needed.

Meanwhile it came time to pay our rent. We telephoned the German Consul to ask to whom it should go, but he said, "It is not our affair. He was not one of us. He had a French passport." We contacted the French Consulate in the Concession and were told, "No, no, he was not ours. His passport was German." Neither country wanted to recognize poor Mr. Ahrens. We left the rent money in the bank and it accumulated for three months.

We paid it finally to a rather weary young man in a dark suit, with a dark felt hat, who climbed the stairs one afternoon and introduced himself as coming from the French Consulate. Mr. Ahrens' brothers and sisters lived in France and had asked the French Government to settle his estate. Sighed the young Frenchman, "It seems we were stuck with him."

Arrangements were made for us to pay our rent every month to the French authorities. I asked what had happened to Mr. Ahrens. Where was he buried? He said he didn't know and had not been asked to find out. Nobody cared now about the Superintendent.

Jim and I counted our teeth and found that none were missing. We truly mourned our friend for the problems he must have had during life and the unhappy hours before death.

15

THE MORE
UNDERSTANDING,
THE FEWER WORDS

-German

WE CALLED HER AMAH, which means mother in Chinese.

She called me Missy and Jim Master, but there was no hint of bondage or ownership in our relationship. The names were simply convenient, recognized handles.

Amah quickly became part of the life which Jim and I were organizing together. At first she was our only, therefore our Number One, servant and went to our wedding with this status behind her. As far as we knew she had enjoyed herself in the kitchen at our reception, with its staff of houseboy, two amahs and coolie, plus the attendants provided by the caterers. We did not see her until we had returned from Hangchow and she brought in the morning tray of tea, with two cups on it instead of one.

We paid her less than a House Boy's wages but more than the average baby or wash amah in white families, who usually paid about three times as much as Chinese families. Amah's dignity expanded with every pay day and she gained considerable 'face' among other Chinese.

In the first weeks her subdued manner and lugubrious expression irritated Jim. "The old girl has to crack a smile or leave," he told me. "I can't stand the wet atmosphere."

Then one day we heard that there had been a shooting in the big apartment house across the court. What was it all about? Jim told me to ask Amah—she was sure to have details via the bamboo wireless. We summoned her

to the living room and Jim asked questions in pidgin English.

"Amah, this big house next door, you savvy?"

"Yes, Master."

"Somebody have shoot somebody."

"Yes, Master."

"How fashion?"

She brightened as she launched readily into narrative.

"This big house have got plenty small house inside. This one-piece small house belong Chinese policee-man. Policee-man have got one sweety-heart. Bimeby sweety-heart husband come, shootee-shoot sweety-heart, shootee-shoot policee-man, velly quick shootee-shoot self."

"Oh, Amah! All have die?"

"Yes, Missy. All have makee die." She broke into deep sepulchral laughter so shocking that Jim and I were startled into laughter too. "Hoo, hoo, hoo, hoo!"

"Ha, ha, ha," echoed Jim.

"He, he, he," I giggled.

"Hoo, hoo, hoo," chortled Amah as she went back into the kitchen.

"Good Lord!" exclaimed Jim, "if that's how she laughs we'd better stay with the gloom."

Little by little we taught her the secrets of domesticity—how to peel and boil potatoes, how to soft boil an egg. And little by little we learned something of her background. We knew that her home was in the hills outside Hangchow. Her feet were bound, giving her a stilted walk, and indicating that she was not of coolie birth. I asked her what her father did and she said he "belong teacher". One day she told me that her husband was House Boy for a Chinese family, and added bitterly, "This husband no good. He all time—" she mimed dealing cards. "All time spend he money, spend my money. He no time have buy me one dless, no buy my son dless. All time I do busy for self, for son."

"How old your son, Amah?"

"Twelve year. My auntie house have got. This husband no belong my son father. My son father have go makee soldier, have makee die. My auntie all time talkee me must catch husband, must catch husband. I no wanchee husband. I can do busy. My auntie talkee me must catch, must catch, must catch. Have catch. All time he spend my money."

I told her that in two days friends were coming for dinner. Would she like to stay late and wait on table as House Boys did? I would pay her extra. She readily agreed. I explained that when I rang a little bell she was to come in and take away the dinner plates, two at a time, and then bring in the dessert. "Kui v'kui"—'Can do, no can do?'

"Kui, kui."

On the evening of the dinner she mysteriously changed somewhere into a clean jacket and pants, with a decorated comb in her brushed hair. We were pleased with her. However, when we rang the little bell after the main course, nothing happened. I rang again. At last I gathered up two plates and took them to the kitchen. All dressed up but wide-eyed with misery Amah pressed herself against the wall. I smiled at her, went back for the other plates and took in the dessert. We paid her the extra money anyhow for staying late and assured her the next time it would be better.

Next time it was not. I rang the bell. Nothing happened. I cleared the dinner plates and then told her to bring in the dessert. We waited expectantly. Suddenly she appeared, shielding her face with her left hand and carrying a plate of dessert in her right. She plunked it in front of me and, putting both hands over her face, scurried back to the kitchen. I passed it on and we waited. In exactly the same way, with one hand shielding her face, she brought in the other desserts, one at a time.

Later we praised her and raised her salary, and there was no more trouble. She became as efficient as any House Boy, even learning to pass the coffee on the correct side.

Amah and I worked together with the babies and, especially during the feeding hours, she told me many things about Chinese customs and beliefs. Coloured bags containing powders and charms appeared hanging at the corners of the babies' cribs, and candles stuck in pans of sand burned outside their window at night. I allowed a certain leeway in such things, feeling that if I went along with her ideas she would go along with mine.

I had her call Ah Zee into the kitchen and outlined to the two of them routines of sanitation: the widespread use of boiling water to scald and sterilize, the anathema of flies, the death that lurked in raw vegetables and fruits. Amah translated poker-faced, but Ah Zee sometimes used a pudgy hand to wipe an irrepressible grin from her face. Nevertheless I persisted in my clumsy pidgin English.

"This spinach"—all greens were spinach—"plenty small somethings have got, no can see, no can wash away. Suppose puttee table, this small somethings walkee-walkee, go inside small hole in table." I walkee-walkeed my fingers across the sink counter and as Amah translated she walkee-walkeed her fingers also. "Bimeby somebody puttee baby spoon or Master cup table-side, this small somethings go walkee-walkee-walkee," away went my fingers and Amah's dutifully followed, "go baby spoon or Master cup, very quick can makee sick, can makee die!"

Amah and Ah Zee boiled everything faithfully.

One day a mad dog was reported on our street and Amah became very excited. She told me, "This dog sickee velly bad sickee."

"I know, Amah. Nobody must go outside."

She said, "Suppose dog catchee this sickee, inside catchee small doggie all time makee jumpy-jump, makee cly-cly."

"Well, no."

"Yes, Missy. Suppose this doggie bitee somebody, this somebody catchee small doggie inside, all time makee jump-jump, makee cly-cly."

"Oh no, Amah!"

"Yes, this is my home-side I have see. This sick doggie bites one countly-man, countly-man catchee small doggie inside, all time makee jumpy-jump, makee cly-cly. Outside one amah hear he cly-cly, no go inside, catchee small doggie inside, velly quick lun, lun, lun, cly-cly. I have see."

We agreed on one point. The dog-sickee was a very bad sickee. It was a relief when the local radio reported that the Settlement police had shot the mad dog.

Amah's Auntie now appeared sometimes in our kitchen. She was a dainty Chinese woman who produced exquisite embroidered slippers and bedspreads for the twins. Amah told me that her own son was now at school in Shanghai. Auntie also had a son, a few years older, who was an orderly of some kind in a Chinese hospital in the city. Amah admired him and sang the praises of her Auntie's so-goodee son.

Following Chinese custom he had been betrothed in childhood, but his betrothed had died and Auntie was now looking for a new wife for him. A young amah whom Amah knew was interested, and I was asked if our kitchen might be used for a meeting with the Auntie. On the appointed afternoon Ah Zee and the Pidgin stayed in the background and the three amahs met, dressed in long, lovely silken gowns, their hair glossy and alive with bright enamelled combs and pins. As they drank tea and talked quietly, a feeling of elegance seeped from the kitchen and pervaded the whole apartment.

However, it came to nothing. The other amah wanted four hundred dollars as the price of marriage and Auntie thought this too much money.

Soon afterwards Amah told me her Auntie had found a suitable candidate and wedding plans were moving ahead. The bride was a country woman who could not speak.

"Oh, Amah! How sad!"

"This goodee," she said complacently. "This kind more cheap. Can do plenty busy."

The wedding would include the traditional three days of feasting at the bridegroom's home, which was the Auntie's house near Hangchow. Some of the bridal fare was prepared in our kitchen and everyone was very happy. Amah was given the necessary days off and Ah Zee and the Pidgin took over our household chores, the Pidgin proving more adept with the tea tray than Ah Zee.

When Amah returned she told me, "My Auntie son no catchee mally, Missy."

"Again! Why not?"

This wedding had been very good, she said. Plenty guests had come with plenty presents and stayed three days and eaten plenty chow. On the third day the bride arrived, but the bridegroom never showed up. The bride was insulted, her family very angry. Auntie had to pay them plenty money.

What happened? Auntie's so-goodie son, imbued with modern ideas, declared that when he wanted to catch a wife he would catch one himself.

Perhaps all this importance inflated Amah's ego a bit too much. She ran into trouble.

Wishing to send a message to a friend who lived about two blocks away but who for some reason could not be telephoned, Jim wrote a note and gave it to Amah with instructions to send it by rickshaw. He gave her a twenty cent paper note to pay the fare.

The paper note was Big Money, part of a fiscal reform introduced by Chiang Kai Shek. Five paper notes made a dollar, always, every day. Foreigners preferred the Big Money, as it eliminated the piles of coppers which plagued the old system, known as Small Money, still used by most of the Chinese. Twenty cents Small Money was a silver coin, and it took five such coins plus several coppers to make up a dollar. The number of coppers varied every day.

Amah offered the rickshaw coolie a silver coin. Because she was wearing her white jacket, suggesting foreign employment, he demanded Big Money. Argument followed and, as usual a small crowd of Chinese spectators quickly collected.

Hearing the sound they were making, I looked from the children's bedroom window and saw a crowd of about a hundred Chinese, three or four dozen rickshaws and several Chinese police from the village around the corner surrounding Amah and the rickshaw coolie, both in shrill voice. Jim, who had been up all night, had gone to bed, but when I saw a coolie on the edge of the crowd pick up a stone, I called him. He threw one look through the window, told me to call the riot van and ran downstairs. I was back at the window to see him pushing through the crowd, which was suddenly quiet. One of the Chinese police put a hand on his arm—out there in the square they were all in Chinese territory—but Jim shook him off as one shucks a wandering fly, and brought Amah back to our doorstep. Since the house was foreign-owned they were now under Settlement jurisdiction.

The crowd moved around making low angry sounds, but Jim ignored them and somehow that cowed them. With Amah silent in the shadows behind him Jim could have been quite alone, admiring the sunlight on the clouds in the blue sky. When the armoured riot van appeared around the corner about a block away everybody in the square disappeared except Amah's rickshaw coolie, who had not yet received even Small Money. There was a short conference, the rickshaw bowled away, the police sergeant climbed back into his armoured car, and Jim and a crest-fallen Amah came upstairs. Before he went back to bed we had a cup of tea on the big verandah.

Jim told me that the sergeant had said to him, "The old girl's a bit of a termagant." We regarded her, so meek and gentle, with new eyes—we had never thought of her as a termagant. The amount of money involved in this incident would have amounted to about 1/6 of a Canadian cent.

16

WHAT THREE KNOW, EVERYBODY KNOWS

-Spanish

LIKE THE DUST-COLOURED sparrows that hopped in the gutters, drab public rickshaw pullers hovered in small groups along the curbs, gossiping amicably as they waited for fares. In fact, they were an intrinsic part of the famous "bamboo wireless," for when they had delivered their fares they did not go back to where they had started from but joined the nearest group of pullers, passing on and gathering up all kinds of information. On their almost endlessly jogging feet news spread around the Settlement much faster than by any other medium.

The public rickshaws, once yellow, were now a dingy gray. The pullers' pants, once blue, were faded, torn but not patched, and frequently worn with one leg rolled up above the knee and the other hanging halfway down the shin. Jackets, if any, were equally derelict, but their hats were a comedy skit for a fashion magazine.

Since city Chinese usually wore only skull caps or headbands the pullers' hats must have been discards from the foreigners. Once acquired they provided scope for all kinds of individual ingenuity. A fedora, dents and creases fisted out, could serve three wearers. The very top, cut off with points or scallops, and sometimes cut out like a paper snowflake, made a skull cap. The side of the crown made circlets of varying widths and stylings; and the brim, pulled down to rest on eyebrows or ears, could be turned up at the side or the back, tipped to one side or pushed back, finished with a feather or nosegay.

Women's hats were adopted with all the trimmings—ribbons, artificial flowers above or below the brims, even one with a pale mauve scarf drawn through slits in the brim and tied under the puller's chin.

During the 1930's sparked by the Rotary Club, an investigation was made by the Municipal Council into the working conditions of the Settlement's public rickshaw pullers. The resulting report is covered in *Life and Labour in Shanghai*, a book written by Eleanor Hinder of the Council's Industrial and Social Division and published by the Institute of Pacific Relations in 1944. The report states that in the Thirties there were about 10,000 public rickshaws operating in the Settlement, all owned by a few very large companies who rented them to sub-agents, who rented them to the pullers for 12-hour shifts. Some pullers shared their shifts which meant that as many as 25,000 or 30,000 men and older boys earned money through this service. Earnings, the report said, were not enough to ensure the pullers a living wage. Under a treaty signed in 1854 and never updated, Settlement authorities could not interfere with the Chinese owners or sub-agents. Their only weapon was a license fee charged for the ownership of vehicles using Settlement streets, and this fee was covered in the rental charged the puller.

While the Rotarians and others worried about them, the pullers themselves brightened the streets with impudent grins and ready laughter, often at the expense of the foreigners. They knew almost every resident foreigner, where he lived and where he worked. It happened sometimes that men who had celebrated too much at a stag party were delivered home, all unknowing, by rickshaw pullers who collected their fee from the men's wives.

One morning before we were married, on my way to the office by rickshaw, I saw Jim finishing his breakfast near the plate glass window of an American-owned restaurant. Since I was early I stamped to stop the puller and joined Jim for coffee. After that not one rickshaw would take me past the window if Jim were there—and he usually was. There was quite a hubba-hubba as the puller drew into the curb, disregarding all my protests.

Other pullers congregated, jabbering shrilly, traffic was slowed, cars tooted, bells rang. I did not like being so publicly delivered and even walked blocks from my little apartment hoping to find a puller unfamiliar with the routine, but it was no use. The pullers knew and liked Jim and were all on his side. I asked Jim to change his seat but he just laughed. "Great fun!" The pullers thought so too.

The simplest way to direct a puller was by stamping. In the noise of the traffic he might not hear a voice, but through the slender shafts of his vehicle he could feel a stamp on the right side or on the left for turning, or in the middle for stopping. There were few people more unreachable than a rickshaw puller lost in a dream, real or simulated, jogging rhythmically along a busy street. I saw a U.S. Marine once, flowing along with the traffic, leaning forward frantically shouting, quite ineffectually, "Whoa! Whoa!"

Another day a British sailor was smiling proudly at his solution to the communication problem. He had a pretty Chinese girl on his knee shrilling directions. Not far behind was his buddy, Mr. Ford, with a better idea. He had a girl on each knee, both shrilling.

Equally pervasive as the rickshaw pullers, though in quite a different category, were the devils who plagued the populace as the Little People used to plague the English country folks. One could never forget the devils; both by sound and by sight we were constantly reminded of them.

Wherever a new building was going up or outside repairs were being carried out, the scaffolding was topped with small branches of trees or shrubbery, so that the devils flying overhead would think it was a glade and not descend to cause accidents. Bridges were built with angles so that the devils, unable to turn corners, would fall into the water. Similarly devils could be kept out of a house by building a gateway, but no wall, just in front of the entrance. The devils would have to fly upwards and over the roofs.

Small boys were dressed like girls and hung with jewelry so that the devils would not bother with them. Loud noises like clanging tin cans or popping firecrackers would frighten the devils away. Even the evil Fox Spirit who dared now and then to try to gain power by swallowing the moon could be driven away by enough bedlam in the streets below. It seemed to me very fortunate that devils were so easily fooled and I wondered if the "foreign devils," so named because so many had the legendary blue "devil's eyes," had been as easily handled by the Chinese of their day.

Devils invaded our own home and sometimes I was able to outwit them. The electric iron was bewitched. "Please Missy, this i-lon all time walkie-walkie, bitee me." I bought a stand which kept the iron in its place and scotched that devil. Then there was the electric stove which Amah said, "All time velly quick makee jump bitee me." This was a puzzle until one day I noticed her shuffling slippered walk. A rubber mat in front of the stove mastered that one.

Soon after we hired Ah Zee, our plump coolie amah, she came to grief because of the devils. She was shaking a rug from our big balcony one morning and suddenly came hurrying inside and through to the kitchen with one hand over her eyes. Moments later Amah appeared to report that "something badee have go Ah Zee eye."

"Dust," I said. "Get this eye wash bottle—"

"No, Missy. This no belong dust." She smiled diffidently. "English Missy no savvy this. Outside have got plenty something badee, have go Ah Zee eye."

I recognized our unfriendly neighbourhood devil. "What do you want to do?"

She explained that she and Ah Zee must go by rickshaw to the nearest temple. "Must pay money, catchee light, makee oil. One dlop this oil go Ah Zee eye, something badee go 'way."

"How long will you be?"

"Please Missy, one half hour can do."

"Okay, 'way you go."

They were back, crestfallen, in twenty-five minutes. The something badee was still in Ah Zee's eye. We tried the eye wash and fortunately it was quickly effective.

Much later, the devils were Ah Zee's undoing. One day Amah reported that Ah Zee was very sick. Standing pink-cheeked in the kitchen doorway, Ah Zee did not look sick. Amah said that Ah Zee had seen a Chinese doctor who had told her that there was no blood in her body, that she would makee die. She must go homeside to the village near Hangchow and Amah must go with her.

"Oh, Amah, how fashion no got blood?"

"This blood all have go way. Yesterday night, Ah Zee loom, one hand have come, touch Ah Zee—"

"Who belong this hand?"

"Nobody belong. Just this hand have got. Ah Zee much fear, no can sleep she loom. Have come my loom, all night stay floorside my loom."

This was a bit beyond me. Amah said they would be away for three or four days. I said I would have to ask Master.

Jim's reaction dismayed me. He said no. Amah could not leave at this time and if Ah Zee was so sick she must be paid her wages to date and leave immediately. He explained to me that the story was obviously poppycock. There was some celebration in the village, perhaps a wedding, which the amahs wished to attend, and while he would agree that they might go if they told the truth about it, he would not be put upon by a story of a devil's hand. Ah Zee, he said, must be off our premises by seven o'clock next morning.

I was horrified. Ah Zee recovered rapidly, her blood miraculously returned. She was all smiles and eager to go to work, but Jim would not relent. Seven o'clock next morning was the deadline and Amah must get busy at once and find a replacement. It happened as he ordered. Ah Zee showed up in the kitchen next morning and hung around wistfully for two or three days but I ignored her and Amah meekly barred her from doing any work. An older cousin of Amah's, quiet and efficient, took her place. However, she too slept on the floor of Amah's room and Ah Zee's room remained unoccupied.

Somehow, too, the devils disappeared. If any caused trouble in our small household, Jim and I did not hear about them.

Chang, Jim's senior Chinese foreman, introduced me to the temples and the gods. The yellow pages of the telephone book listed more than thirty Chinese temples in the Settlement, and there must have been many more gods that did not have temples.

Chang was thin, knock-kneed and cross-eyed and remarkably erudite. At one time he had been married to a Russian woman and spoke that language fluently. He also had a working knowledge of each of China's thirty district dialects. Now he had two Chinese wives, the Russian having left him for another husband. He assured Jim that having two wives was a very good idea. "My two wives like sisters, all time talk together, no bother me." He brought his Number One wife to visit me but explained that his younger Number Two wife did not rate this privilege. Number One gave me a very beautiful green jade and gold ring, saying in her gentle hesitant English that it was her own and she liked it very much but, "I wish to give you something near my heart." I gave her a Spode plate that had been cherished by my mother. Amah served tea and small Chinese cakes she had been commissioned to buy. She brought, too, some white lilies for Chang's Number One wife and made the whole occasion exquisite.

By Jim's arrangement, Chang came one afternoon with Jim's Council car and chauffeur and took me to a small temple in Chinese territory. He said it was not the biggest but he thought it the most beautiful in Shanghai. It was dim, fragrant with incense and richly carpeted. Everything in it was painted dark red or green or gleaming gold.

One wall was entirely occupied by a giant figure of Buddha—Gautama Buddha, the Great One—its head lost in the shadows of the ceiling but the whites of the eyes showing. In front of the Buddha, four on one side and four on the other, were life-size figures of other gods. Said Chang, gesturing, "He is the great Judge, and these—these are like the lawyers."

Mr. Choy in Fred Baker's office had introduced me to the eight Major Deities of his faith. I had been fascinated by what he told me. Now I was able to recognize and identify them easily. Chang expanded on what I knew. The gods included the terrifying God of Thunder; the hideously grimacing God of War who was also the god of

money; the God of Hell, also the god of sorrow; the God
of Literature, patron of scholars, also the god of water. I
could not see this connection and Chang could not explain it. Opposite these were the God of the Eastern Sky,
sunrise and the beginning of life; the fat, well-satisfied
God of Earthly Happiness, signifying children; the God
of Fields, Soil and Grain; and Kuan Yin, Goddess of Mercy and spiritual purity, the mother figure.

Mr. Choy had told me, "Some scholars argue that she
should be a god, not a goddess, for it is not fitting that a
woman should rank among he gods. But the Chinese
people have always said no man could ever be as merciful
as Kuan Yin. She is the marriage of the earth and the
sun, loving all things and bringing fruition."

Kuan Yin was sometimes called the Lotus Princess. I
had read that she lived on an island in the Yangtse Kiang
called Pootoo which was so swampy it was covered with
lotus plants. The goddess is often depicted sitting cross-
legged on a lotus lily pad holding on her crossed open
palms the lily bulb. On our country walks Jim and I often
saw the lotus growing in village ponds which drained all
surface water. There would be patches of thick green
scum, ducks paddling busily making soft throaty noises,
a woman at the pond's edge washing clothes in a froth of

150

soap chatting with a neighbour who rinsed rice or greens held in a sieve of split bamboo. A few feet away floated the lotus leaf, large as a dinner plate with a stem the circumference of one's little finger rising two to three feet and bearing the fragrant bloom of waxen flawlessness, white pale rose or tender yellow. The saying was, that just as the lotus rises above the pond to bloom in perfect purity, so should the human spirit rise above the troubles of every-day life to flower in spiritual beauty.

Chang had a more earthy story to tell about a very different God. Lightly brushing with his fingertips the polished swollen belly of the God of Earthly Happiness, or Prosperity, he said, "He used to like to walk among the people as a man. One day he came to a river where women and girls were running in and out, in and out again. He asked why they did that and they said it would make

151

them fertile. The God laughed and asked, 'Would it do the same for me?' He too ran into the river and came out as you see."

Smiling into the roguish face of the Happy God, Chang added softly, "At least seven months, I would say."

17

THE WILD GOOSE
NEVER LAID
A TAME EGG

-Irish

RESTLESS AFTER MORE THAN four years service during the First War, Jim went to China in 1922 with an introduction in his pocket to Major Hilton-Johnson, deputy Commisioner in the Shanghai Municipal Police.

Also in his pocket was a British Columbia Teacher's Certificate, an appointment to a school in South Vancouver and $200. His trip to China was made on impulse. Four days before school opened—a prospect Jim did not find alluring—he happened to meet a man who served with him in the trenches and who had signed on for a trip to the Orient as a crewman with the Canadian Marine Service. "We need men," he told Jim. "Why don't you come along?"

Jim went with him to the wharf where two hundred unemployed had collected looking for work. The ship's boatswain came to the rail and picked three men—the third was Jim. For thirty days he shovelled coal as the ship moved up the B.C. coast loading lumber and then sailed across the northern Pacific to Japan and China. At Shanghai, last port of call before the return home, the ship anchored in midstream of Yangtsepoo.

After shore leave, Jim returned to his Captain and asked for permission to sign off. It was refused: the crew had been hired for the round trip. Jim told the Captain he could keep Jim's pay. Finally it was agreed that Jim could "go over the side" provided the Captain did not know, and a replacement was made for the trip back to

153

Canada—the ship sailed with a convenient stowaway.

Jim presented his letter to Major Hilton-Johnson. The Major turned him down. "Canadians and Americans are unreliable," he said. "They sign on and then in a couple of months find things boring, get drunk, start brawling. We have to fire them and ship them home, and it isn't worth the money."

Jim assured him this would not happen, and posted as security enough money to cover his passage home if needed. He was hired by the force and sent to training school.

Major Hilton-Johnson, whom Jim described as a small man with a big brain, had been commanding officers of the Wei Hai Wei regiment at the British northern naval base. All members of this regiment were northern Chinese at least six feet tall, and under its rather diminutive c.o. it earned an enviable reputation for efficiency.

Some famous men came from the Shanghai Police Force. Inspector Fairburn, who was in charge of the Police Training School in the 1920's, wore the brown belt of Japanese Judo: he was later instrumental in forming the Commandos of the Second World War. Paddy O' Neil, also a Brown Belt, became instructor in self-defence for the New York Police. Elementary Judo was one of the first skills taught at the Police Training School.

The force of six thousand men was semi-military in organization. Men of all nationalities could apply, but entrance requirements were strict. Rigorous discipline in all ranks, relatively poor pay and unquestioned authority in maintaining law and order in the Settlement ensured that those who served with the police were dedicated men.

Single men lived in barracks attached to ten police stations located in various districts. Each barracks had its own mess, contracted for its own food and engaged its own cooks. Men were usually assigned to the barracks according to their nationality and the predominant nationality of the surrounding district. There were Japanese policemen in Hongkew District. All over the Settlement there were hundreds of stalwart Chinese policemen most from northern China, taller and heavier built than their countrymen in the south.

A Chinese university student once told me that "it was said" by scholars that those raised in a northern climate and fed on wheat and millet rather than rice grew up to be soldiers, robbers or policemen.

The religion of Southern China was mainly Buddhism, but the northerners were followers of Islam, one of the world's fighting religions. The spirit of Genghis Khan and his Mongolians was tamed when Buddhism and rice were introduced into the north, the student said. The true Buddhist would not take life although in defence of his beliefs he might sacrifice his own.

Other Moslems on the police force came from the northwest regions of India. There were also about seven hundred Sikhs, British army-trained and valued for their loyalty and discipline, maintained as a reserve in case other police elements ever went on strike. The Sikhs and the Moslems did not get along: when they came together there was trouble, Moslems knives flashing readily. So the handsome, bearded Sikhs, in navy blue uniforms with bright silver buttons, were kept in Central District on traffic duty, while the Moslems were employed as wardens in the gaol on Ward Road in Wayside, south of Hongkew. "Biggest gaol in the world," some boasted: six thousand prisoners and all put there by Chinese magistrates.

These were the magistrates of the Mixed Court who tried Chinese offenders and others, like the Russians, who had no extra-territorial rights. A British magistrate always sat on the bench of the Mixed Court, playing no official role but ensuring justice by Settlement standards. Offenders who did have extra-territorial rights were tried in their own courts, and kept if necessary in cells at the consulates for short terms or shipped out to serve longer sentences in Hong Kong, Manila, or Portuguese Macao.

Jim always hailed the Sikh constables on the traffic islands with a cheery greeting, calling them "Gemidah," promoting them to Sergeants which made them grin. One day as we waited to make a turn in busy traffic he raised the rank.

"Afternoon, Havidah."

The familiar grin beneath the turban vanished. "No,

A Settlement Mounted Policeman on Bubbling Well Road.

no, sahib," sighed the imposing looking officer. "No can poor Indian man do superintend police!" Then he stopped the steady stream of traffic and sent us on our way.

Most British members of the police force were assigned to special duties. Soon after he left training school Jim was loaned to the Health Department as a guard in the mental ward of the nuns' big General Hospital. Patients included religious melancholics, who were often Eurasians; alcoholics and syphilitics 'with brains permanently damaged,' and once a man from the interior who had contracted rabies, "the most terrible death," said Jim, "that I have ever seen."

He stayed on this job for eighteen months with only one day off in all that time, but he said he did not mind it. He knew nobody in Shanghai, nuns and nurses were pleasant companions and he had time to study his Chinese. He became fluent in the Shanghai dialect, said to be a polyglot of the thirty other dialects spoken in the rest of China. His knowledge of colloquialisms and some rude phrases made him popular among the rank and file with whom he later worked. He could call a man a "bung nautse," or stupid brain, for instance; or "gong du," hollow head; or "huh shing," black heart or cruel man. These expressions were not found in the text books. Another which he admitted he did not learn from the

156

nuns was "ts-nu-pi," a braggart, literally a man blowing wind up a cow's backside. When he suddenly came out with such unexpected street talk, always said with a grin, the Chinese laughed gleefully and loved him. When his required term of three years ended, Jim transferred to the Food Control Division in the Health Department.

On one occasion a Chinese loafer was lounging against our parked car. Jim told him to "chi-chi-ley," or get away, and the man, staying where he was, answered rudely. The instant crowd surrounded the two men. Jim, not grinning now, said one word and the loafer slunk away sheepishly while the crowd roared approval. As we drove away I asked Jim what he had called the man, and he said, "The worst thing you can call a Chinese, just 'a Thing'."

Augmenting Settlement defenses was a British regiment, which changed every year, and a detachment of U.S. Marines. These garrisons had only been stationed in Shanghai since 1927 when they were rushed in from Singapore and Manila as Chiang Kai Shek's army approached the city. They were not needed: the Settlement was not molested and Chinese areas around it surrendered readily, conquered, they said, by the Generalissimo's honeyed words. However, the garrisons stayed.

The popular feeling of security rested with the Volunteer Corps. Tensions and war scares flared periodically, but the Corps was the barometer the people trusted. No situation was really serious unless the Volunteers were mobilized.

Some three thousand unpaid members drilled hard. Jim belonged to the artillery and paraded three times a week. Every Tuesday night there was riding school, every Thursday gun drill. On Sunday mornings, rain or shine, the artillery was in the country outside the city for field drill. Jim's work often kept him up all Saturday night but that made no difference. He never missed Sunday morning field drill.

The Artillery were equipped with four horse-drawn 4.5 Howitzers on loan from the British Army. Four men were attached to each gun, Number Four man being the man who actually fired the cannon. Jim was Number Four man on Number Three gun. On special occasions when the big guns fired a salvo, I learned to count the seconds between the booms and was triumphant on the day that I detected that Number Two gun misfired and Number Three filled in a split second later.

When the British reclaimed the Howitzers and the artillery was disbanded Jim joined the Transport Company because, he said, he wanted to learn to drive the giant army trucks.

Various units of the Volunteers drilled separately, but once a year the Corps paraded and crowds lined Bubbling Well Road the entire length of the parade route from the big Bubbling Well Police Station to the final disbanding at the Race Course. Since Jim held non-commissioned rank we did not have to stand on the street but were admitted to the special enclosure near the saluting base in front of the British Country Club. For a wife like me, plagued with either pregnancy or small children, this was a great boon.

The Chairman of the Municipal Council, whatever his nationality, took the salute. With him on the dais was the Corps' commanding officer, detached from the British army and specially sent from England with adjutant armed sergeant-major to supervise the training of the Volunteers.

Several bands marched with the parade; the U.S. Marine Band, the British Navy Band, the fife and drums if they were in garrison, the Municipal Firemen's Band, the Cadets' Band, the kilted pipers and several others.

First Militia unit following the lead band was always the Light Horse, nearly all members of the Race Club, spruce and disciplined, on Mongolian mounts groomed till they shone like polished leather. Immediately behind them came the American cavalry unit, similarly mounted, similarly disciplined, wearing broad-brimmed hats. After a brief pause the horse-drawn Howitzers went by at a lively gallop.

Next came the Armoured Cars, the Machine Gun Company close behind carrying their shining Lewis machine guns. Many of those in the Machine Gun Company were Swiss, German and other Europeans not numerous enough to form units of their own.

The turbanned mounted Sikhs carried lances with pennants flying.

There were seven companies of infantry. Two were British, one American, one Portuguese, one Japanese, one Chinese, and the paid Russian permanent force. The Russians were mercenaries ready for combat anywhere in the China Seas they might be needed. Twenty to thirty of these men were regularly employed by Canadian Empresses and other passenger vessels sailing between Nagasaki and Hong Kong in case pirates, aided by other Chinese shipping as third-class passengers, tried to take over the ship. The professional Russians, who usually came last in the parade, were by far the best marchers. The sound of their feet was like the sound of drums and the deepening beat could be heard approaching long before they came into view.

We were proud of the Shanghai Volunteers. To his Military Medal and service medals of the First World War Jim added two more from the Volunteers.

18

A MAN
IS NOT KNOWN
TILL HE TAKES
A WIFE

-French

BEFORE THE TWINS WERE BORN, while I was still at Baker Agency, Big Alice from the library phoned and asked me to tea. I was casting about for the most courteous "no"—something which never bothered Jim—when Alice added that Mrs. Fairfax was coming and wanted to meet me. Mr. Fairfax was the head of the print shop at the Agency. We worked together sometimes on matters of type-face and white space, and I was interested in meeting his wife.

Alice said arrangements had been made for the next afternoon and since her place was hard to find it would be best if I came to the library when it closed at four-thirty and followed her rickshaw to her apartment. Jim could pick me up at six-thirty. I demurred on the grounds that our office did not close till five, but she answered, "Ask Freddie—he won't mind," and seemed to feel the matter settled. I did ask Fred Baker who agreed readily. He said it was just as well to be friendly with Alice—her tongue circulated as well as her books.

Our rickshaws travelled north, crossed Avenue Edward VII and entered a series of narrow streets in the French Concession. The address had a lane number, as well as a street name and house number. A terrace of miniature houses were fronted by tiny gardens enclosed in high, woven bamboo fences. Our rickshaw stopped beside one, Alice paid her puller for both of us and opened the gate for me. About six steps took us to the front door. It all seemed incongruously small for anyone as big as Alice.

The house had two rooms, one on the ground floor, one on the second. There was no hall. A rather delicate stairway hugged one wall to a landing where two doors opened, one to a little bathroom, one to the bedroom. Downstairs, the kitchen alcove was under the bathroom.

I left my hat on Alice's bed, washed my hands and combed my hair and followed her down the stairs again. It was harder going down than up, the stairs appeared more fragile, and it seemed unsafe for the two of us to be on them at the same time.

Mrs. Fairfax, a blonde English woman, stood up from a chair in one corner, and another young woman whom Alice introduced as her assistant, Louella, was also introduced. Like Alice, she was Australian.

The furniture was mostly of wicker with several small tables crowded with Chinese oddments. Alice waved us to seats and lowered herself onto an ottoman which she overflowed like the cap of a fat mushroom on a short stem. A Chinese Boy unfolded legs from a teatray and set it beside her and she began to fill cups which the Boy passed to us.

"You must excuse the furniture," Alice explained to me. "It's all Bobby's. I'm sure he picked it up at the second-hand stores on Peking Road, anything cheap—you know how men are. The lease is his, too, and he pays the rent, so I can't complain."

In Shanghai, foreigners could not buy a house, only a lease which would expire when the Treaty expired. As the Boy passed us exquisite hot biscuits Alice went on explaining.

"I have a Sea Captain friend, Aussie like us. He's Deep Sea so he only gets into Shanghai about twice a year. He was sending me money to pay for an apartment where he could stay with me when he came to town. I just couldn't find a place I liked until I found these little houses, but all of them were booked up. Then I heard that Bobby wanted to sell his lease, but when I found him he said no, he didn't. He suggested I move in with him, bank the Deep Sea's money, then when he wrote that he was coming, go out and rent something posh. It sounded like a good idea, so that's what I did."

"Would have been good, too," Louella asserted, "if the Deep Sea had given you warning."

"Yes, but you see, he didn't," Alice told me. "Suddenly one morning the Boy told us his ship had arrived in the river. It was Saturday, too, no chance to go to the bank, no chance to do anything. I told Bobby he would just have to clear out to the Y and he got sticky. I was frantic. Finally he went and the Boy and I just flew around trying to get rid of any trace of him. I'd given the Deep Sea this address to send the cheques to, thinking I would say I'd moved when he came—all he had to do was arrive any minute."

Louella nodded. "I helped. I had to rush around waving one of Bobby's handkerchiefs soaked in eau de cologne to get rid of his pipe smell."

"It would have been so much easier," Alice said, "if Bobby smoked cigarettes but he stuck to that haystack pipe of his."

I saw Mrs. Fairfax looking at me sideways to see how I was reacting to all this and since I did not know her at all I tried to be noncommittal. "It does seem a bit inconsiderate to smoke a pipe under the circumstances."

"However," Alice continued, "we managed. The Boy cooked a nice dinner for the two of us here, and the Captain was pleased I had such a nice place. He even said it would be a good place to retire to, which he plans to do in about three years. Then, about two in the morning, Bobby came back. He stood out in the lane and shouted and shouted and the neighbours opened their windows and shouted things too and the Deep Sea wanted to call the police. I didn't want that because then Bobby would say it was his place, so I told him Bobby was a syphilitic who did strange things when the moon was full, and after a while things quietened down and Bobby went away."

Louella nodded, "Smart!"

Alice said moodily, "It would have been if I'd left out the moon, perhaps. I should have remembered that as a Master Mariner the Deep Sea would know when the moon was full. He was cool all day and that night, but Bobby came back with a cornet which he blew, and the neighbours called the police, and Bobby did say it was his place. So the Deep packed his bag and walked out."

Now *I* was looking sideways, but nobody was laughing. Louella looked sorry for Alice and Mrs. Fairfax was studying a plate of lemon cake the Boy was offering her.

Mrs. Fairfax began to talk about the problem of women when their children reached nine or ten years of age and had to go away to boarding school. They wanted their children in private schools and the only close one, on Wei Hai Wei Island off the northern coast of China, was often full. So mothers had to take their nine-year-olds back to England or the States and settle them in. school there. This left their husbands alone in Shanghai.

Even before the *Empress of Russia* had reached Shanghai, fellow passengers had told me about the Russian women who, being stateless without the security of any government behind them, were desperate to make a foreign marriage—Portugese, perhaps, or British or American. Before a wife's ship was out of the river, it was said, there would be a Russian woman in her bed. You couldn't blame the husbands, I was told: it was the climate. It did something to men.

Now Mrs. Fairfax told of a tragedy that had happened in her apartment building only a week earlier. A mother returning from England with her two youngest children had not been met at the ship by her husband. Thinking him delayed by business and anxious to get the children home she left the luggage to be collected later and took a taxi to the apartment. A Russian woman in a dressing gown was sipping coffee in the dining room. The wife did not wait for explanations. She took the two children with her in the elevator as far up as it would go, walked the short flight of stairs to the roof of the ten-storey building. Holding a child's hand tightly in each of hers, she jumped off. The story had not been told in the papers.

You couldn't blame the men, said Louella—it was the climate, and it affected all of them. She had a friend who lived in an apartment where the bathroom walls were just partitions, not reaching to the ceiling. There was about a foot of open space and one afternoon when she had nothing to do, she relaxed for a sit-and-soak bath.

As she lay back she happened to look up and there was the cook-boy watching over the wall. She realized it was probably not the first time he had done it—he had been so quiet and organized. He must have had a ladder hidden nearby. When their eyes met, he smiled merrily. She didn't know what to do, as he was a good cook-boy and her husband liked his cooking. She didn't want to fire him, but decided to show him that he did not count as a man with her; his function was that of cook-boy. She told—not asked—him to prepare coffee as quickly as possible and serve it in the living room. She was in a hurry to go out. He disappeared and she dressed quickly, drank her cup of coffee and spent the rest of the afternoon looking for an apartment with ceiling-high bathroom walls. Then she persuaded her husband to move.

On the drive home Jim did not laugh about the Sea Captain and Bobby's cornet. He said he knew Bobby, a gutless wonder who must have been drunk to go as far as he had. Where was he living now? I had asked Alice the same question and she had said that she "let him come back." After all, he paid the rent.

Jim wondered whether Alice was a nice friend for me, but he had nothing to worry about. She and I were not drawn to each other and though we met cordially our friendship went no deeper. About a year after the tea-party she went to New Zealand and we heard later that she had found her Sea Captain again and they were living happily together there in his retirement.

I did not think that it was the weather that gave Shanghai its worldwide reputation for immorality. I felt it was the fact that nobody really cared. Public opinion is the most powerful legislator, and in a community where so many varying customs and codes were conscientiously tolerated, each lived by his own moral code. Perhaps some of it was due to the lack of organized religion among foreigners.

Shanghai, city with so many names, bright lights and sinister shadows, could in no way be described as a city of churches. The telephone directory, my personal mirror of life in the crowded metropolis, listed only thirty— including mosques, Russian Orthodox churches and missions, Christian Scientists, a Japanese church and several synagogues.

Out in the country small temples were distinguished by their colour. They were built like the country people's homes, but with three walls only, usually painted orange or bright yellow. They contained only a Buddha figure with a kneeling bench in front of it. Worshippers stopped there any time, it seemed, day or night. We learned that there had been such a temple beside the Bubbling Well since Christ walked the hills above Jerusalem. It was listed as the earliest historical site in Shanghai.

Jim was born a Roman Catholic, but the First War had turned him away from any concept of a divinity: "If there were a God He would not allow such things to happen." My parents were devout Anglicans, and the simple faith I had met in country churches on my visits to England warmed and attracted me; but I was also impressed by the quiet unwavering regard for long-held traditions practised by Jews I had known and the burning zeal shown by Hindu leaders.

In Shanghai, faith was apparent in many unexpected places. Although there were only thirty churches, on nearly every street in the huge, busy city a small shallow shrine containing a statue of Buddha would be sandwiched between adjacent stores, and men and women in the jostling crowds would reach out and touch the Buddha as they passed. The bases of these statues had all acquired a high polish from the light pressure of countless fingers.

When, soon after my arrival in Shanghai, I had sought guidance in the big red-brick church, I had been dismayed by the clergyman's purely secular interpretation of my moral dilemma. As I grew to know Shanghai better, I ceased to be surprised by the role of his church in the community. The social columns of the newspapers often included items about parties or dances held at the church, listing the names of prominent people attending them. The name of the minister often appeared among those at fashionable cocktail parties.

Those who did "belong" to various churches found satisfaction in them. It seemed to us that this satisfaction was too often a cloak of respectability, or a protective mantle to shut out fears. Sometimes it was a relaxing outlet for the emotions. In the Russian churches where we went infrequently with Onya and Bloomie there was no organ and seemed to be no leadership. Everybody sang with fervour. Onya sang with others around us in Russian: she knew the words. Bloomie boomed in a happy bass, belting out la-dee-da's or o-da-dee's. Even Jim who might have been an Irish tenor if he had been taught when young, sang along something of his own—sometimes even rather bawdy army songs. I found myself repeating in a silent rhythm, "If you are anywhere help me to see."

I felt that true religion was best expressed by those unnoticed few of many different faiths who tried to offer service to their fellows. They had no money; nobody wrote about them or talked about them; they were shabby young clergy, or nuns, or priests following different prophets, or Salvation Army personnel. Father Jacquinot, one-handed shepherd of the Roman Catholic church in Hongkew, was known to work devotedly among the poor, but the numbers of the poor were overwhelming. He was a very small wave fighting a mighty current.

Secretly I resolved that if I were ever left alone in Shanghai I would dedicate myself to the beggar babies, but I never was left alone. Once married, my innermost need to be of service was fully occupied. We agreed to "belong" to no church.

19

A WRATHFUL MAN
STIRRETH UP
STRIFE

-King Solomon's Proverb

OUR FIRST HOLIDAY IN JAPAN, which we counted as our official honeymoon, was a tale of enchantment.

We went in 1934—before the hostilities of the late thirties—taking the *Shanghai Maru*, an overnight ferry to Nagasaki, then the small Japanese train which followed the western coastline of Kyushu Island northward. At a shed-like station several hundred feet above the narrow coastal plain, a Japanese in coloured cotton coat bowed and smiled us to an open touring car and drove us to the sea.

The hotel was built on the sand in a grove of long-limbed but low-standing pine trees which had been twisted into grotesque shapes by the sea winds. There were two wings in the hotel, one for foreign guests with foreign-style furniture and flush toilets which did not work too well, and one for Japanese guests where everything was Japanese style and worked perfectly. There was a connecting wing containing six rooms on two floors, Japanese in style but available to foreigners. After two nights in the foreign wing, we were able to move to a second-floor room in this central wing. It opened through sliding panels onto a narrow balcony which overlooked a rock garden where black and gold dragonflies danced by day and glow-worms jigged at night. The room contained no furniture except a child-size bureau with mirror and a jar containing a spray of flowers in an alcove raised about six inches above the floor. In the

167

evening Japanese maids or Nei Sans in bright flowered kimonos pulled quilts from behind sliding panels in one wall and spread them on the springy tatami floor.

Beyond the twisted pines on the white sand beach was the sky-blue Sea of China to the west, and to the south a soft smudge which was the small city of Karatsu. We were told that Chinese writing and other culture found its way to Japan during the sixth and seventh centuries A.D.

We swam, lay in the sun, walked for miles in our identical outfits of white cotton shorts and shirts, straw hats and sandals. At the opposite end of the beach from Karatsu a small fishing village cuddled under the hills like leaves blown together in a hollow in autumn. We prowled the narrow lanes among the little homes with their individual gardens designed, it was explained to us, to express the owner's philosophy or life story: hills and hollows, rough pebbles or smooth raked sand, rivers of prosperity marked by white stones.

Early in the morning, a fishing fleet of five or six boats put out to sea. Late in the afternoon, when the women were on the beach with their small children, all golden naked, the women's hair gleaming in puffs and coils on their heads, the boats came home again. (I learned since, that in the 7th and 8th centuries when Chinese culture entered Japan through the port of Karatsu, Chinese women were wearing their hair in just such puffs and coils. The fashions changed in China but persisted in Japan for 1200 years.)

Everyone, including us, went into the sea thigh-deep to help haul in the nets. To us the catch seemed extraordinarily meagre, but all the Japanese were pleased. Always they made the same comment, which we memorized and learned meant, "All in the village will eat tonight."

Twice we went with other hotel guests by chartered bus to Karatsu, once for suki yaki and another time to see the Lantern Boats; but all these pleasant outings were interrupted by a dramatic event.

Among the guests in the foreign wing were an American and his Russian wife. She had a wardrobe of fashion-plate clothes, broad-brimmed hats, floating scarves, silks and chiffons and nearly always a matching inflated beach ball. Her attitude to domestic discipline was simple: if her husband displeased her she went to bed and stayed there until he was able to placate her.

We heard the Emperor's two brothers were coming to stay in the Japanese wing and the Russian woman urged her husband to transfer to that wing so that they could later say they had stayed in the same house as Royalty. Security was tight and the management unwilling, but somehow they managed it. The husband went to Karatsu by himself and came back with a set of clothing which he said was a countryman's outfit. The foreign guests admired it but his wife was furious. She stormed "I try to dress like a lady and you—you dress like a coolie!" and then retired to bed. Jim and I wondered if she remembered that her bed was now on the floor.

But the little Nei Sans tittered softly together when he went by. I had made friends with one who spoke a little English and she explained that the outfit he had chosen was actually cold-weather underwear. It was as though he was parading proudly in long johns.

As long as he wore his peasant outfit his wife stayed in bed and he walked morosely among the pine trees by himself. Then one morning he came across a large snake and killed it. Suddenly, most of the foreign guests deemed him a hero, and his wife came down to breakfast....

But the Nei Sans were crying and the men of the staff were glum. The manager Hironda San told us all that the snake was a pet and had lived under the hotel for more than twenty years. He said it was to be given a ceremonial burial: would the guests please stay away? From a distance, we watched as the staff gathered around a tract of sand about ten feet square which was then enclosed with a fence. All the women were crying.

An announcement was posted at the office door. The death of the snake was a great tragedy, and since bad things come in threes, guests were asked not to leave the premises, not to go swimming, nor fishing, until the other two accidents had happened. The rowboats were locked up; a wire was sent to the Emperor's brothers advising them to postpone their visit. Of course the Russian wife went back to bed. The bored guests, with the

exception of Jim, soon ostracized the unfortunate American. Jim shared with him a common glee in the Russian woman's displeasure at having her bed on the floor and from that went on to other interests. He was a cigarette salesman and had stories to tell of his adventures in China's interior provinces.

Two dull days crawled by. Then a motorist ran into a tree on the road in front of the hotel and had to be taken to hospital. Tension increased as we waited for the third disaster. It happened on the third day at dinner time. The head cook spilled a pot of boiling soup over his arms and was badly scalded.

We could not help ourselves. We were overjoyed. The little Nei Sans, smiling, said the cook had done it on purpose and was a hero. They started a collection for him and everyone responded generously. The rowboats were unlocked; some men went fishing in the dusk; we heard that the Emperor's brothers would be arriving next day—and the Russian wife dressed and appeared for dessert.

Jim ordered two horses with western saddles and said we were going for a cowboy gallop along the beach. I was not a very good rider and afraid of a linguistic problem between my horse and myself. Both mounts were unshod stallions who snapped and kicked at each other if they came too close. Fortunately, the low-tide sands were hard and smooth, and my horse and I got along quite well.

Hironda San, the hotel manager, had a problem. Each night after dinner, with his kimono tucked up into his waistband, he went off among the twisted pines with a bottle of saki in each hand and came back staggering. However, he never forgot his responsibilities to his guests and when some of us, jubilant in our release from the Bondage of Doom, elected to go to Karatsu by bus with some of the Nei Sans to see the Lantern Boats, Hironda San came with us.

The Lantern Boat Festival was celebrated when the moon was full at the end of August. It commemorated sailors and fishermen who had died at sea. The boats, big and little, were made of straw, furnished with short candles in paper lanterns and carried greetings and gifts of cakes and rice wine. Anyone who had lost a relative or friend could make a boat, or pay to have one made, and launch it when the tide was high and ready to turn to sea again. At Karatsu in 1934 that time coincided with the moon rise. There was not a cloud, no wind. The unruffled sea shone like glass and the incredible moon, as big as a wagon wheel, hung just above the horizon as men, women and children in their bright traditional costumes waded into the shallows and launched their light boats. The hope was that the boat would stay afloat on the tide until the candles burned low and straw and paper lantern went up in flames, but this did not happen too often. Too many boats capsized and sank too soon, but no one ever seemed to think their mission had not been accomplished. It was a happy crowd.

Unable to express our pleasure, Jim and I stood unobstrusively holding hands; and then my Nei San was beside us, bowing not to me but to Jim. "Please! Hironda San!" It seemed the bus was ready to take us home, most of the passengers were on board, but Hironda San was not—the young girl mimed drinking from a bottle.

Jim told me he would meet me at the bus and went off to get help. I was in my seat when I saw him coming with another tall man, each with one of Hironda San's arms over his shoulder, actually carrying him, his feet just clear of the ground. They put him in the front seat, where he sat meekly. At the hotel two Nei Sans guided him indoors, his knees bending and buckling so that he sagged first against one, then against the other. We heard him say, in English, "I am so-o-o tired."

At 5:30 the next morning we stood again at the high railway shed, the hills around us and the sea below all tinted by the sunrise. Bare-legged, kimono hem tucked into belt, Hironda San approached us, his little bald spot touched by lavender rays. In each hand he carried by the neck a large bottle of beer. With a deep bow he thrust one at Jim and drank from the other.

"Beer before breakfast!" exclaimed Jim. "Thank you, no!" But the manager backed away and the train came gasping and rattling around a bend and we carried the bottle on board. The coach was divided, European-style,

171

into compartments. Jim headed down the corridor and gave the bottle to the first white man he saw. The man was travelling with three gracious ladies and when he accepted the beer eyes wide, all four faces expressed open-mouthed astonishment.

Two years later, in 1936, we again took a short leave to Japan, hoping to avoid the searing heat of August in Shanghai.

The twins were almost fourteen months old, old enough to travel safely, we felt. We asked Amah if she would like to come too, and she agreed readily. Again we took the overnight ferry, but next morning instead of the day-long train trip to Karatsu, a taxi took us in twenty minutes from the Nagasaki dockside to a small fishing village called Mogi (not to be confused with Moji, a large seaport further north). In Mogi there was a hotel popular with Shanghai foreigners and again we booked a Japanese-style room.

There were only four or five lane-wide streets in Mogi. Nearly all the men were fishermen, in and out of the water most of the day as they worked around their boats. They wore only loin cloths tied up in front like puddings.

Amah was prepared to disapprove of everything Japanese and quickly voiced her disdain.

"This Japanese man all time no get clo'es!"

I agreed that it was so.

Amah said severly, "My homeside suppose somebody go this fashion, maybe somebody can smackee he."

"My homeside too, Amah."

We had little time, however, to compare travel notes. The twins had taken ill.

It was a nightmare experience. They sickened so rapidly—feverish, crying, retching, straining. By noon we were asking for a doctor. Concerned, the manager, who was also the owner of the hotel, explained that the village doctor was away. He would put in a call to Nagasaki, but it might be tomorrow before the doctor could come. Remembering Baby Row in Bubbling Well Cemetery I was sure that by tomorrow the babies would be dead. During that night they began to pass blood. Amah, Jim and I stayed with them all night, easing them and each other as best we could.

Very early in the morning I slipped away to the hotel dock for a dip in the clean refreshing sea, for there were no showers in the Beach Hotel. Another white woman was there, not swimming, just taking the air, she said. She was a large motherly woman, square-shouldered, square-hipped, and soon I was pouring out my anxieties. She told me, "Well, I'm not a doctor nor even a registered nurse, but for years I've been a practical nurse in Tientsin, and I can tell you how we've saved hundreds of babies.

"Half a teaspoon of powdered raw arrowroot in a cupful of boiled water," she said. "Offer it in a baby bottle. Even though they are long weaned, little ones find comfort in a bottle. Then a very little grated raw apple. Even half a teaspoonful of grated apple would help. Ask Susie San, the housekeeper, about the arrowroot. She'll have some, or get some—the Japanese use it in cooking."

I rushed to tell Amah, who rushed to find Susie San. Impossibly soon, the two women appeared with two baby bottles and a small covered china dish. The children, who had refused to eat or drink anything since we arrived, took the bottles eagerly. Susie San held one baby, Amah the other. Jim and I just sat and watched.

The babies were more comfortable. They even slept a little, curled on the quilt beside me. Amah and the housekeeper departed with bottles and apple jar. Jim, who always wore a blue and white cotton Japanese kimono at home as a robe, donned one now and went to find a place to shave. In two hours, on the dot, Amah was back again with fresh arrowroot and apple. The children slept again, Jim went down to breakfast and Amah brought a tray for me. The doctor's visit was cancelled.

During the morning the nurse from Tientsin came to see us. She said she thought the children would be all right now; we could try a little—a very little—clear chicken broth. She stressed to Amah, "Absolutely clear. Not a shred of meat, or skin, or salt, or herbs." Amah said she savvied.

The nurse also said that her holiday was over and she was leaving at noon to return to Tientsin. If she told me her name, I was still too shocked to remember it. The whole episode seemed like something imagined. I tried to thank her, and she said, "All I did was pass it on." Then she left.

As fast as they had sickened, the children now rallied. Two days later we carried them down to the garden where—since this was clean Japan—they could sit on the grass to play, a pleasure we could not allow in China. In a week they were splashing in the sea.

Susie San was a quiet young Japanese woman who wore a gray kimono and brushed her shining hair off her face to coil on the back of her head. She and Amah were about the same age and the two became great friends. There was no more criticism of the Japanese from Amah, and she seemed very happy.

In the garden the children's constant companions were a flock of tame pigeons. This was a picture I longed to snap but could not, for Mogi was within a security zone where no picture-taking was allowed. The owner explained, smiling, "If you take a snapshot here you both and also I and my wife will go to jail."

He was a plump, smooth man of about 60, very Western in appearance. Susie San told us he was extremely wealthy and well-known in Japan's business community. He usually wore a well-tailored suit and small bright-coloured bow tie. We never saw his wife, but his grand-daughter, Nikki-ko, came next to the pigeons as the twins' playmate. She was a pretty, bright child of eight or nine, and a favourite of all the foreign guests. She spoke excellent English.

First thing every morning I liked to go down to the dock for a swim (Jim thought this as abhorrent as drinking beer before breakfast). No other guests were around at that hour, but a gardener was always around, carefully raking the white pebbles that covered the paths and flowerbeds between the shrubs. He wore the same scanty costume as the fishermen. One morning I stopped to admire the artistic swirls he contrived in the pebbles on the flowerbeds, and when he replied to my comments I suddenly recognized him as the owner-manager —clearly a busy man!

Another morning Amah brought me a large ripe fig

which she said "this my flen', this gardener-man" had given her. I had known ripe figs as a child in South Africa but never in Canada. We had small figs in Shanghai, but they always had to be stewed. Here in Japan, where sanitation was almost an obsession, they could be eaten raw. I was ecstatic. Every morning after that, Amah came with a bowlful, gathered with the help of the gardener-man. When we were leaving I wished to leave a tip for him and spoke to Susie San about it, but the housekeeper smiled and shook her head. I wondered then, and wonder still, if Amah's gardener friend and my raker of pebbles were not the same person, the respected business executive, wearer of tailored gray suits and red and blue bow ties.

However, there was trouble, too. There was the stricture against cameras. Jim and I found that in the village stores all the toys were warlike—tanks, army trucks, fighter planes, gas masks, toy guns and cannons: the dolls were dressed as soldiers or nurses. Susie was the only woman on the staff who wore a kimono. The maids, like the clerks in the village, were dressed in white middy blouses and navy blue pleated skirts, their hair cut short or pig-tailed. There was none of the picturesque beauty of the flower-like Nei Sans at Karatsu. Every now and then in the village all work stopped and the young people, wearing gas-masks, rushed out to do a kind of drill in the street, calisthenics, or taking cover, or going through motions which looked like the loading of an imaginary gun, perhaps anti-aircraft, for they looked frequently skyward.

Jim and I noticed that on our evening walks after dinner we were followed. Jim spoke to the owner of the hotel about this and was told, with a smile, "Intelligence! Because of the colour of your hair and the way you stand, so straight, they think you might be a Russian spy."

Russia, whose Sahkalin Peninsula jutted out into the sea like a dagger thrust at the northern Japanese island of Hokkaida, represented a major threat.

A diminutive Scottish woman, Mrs. Mac, whose husband was expected later in the month, took her two children to bathe on a beach beyond the ridge of rock and trees behind the hotel. Once a group of teenagers threw

rocks at them and chased them back to hotel property. After that, as at Karatsu—but this time because of human, not occult, menace—guests were asked not to leave hotel property unless accompanied by a member of the hotel staff. Jim and I protested and were permitted our evening walks but never too far, please, from the Beach, and we were always followed.

Everything was so small! Here there was no flat plain between mountains and sea; the land came sheer to the water. Steep little trails led up the slopes, flanked wherever there was room by tiny fields built up with rocks and filled with soil carried in sacks from the valleys. When heavy rains washed them away, they were painstakingly built up again. Some were only about three feet wide and six to eight feet long. In some, rice was growing. Since rice, and other crops, need water, this too was carried up—and up—and further up.

"Japan is so terribly overcrowded," Jim commented. "She will have to do something one of these days."

We saw straw lantern boats being built in the tiny gardens of many homes. Big ones, up to twelve feet long, were carried to the water on poles by six or eight bearers. They came from villages high among the hills, cooperative offerings winding down the narrow trails, bearers singing. Others came from "guilds" in nearby inland cities.

One guest was staying all summer at the Beach. He was a retired British army sergeant, bluff and rusty-coloured, with a huge bristling walrus moustache framing his mouth. Jim said he was a familiar figure in Shanghai and was universally known as Bug-whiskers. A very old wisteria vine had been trained as a garden-house over rustic wooden seats on a red cobbled floor. Bug-whiskers, pipe smoking, read his papers here each morning. I was nearby knitting and watching the twins when Nikki-ko came running. While staying with him earlier in the summer, one of Bug-whiskers' dearest friends had died suddenly, and Nikki said that she was building a boat for him and wanted Bug-whiskers to write a greeting to him.

With a sidelong glance, as though he felt a little foolish, the Englishman demurred. He pointed out that his friend had not drowned but died on shore, but the pretty child insisted that his spirit was "just out there", no doubt waiting for the Festival. At long last Bug-whiskers took the proffered pencil and piece of paper, wrote about three lines, folded it, put it in the envelope which she had ready and sealed it securely. Happy as a butterfly she carried it away.

That night the moon was full and up by midnight. A slight breeze ruffled the sea. Once again we watched the lovely launching of the boats, bright lights bobbing up and down as the waves withdrew from shore. The larger boats survived the longest, but some of the little ones soon capsized, among them Nikki's.

Next morning the tide was still well out, and I had to walk some distance among the rocks to find water deep enough to swim in. I passed Nikki's boat about twenty feet away, lying on its side all sodden in a tide pool, doll-sized bottle of rice wine still tied to the deck, white note tucked among the straws. I longed to read that note but respect for tradition and for Nikki would not allow it. But still I wondered what Bug-whiskers wrote there under the aged wisteria vine, where the two old men had smoked so many pipes and talked of so many things.

This visit had shown that the Japanese were training for war, but not, we thought, against us. Their enemy was Russia. It would be most convenient for Russia to swallow the small archipelago and gain a strong front on the Pacific Ocean. On the other hand Japan needed fertile land and saw it on the plains of the northern mainland.

The two nations had been at war, signed peace treaties and still made war since the 1890's. Russia's munition factories and other sources of supply were far to the west, where the government was plagued with revolutions. A single railway track, recently completed across the Siberian wastes, was the only link between Moscow and Vladivostock. Japanese victories against her mammoth foe were surprising and heady. In 1902 the Russian naval base at Port Arthur, after weeks of blockade by a Japanese fleet, had to surrender. A few months later the Japanese attacked and sank thirty-two naval vessels with full complements of a fleet completing the

long voyage to Vladivostock from St. Petersburg.

At the beginning of the First War Japan was a treaty ally of Great Britain and France and quickly moved to take over German and other interests in Tsintao and Tientsin in Shantung Province north of Shanghai. Post-war peace talks confirmed her ownership. With growing confidence the nation pursued what Tokyo termed its "peaceful expansion" on the mainland's "friendly soil." Their claim was that they needed strong bases from which to help the Chinese combat the Communists in the northwest. In 1932 Manchuria, re-named Manchoukuo, was recognized as an independent state by both Chinese and Japanese. The former Chinese child-emperor, Pu Yi, who had been living in the Japanese (formerly German) concession in Tientsin ascended the throne of Manchoukou, surrounded by Japanese advisors and pledged to support Japan's interests in his country and fight with the Chinese against the Communists.

Although the many Chinese generals continually battled among themselves it was generally felt in 1936 that the Chinese were not good fighters. There was even a Chinese saying: one does not use good iron to make nails, nor good men for soldiers. Militaristic Chinese Communists under Mao Tse Tung and Chou En Lai were confined in the northwest mountains, well supplied with food by their peasant neighbours but lacking arms. Chiang Kai Shek equipped armies to send against them. His men had good uniforms and rifles but no soup kitchens. They were expected to forage for their own food.

They found plenty in the Communist camps where they were kindly received, well fed, given $3 for their uniforms and rifles, and set free. Three dollars was a lot of money to a Chinese soldier.

We did not think that any of the three nations involved in these hostilities would want to take on any of the European powers as an enemy. We who lived in the international communities felt secure in our strong neutrality.

What we did not recognize was the nearness of Adolf Hitler. Japanese master-planners were already in close step with his visionaries and advisors. Top men in Tokyo were planning not only a buffer state between themselves and Russia but an expanded Empire to be consolidated while the Western Powers were entangled in a Second World War. The new Empire would include Shanghai, Hong Kong and the Pacific Islands and drastically concern Pearl Harbour. It nearly happened.

20

THE EYES SPEAK
AND THE EYES CAN
UNDERSTAND

-English

THE TWINS WERE INCREDIBLY perfect and soon knew it. You could see them start to preen themselves as soon as anyone approached. There had to be another child to take some of the attention away from them, and the new baby was expected in early June.

The ground floor apartment of our house was not re-rented after the German couple moved but remained empty all that winter and through the humid spring of 1937. A river boat captain, his wife and their two sons aged six and eight years old, moved into the second floor apartment. We knew them slightly but were not close. He was away a great deal with his river steamer up the Yangtse River to Hangkow and beyond, and when he came home they had lavish, and noisy parties. They seemed to have many friends.

Our friends, Phyllis Ayrton and Louie Stops, retired to live in Peking in a small house near the Forbidden City. It was planned that we would visit them as soon as the new baby was old enough to risk the journey and this seemed the perfect way to see Peking.

Fred Baker had taken Fran and their three small children, with whom my children spent many happy hours, to England for a holiday. During their absence I made a strange friendship that remains one of my warmest memories.

As the days warmed towards spring I often took the twins to Jessfield Park and sat on a bench while they ran

The approach to Jessfield Park Tea House viewed from inside the moon door. The path is flanked by vivid flower beds and ancient stone lions.

and played nearby. The clatter of the palm fronds in the beds of shrubbery and whisper of the fresh bamboo leaves made a sweet symphony of welcome. One day I saw a tall white woman standing a short distance away, a little behind me. She had straight, tawny-coloured hair drawn back from a beautiful face and I thought her expression sad and somewhat hungry. She did not look at me nor come too close, keeping her attention focussed on the twins and a Chinese child of about the same age whom she had with her. The child was well dressed and I realized that it was the barrier between us.

She might have been its mother, for there were several white women in the Settlement married to wealthy Chinese—they lived in the same district and maintained a community of their own. Or she might have been a governess. I felt it obvious that the colour bar, more keenly practised by well-born Chinese than by whites, must not be breached. If her child approached the twins she called it back sharply. When I stood up to take the twins home she moved away across the grass and I had no opportunity to speak to her.

On our next visits to the park she invariably reappeared, always remaining just too far away for me to speak, never meeting my glance, watching the twins sometimes but never sharing a smile with me. She seemed to like being near us, but that was all and I found a comforting companionship in her presence, her beauty and her just

181

being. If she didn't come soon after we did, I missed her. Then there she would be, aloof, but clearly aware of us. It was always she who found us. I felt she liked us as I liked her, or why should she bother?

If we had spoken, we might not have understood each other. She might have been Swiss or French or Scandinavian. The language she used with the child was unfamiliar to me, perhaps Chinese, but they were never close enough for me to be sure. If we walked her way she moved away, but never too far. We were near each other —that seemed to be enough—and for weeks we shared in this manner our outings with the children in the park.

I thought of her even when not at the park and the mental picture of her—tall, quiet, honey-coloured—was as soothing as the actual handling of amber or yellow jade. I determined that when the new baby came I would take it to the park so that she could see it, even at a distance. I would wrap it in a blue blanket or a pink blanket to let her know its sex.

It did not occur to me that I would never see her again, but so much was to happen after the baby was born that our paths never crossed again.

Amah was to be in charge of the household while I was in hospital. Her Auntie was engaged to help her, we hired a new coolie amah and Amah eagerly assured me that I had nothing to worry about.

"I savvy plenty, Missy. This other Missy (her former employer) I have go, she belong English Missy. She have go hospital for catchee baby. I looksee her son, Lemons."

Lemons? "Leonard," I suggested.

"No, Missy. Lemons."

"Clements, perhaps."

"No, Missy. Lemons. Same this ice box have got."

Lemons it had to be. "This outside plenty baby have got plenty measle spot," Amah continued earnestly. "My other Missy fear Lemons can catchee measle-spot. I puttee on led-dee libbon Lemons arms. Baby have got this led-dee libbon, baby no catch measle-spot. Have go park—Lemons no catch."

Very, very firmly I told her that with or without red ribbons on their arms the twins were not to go to the park nor even down the stairs from our apartment while I was away. In my imagination I could see other amahs and other children crowding around, eager to see the two-piecee baby, the girl with her big brown eyes and dark curls, the blonde boy with his strange light devil's eyes. Crestfallen, Amah promised.

Back from England, Fran vowed to come every day, unexpectedly, morning or afternoon, or both, to make sure everything was as it should be. She did, too, and found nothing amiss.

With the new baby came the heat again. The temperature soared to the high nineties and even at night did not drop more than two or three degrees, and humidity was at saturation point. For all its fine streets and buildings Shanghai was still a bog land.

Nobody slept much in such weather. Bedding was put away and straw mats covered the mattresses. The twins were bathed twice daily in mild soda baths to guard against prickly heat. In such a climate one does not recover easily from the baby business and Amah's Auntie stayed on with us after the new baby girl and I came home. We named her Norah for my Irish grandmother and Amah called her "dolling" (darling).

One of us would take the twins down to play in the shaded garden at six each morning. By eight the sun was too hot and they had to come indoors. It was too hot for them even on the big tree-top verandah. The amahs always wore their black pants and white jackets, but I discarded everything possible in the apartment, wearing only briefest shorts, handkerchief halter and straw sandals.

Almost everyone who could, left the Settlement for cooler resorts in northern China or Japan—all the big houses around us were empty.

One morning, as I was talking on the phone to Fran, unbelievable sounds erupted in our living room. I rushed in to find my year-old son jerking and frothing in convulsion while the three amahs, each holding some part of him, tried to exorcise whatever devil possessed him by shaking him and shrieking imprecations.

I had read in a baby book that a tepid bath could calm convulsions, and after telling Amah to "catchee warm water"—fill the bathtub—I tried to call our doctor, holding the jerking little body on my shoulder while Twin Sister clung to my knees. The doctor was away on holiday; his partners were unavailable. Amah came with a half a cup of warm water.

I rushed to the bathroom, Twin Sister stumbling with me. We ran the warm water.

"Call taxi, Amah. Then please call Master office, talkee boy find Master. I go hospital."

The tepid water stilled the spasms but the child was in deep coma. We wrapped him in towels and a blanket, left Twin Sister sobbing in Auntie's loving arms, and the sympathetic taxi-driver sped us to the country hospital. My son was so still—I could detect no breath in him and thought him dead.

Jim joined me in the waiting room just before the doctor came to say the child was better. "This does not mean he's crazy, you know," the medical man reassured us. "These fits are usually just a symptom of serious disease. We will have to keep him here for observation." He told us the boy's temperature when admitted was 105 degrees, but was now falling. The best they could hope for was malaria, which would mean another temperature rise in three days. We were allowed to peek at the baby ward through a window and saw him lying in a crib with his eyes open, tears on his cheeks. We were asked not to go in as it would disturb him.

Only then, as I turned, crying, towards Jim's car, did I realize how little I was wearing. In 1937 women did not appear in public so 'unclothed' and some people in the big crowded foyer looked at me as if I were nude. For once I would not have cared if I had been.

The expected malarial cycle did not happen and after three days the hospital telephoned to say we could take him home. He was dressed and on a shaded porch in his crib when we arrived and when he saw us it was as though an incandescent bulb was turned on inside him. He made no sound, just stood on his toes and held out his arms. At home he ran from room to room, his sister at his heels repeating happily, "Dei-dei come! Dei-dei come!" The three amahs followed, wreathed in smiles.

We planned a full examination when our doctor returned from his vacation, but again there was no time for that. The best diagnosis we were ever able to glean was that his seizure had been caused by the heat, and perhaps a new tooth coming through.

The heat stayed with us through July. Tempers were brittle, for everyone was short of sleep. We were especially irritated by the Japanese, who once again were indulging in strutting and sabre rattling. The pattern had been Japanese trouble every five years. The last had been in 1932 (and 1927 before that) and here it was 1937—so away we went again. Ugly incidents speckled the news although they were far away around Peking, newly renamed Peiping by Chiang Kai Shek's regime. We were concerned for Stops and Ayrton, who had retired full of dreams to the fabled northern city.

Events were confusing, names and places unfamiliar. Half a dozen Chinese generals seemed to be fighting in northern China—Chiang, Yang, Yu, Sung, Sun, Chou, Mao, Wang and other Chiangs. Sometimes they were good guys, sometimes bad. Then there would be a sudden change, and the good guys were apologizing while the bad guys were being appointed to high Government posts. The generals fought against each other, or against the Japanese, or against the Communists. At a small walled town called Wanping not far from the old capital, Japanese troops engaged in exercises knocked at the gates one evening after they were closed for the night and demanded entry. They said that one of their men was missing and they wished to search the town. When town authorities refused, the Japanese fired on the gates, and the Chinese returned the fire. Next morning higher-ups apologized and a cease-fire was ordered but the troops continued to fire sporadically at each other. This was called the Lukouchiao Incident and seemed a silly episode. One felt like calling the radio station that reported it and asking "Who cares?"

The call letters of the radio station were RUOK and they were always spelled out, never pronounced as one word. They had been selected in a contest a few years previously, the prize going to a young Scotsman. The call letters had a warm friendly feeling and the days seemed launched to a better start when the familiar cheery greeting, "Are you okay?" preceded the daily news summary.

We were expecting the Peking trouble to be over and things to return to normalcy, though trouble with the Japanese might be said to be normal. Crops were nearly ready for harvesting and men would have to forget their military exercises. Then early in August the fighting came nearer. RUOK reported that during the night twenty-eight Japanese warships had arrived in the Yangtse and anchored near the mouth of the Whangpoo. Secure in our extra-territorial rights we found this a tiresome extravagance, more gold braid and show-off on the part of the Japanese. If they wished to inflate their egos after the confused campaign in the north by once again flattening the sorry Woosung forts, surely three ships would have been enough! Why send twenty-eight?

Jim went to work as usual. About eleven o'clock he telephoned. "The Japanese have landed troops on the east side of the Whangpoo near the sea. You may hear the big naval guns firing. Refugees are pouring into the city by the thousands, but don't worry. This is just between the Japanese and the Chinese—we won't be involved."

Soon the sound of guns began ten or twelve miles away, and quickly grew heavier and nearer. I had never heard big guns before, except for the Volunteers' Howitzers. I found this frightening. Even the twins noticed the noise and stopped their play every now and then to exclaim "Big Bang!"

Fran telephoned to say that Fred was moving their family from the big house on Hungjao, west of the Settlement, to a suite in Cathay Mansions, a new apartment building inside the Settlement. "If things get too bad where you are, come to us—we'll put all the kids on the floor."

Amah came to say her Auntie had much fear and wished to go home to their village. I told her Master had said not to worry, but still the Auntie went home. Amah, the coolie amah and the Pidgin stayed.

When Jim came home for dinner he reported that the Volunteers might be mobilized to keep the fighting out of the Settlement. He brought a case of canned milk, because he said Japanese planes had been machine-gunning the Districts' precious dairy herd, claiming they thought they were troops.

So many refugees were streaming in from the country that Settlement Police had been withdrawn from outside areas such as ours to keep order in the refugee-crowded downtown streets. "Whenever there's trouble the whole countryside tries to cram into the Settlement."

Father Joachim, the one-handed priest from the Hongkew church, was doing wonders calming the crowds that stormed the gates of the French Concession.

Jim took his Volunteers' uniform from the cupboard and polished buttons till they shone like stars, leather till it gleamed like satin. He told me to keep all doors and windows barred and not to allow any Chinese into the house on any pretext. "The Chinese refugees are more our enemies than the Japanese—they're starving, and men will do strange things when their children are starving."

We checked our own provisions and decided that we had enough for the moment.

"This may all be over in two days, especially if the foreign powers take a hand."

The mobilization order came on the telephone just after ten o'clock at night. We had been out on the big

verandah listening to the guns—the chatter of machine guns could be heard now too—and watching the flares in the night sky from burning villages or straw-filled ice houses. Jim was ready to leave in five minutes.

I stood at the top of the stairs as he started down. He stopped and looked back. This time it was not cotton wool in his ammunition belt, as on the weekly parades, but live ammunition.

"Are you frightened?" he asked me.

"A bit, yes."

"Remember the navy is there in the river watching out. Neither they nor I will let anything happen to you."

A transport truck had called for him, leaving our car in the garage. I had thought Amah in bed, but she was still in the kitchen when I went back and brought tea for me to the chair beside the radio.

All that night I sat beside the radio listening to disc jockey Carroll Allcott alternate vacuous popular recordings with messages of urgent importance.

"A message for Mr. Peacock, Al Jones, Sidney Eversham at Blue Ribbon Dairy on Tunsin Road—do not leave the building where you are. Prepare to spend the night in the office. You will be brought in under escort in the morning."

"Dr. Corritt! Dr. Corritt in Tientsin! We hope you are listening. Your wife and children are safe but conditions approaching the Settlement are not good. Do not attempt to return."

"To all foreigners on holiday from Shanghai. Plan to stay where you are. Do not come back to the city. Repeat, do not come back to Shanghai."

Allcott eased the tension these warnings invoked by playing "I want to get you on a slow boat to China", "Baby Face", "Shuffle off to Buffle-lo."

He told us that the Japanese had landed a strong force south of the Whangpoo, with their naval guns along the river pounding the countryside between Shanghai and the Yangtse Kiang where Jim and I had walked on the houseboat trip. Chinese troops were resisting stubbornly but were not as well armed as the invaders. Reinforcements were slow in coming because Chinese authorities were sinking a line of ships across the Yangtse Kiang to prevent the Japanese from sending warships further up the river toward Nanking and Hangkow. This boom would also hamper the normal flow of food to Shanghai from the interior. Food supplies in the Settlement were adequate for two or three days for residents, but could not possibly support the tens of thousands of refugees who were flooding in from all directions.

Big iron gates leading into the Settlement and French Concession from Nantao, Chapei and other surrounding Chinese areas were now closed and barred. The refugees were the responsibility of the Chinese government. They could not be supported by the foreign powers, who had their own nationals to protect and therefore chose not to become involved with either side of the two warring parties. All rice shops and other food stores in the Settlement and Concession were closed and under heavy guard. Vacant stores and office were being thrown open to the refugees for shelter, but most had to camp in the streets. Priests from various temples were attempting to help police establish some kind of control.

The Volunteer Corps and troops in garrisons were manning the perimeters where possible, to keep soldiers of either army from entering the foreign concessions. Nonetheless Settlement hospitals were overflowing with wounded, both Chinese and Japanese, who were being brought in by truck.

I wondered if these were trucks of the Transport Company. Also, we were on an Outside Road, and I knew that there were no iron gates barring us from the boundary at the Temple of Tranquil Repose. Nor were there gates between us and the teeming village of Jessfield two blocks away. Hopefully the fighting would not come that far.

"A message for Mrs. Leavitt—Mrs. Ada Leavitt— your husband is safe but you and the children must stay where you are or go home to the States. Do not come to Shanghai. To all foreigners wherever you are, do not try to come to Shanghai. Now some music—'My Little Cockroach'. Anybody want to tango?"

At half-past five as daylight was spreading over our convulsed, shuddering world Amah brought me the morning cup of tea. The new baby must be nursed at six o'clock.

21

FEAR
SPRINGS FROM
IGNORANCE

-American

AFTER BREAKFAST I TOOK the twins with me and went out in the small maroon car to see what could be seen. On a lucky impulse I filled up the gas tank at the service station at the corner of Edinburgh and Yu Yuen Roads.

The streets were absolutely deserted. We turned down Yu Yuen road to the Settlement boundary by the Temple of Tranquil Repose on Bubbling Well Road. Now I could see why gates were not necessary: in the middle of the street, beside the Temple, an armoured car was parked with machine guns trained on all five approaching roads.

Down these roads country people plodded toward the Temple and Bubbling Well, heads down, pulling small carts laden with cooking gear, bedding, old people and babies. Country women straggled behind the carts, holding strings of children linked hand to hand. One man was pushing a wheelbarrow on which a wizened yellow old lady sat among bundles tied up in straw. Nobody stopped them.

The heat had broken, the temperature was dropping and a thin rain was falling: wet black hair framed stoic faces.

Across the road from the Temple a bamboo fence had been taken down, exposing a heap of coal beside the old building that had housed St. George's Night Club. It still stood there, apparently empty and unused, soon filling

... like the long, lean tail of a dejected blue dragon.

with refugees. On top of the pile of coal British regular troops were mounting another machine gun pointing up Yu Yuen road in the direction from which we had come and in which we would go again on our way home. On the side of a grave mound nearby, which had been hidden by the fence, a family of five now camped under a yellow, oiled-paper umbrella. They were sharing a bowl of cold rice.

In an alley behind the Temple, in front of a shuttered rice store, a long line of sad-faced men, women and children queued, like the long, lean tail of a dejected blue dragon. The store was guarded by a solid semi-circle of stone-faced turbanned Sikh police.

I drove towards Hungjao Road where more British troops were stringing barbed wire, chatting happily. I stopped the car so that we could watch them. An officer saw us, scowled and said something irritable to the men with him. The chatting ceased and they all stopped stringing wire and scowled at us. Obviously women and children were not welcome there, and I turned around and went back along Yu Yuen Road, under the sharp black nose of the machine gun on the pile of coal, until we could turn into Edinburgh Road. All the gardens here had high walls between them and the street. We saw nobody, garaged the car and climbed the two flights of stairs, at the slow pace of the two-year-old twins, until we reached our third-floor home and Amah and the new baby.

Amah told us that one of the small boys from the apartment below us had come up to ask if I would go and see his mother. I went down at once and found Mrs. Laine, the sea captain's wife, lying on the couch in her living room. She was a small woman, but her legs were swollen almost the size of stove pipes. She told me that she was expecting triplets and was afraid the incessant hammering of the guns might bring on a premature delivery. Plans had been made for her in the hospital, but her chauffeur had just told her that they had no gas in their car. Her husband and his river steamer were trapped up-river behind the boom of sunken ships. She had sent her chauffeur to get gas at the service station on Yu Yuen Road but he came back to tell her that it had closed in order to conserve fuel for the military. A radio announcement had just said that all service stations had been ordered closed by the Provincial Government. Gasoline storage tanks were in Chinese territory and therefore endangered by Japanese shell fire.

Since we had a fresh tankful of gas, I was able to promise that if anything happened I would get her to the hospital, day or night. Curfew had been imposed for nine in the evening but surely under such circumstances we would be allowed to get to the hospital.

Mrs. Laine had other problems. Her two sons sat together on a hassock, looking pale and tired but listening with interest to everything we said. Their wash amah and two young Chinese men huddled by the kitchen door, their faces green with fright. Mrs. Laine said the House Boy, who ran the kitchen staff, had run away. Of the three remaining servants, whom she was expecting to flee at any minute, only the chauffeur spoke any English and that was very little. Neither he nor the amah could cook, and the other man, who was the cook's assistant, was paralysed with fear. She herself could hardly walk and none of them had had food since noon the previous day. She had always left everything concerning the kitchen to the Boy, as the custom was, and she did not even know what supplies they had on hand.

Mrs. Laine was very tired and very frightened, but

managed to make a little joke about her coming triplets, saying that when her doctor heard we lived upstairs, he said, "Those Canadians! Living under the same roof you're lucky it's only three!"

The two little boys came upstairs with me to see the new baby and to get a jar of jam. Amah went downstairs and straightened out the green-faced help. By the time the boys and I went down again, Amah had tongue-lashed the cook's helper into contriving toast and scrambled eggs, and the wash amah had brought a brush and was smoothing her lady's hair.

As Amah and I returned upstairs to our own three children—left for the first time ever to the guardian eyes of the coolie amah and the Pidgin—we said nothing, but I felt that we both realized that we now had a very large family to care for.

The telephone brought a cable from a Toronto newspaper asking for 300 words on conditions in Shanghai. This pleased me for two reasons. First, I had always wanted to work for a newspaper and this seemed to me a good challenge, for it would not be easy to compact into 300 words all that was happening in the International Settlement, and convey our own sense of security under the extra-territorial treaties. With all China to fight in, neither side would want to invoke the wrath of the big powers by interfering with the Settlement or French Concession.

This security was the second reason for my wanting to do well with the newspaper story. I knew that it could assuage the anxiety of my family, and all those others who must be worrying about relatives or friends in China. We were at the heart of a hurricane but in a cell of safety.

Jim telephoned to say that he had two hours leave but would not try to get home. "No buses are running because of the gasoline freeze and the same thing applies to taxis. Rickshaw coolies are in hiding—there isn't one to be seen anywhere."

I told him about our full tank and offered to go and pick him up, but he said no. "We may need that gas. I only have two hours anyway, so I'll try and snatch some sleep on an army cot at headquarters. I've had none since

I left you."

"What have you been doing?"

"The Volunteers are guarding part of the boundary. British regulars and U.S. Marines are guarding the rest. Of course the Navy is patrolling the river, but there's no way they can regulate Jap marksmanship in Pootung— the Bund is catching it. Some of the buildings have holes in them already and all the banks and offices are closed. We in the Transport Company are distributing supplies or rescuing people caught in out-lying places. We've brought the Chinese Blind School in from Hungjao Road and evacuated an old people's home from out there too. I've been out a few times, but mostly I've been here at headquarters in the Municipal Building on despatching duty. It's hectic. I'd sooner be out with a truck—they're big ones, good fun."

It seemed important that the cable to Toronto should stress to those who were personally interested the safety of their relatives in Shanghai. I described the floods of refugees, the barbed wire, the guns and the line of warships in the river that ensured the inviolability of neutrals. When the skeleton message seemed to say all it could, I checked it with Fred Baker.

The cable office was on the top floor of a large building just around the corner from the Bund on Avenue Edward VII. The operator in charge was alone and could take no messages by phone, so I must deliver it in person. The new baby was being breastfed, and my trip must be timed between feedings. I planned to leave the key of our car with the Downstairs Missy so that her chauffeur could take her to hospital if necessary. We sent the Pidgin to find a taxi and miraculously he did so, leaving by rickshaw and returning in state.

The taxi driver spoke some English. Inside Settlement boundaries, traffic lanes were being kept open only on the main thoroughfares. All the side streets seemed to be rivers of people. Not a rickshaw, not a bus was in sight and other cars seemed to be carrying military personnel.

On Avenue Edward, seven lanes wide, only the two centre lanes were open. The rest were solid with people,

Rickshaw coolie waiting outside a telegraph office.

their heads like wall-to-wall carpeting around the buildings. Planes zoomed overhead. Against the background
of big gun fire sounded the clatter of machine guns, the
spitting bite of rifles. The chauffeur remarked, "Too
much fightee-fightee." An understatement if I ever
heard one.

At certain depots, especially the temples in side
streets, Settlement police were loading refugees into
trucks. My driver said they would be taken countryside, long way.

The wide intersection at Tibet Road and Avenue Edward was a mosaic of faces. Refugees even crowded the
traffic islands, pressed so close along the curb I could
have touched them through an open window. I noticed
particularly an old man leaning on a countryman's long
stick, his skull-like face strung with straggling whiskers,
and a tiny girl, perhaps four years old, clutching a big
thermos bottle that reached above her chin. Above it her

eyes were jet buttons.

Two blocks from the cable office my driver stopped. He said he would go no further. Missy can maybe walk self? I asked if he would wait for me and take me home again. He hesitated, then said he would. In case of accident I paid him the one-way fare anyhow.

I was at the edge of the crowd—Avenue Edward from here to the Whangpoo River was absolutely empty, and the Angel of Peace who faced the river seemed to turn her back on a stage without performers. Then above the Angel's head, against the gray backdrop of the sky, small clouds bloomed like flowers, dissipated and bloomed again. I must ask Jim what caused those flower-like clouds, I thought, then realized a moment later that they were connected to the shrapnel, which clattered up the middle of the street. I had never seen shrapnel and thought the racing showers like pixie dancers in a bizarre stage setting.

The building that housed the cable office seemed almost deserted. There was nobody in the offices, and the elevators were not running, so I walked up several flights of stairs to reach the lone despatcher on the top floor. He checked my copy and I walked down the stairs and back along the sidewalk beside the pixie ballet to find my taxi waiting where the crowds began.

Yellow planes were snarling close above us. We had just crossed Tibet Road Square when we heard a sharp, loud crack behind us. It was a sound like no other I have ever heard—as if the skies had been ripped by lightning without thunder.

"Driver, what was that?"

"I think-so two airplane have fightee. I think-so one airplane have down."

The driver's head turned from side to side, the taxi slowed—I felt he was going to bolt and leave me stranded. So I moved to the seat behind him and put my hands on his shoulders.

"Chauffeur," I said, hoping to make him feel he was one of the family—actually, finding him waiting there on the edge of the crowd had made me feel that he was. "Chauffeur, homeside I have got three small baby. Suppose you no wanchee drive, okay, pay me key, I drive, but I must get home to my baby."

He steadied and drove on, all the way home, with my hands on his shoulders.

The telephone was ringing as I climbed the last of the stairs to our flat. I reached it before Amah did and answered without taking off hat or coat. It was Fred Baker.

"Have you sent your cable yet?"

"I'm just back from the cable office."

"You'd better get right back down there. They've bombed the Settlement. Bombs have fallen on the Cathay and Palace hotels and on the corner of Tibet Road and Avenue Edward VII."

"But I've just come from Tibet and Avenue Edward, and I saw no sign of bombs."

"You must have just missed it. My foreman is here and told me. He saw the hotel bombing and heard about Tibet and the Avenue."

I told Fred about the sharp sound we had heard and he said, "You must have been too close to hear the reverberations. You missed by inches. There are hundreds killed."

"Foreigners too?"

"Hundreds."

I called the cable office. "Have you sent my cable?"

"It's on the wires now—They're still open. You can add anything you like." But what could I say? Bombs on the Settlement... hundreds killed including foreigners... the countryman, the child with the thermos... I couldn't do that to those people who cared so much. Let someone else do it, someone who had more facts.

"Let it go," I said; but I stayed there by the telephone, purse under arm, hat pushed back, forehead pressed against the wall, knowing that I would never be a great newspaper woman. This had been my big chance, perhaps the first word of the bombing to leave Shanghai—and because I was soft I had failed at it.

The twins had their lunch and settled down for afternoon naps. From our high verandah I watched the planes in their contest of dip and flight over the downtown area. They came from the south where the Chinese aerodrome was located, zoomed low, rose and fled before the onslaught of gunfire from Japanese warships and shore batteries. The Chinese were trying to sink the *Idzuma*, an old cruise ship dating from the Russo-Japanese war. She was anchored almost at the mouth of Soochow Creek near Garden Bridge in front of the Japanese Consulate, a block or so from the Astor House. The Cathay and Palace hotels were nearer the centre of the Settlement Bund a block away from Nanking Road.

I could see the shadowy bombs that floated below the planes, down, straight down. Down there were the crowded streets and headquarters of the Municipal Council, where Jim was on duty.

I panicked to the telephone. "May I speak to Sergeant Carney?"

"Sergeant Carney is on duty."

"Can you please tell me where?"

"I am sorry, no. He is on duty... "

It was answer enough. If he had been in a safe area, I thought, the information would have been given.

In her basket the baby girl was making sucking noises. She was a good child and seldom cried, just lay quietly anticipating, trusting... I loved her deeply but in that moment felt I could not feed her. I was capable of any wild act. If I picked up that tender helpless morsel something bad would happen to her. As usual in any time of tension Amah was hovering near.

"Amah, I much fear for Master. I no can pay chow this baby girl."

"This baby girl all-li'," said Amah, smiling and picking up the baby, full of love. "More better Missy chow tea first."

She bore the child, just eight weeks old, away to the kitchen and moments later the coolie amah appeared with lacquer cups and flowered tea cosy. Soon the baby was in my arms again, sweet and warm, both taking and giving comfort.

22

ORDER
IS HEAVEN'S
FIRST LAW

-English

J IM TELEPHONED: he had eight hours leave and would
come home if I could go and get him.

"Of course I'll come. What time and where?"

"Eight o'clock. I'll have to be back at four o'clock tomorrow morning."

There was beefsteak in the refrigerator—his favourite dinner. He was waiting at the appointed corner near
the Municipal Buildings, a block from the Bund. The
planes had given up their attacks for the night and the *Idzuma* still lay anchored in the river. Jim was showered
and spotless in clean khaki shirt and shorts but he looked
very tired. He told me that he'd been on clean-up duty at
the two hotels.

The bombing of the Settlement had been accidental.
The bombs were Chinese, fallen from a plane trying to
escape from, and perhaps damaged by, Japanese anti-
aircraft fire. Those I had watched that afternoon had fallen harmlessly in the river. By far the worst disaster had
been at Tibet and Avenue Edward where one bomb had
set off another just behind it, which had exploded while
still in the air. Bodies were "stacked along the curbs like
cordwood" until they could be loaded into trucks after
the wounded were looked after. We learned later that
the death toll exceeded 1200, including two Americans
sitting in their car and dead from concussion.

Somehow Jim brought with him, hidden from me, his
blood-soaked uniform and smuggled it to Amah, asking

her to have it washed but "no pay Missy see." He did not eat his steak. At last I had to break the unusual silence.

"Jim, was it very bad?"

He drew a deep breath. "I was sent out in charge of six trucks," he said, and stopped. "We filled them all." He stopped again.

"Many white people?"

"At the hotels, yes. There was a white man's foot, a headless body... " It was no use. He could not go on and I asked no more questions. Afterwards he told me that a foreigner had called him and his fellow Volunteers into the Palace Hotel Bar, not for a drink but for a wash, using an unusual disinfectant. "He poured bottles of brandy over our hands. First time I ever washed in brandy. Of course it was disinfectant too."

We set the alarm for three but it was unnecessary. I had lost the habit of sleep, and the gunfire was a constant reminder of reality. I remembered the Pixie Ballet on the empty blocks of Avenue Edward VII—Pixie Ballet! Those had been the fingers of death beating their sharp tattoo, and reaching—how was it they had missed the figure in the blue-and-white checked summer frock and wide-brimmed hat? I must never tell Jim. He must not know how naive I had been: he must feel he could trust me...

Before we left, I knocked on the door that led to the servants' quarters and Amah came to stay with the children.

In the pre-dawn the downtown streets were filled with a blue light, the sidewalks rippled with the bodies of refugees sleeping on the concrete.

Jim said, "Those are our real enemies, all these thousands of starving refugees. There simply isn't food enough."

I thought of our unpoliced streets and the crowded Chinese village of Jessfield just around the corner. As he stepped from the car at the Municipal Buildings and I slid into the driver's seat he asked, "Are you afraid?"

"Yep."

He said, "Drive straight home and don't stop for anyone except the British Army. Keep listening to the radio. You may have to evacuate."

There was daylight on the way home. The ripples on the sidewalks were unfolding into people. Several small children were holding paper Union Jacks or Stars and Stripes. A wheelbarrow coolie, forlornly trundling his empty vehicle up the middle of the street, had a Union Jack flying from the axle.

During that day I went into the bedroom and took Jim's old army pistol from the bureau drawer; but I had no idea how to use it. There was ammunition in the same box but how and where did it go into the pistol? After a few minutes I put it back in the drawer. In my inexperienced hands it would be more dangerous than defensive. Still, one must have a weapon. The hammer would be a good one... but something else was needed. A quick, deft enemy could wrench the hammer from my right hand unless something in my left could fend him off; a wire coat hanger offered itself, stretched out to make a handle; the hook could be a nasty threat, swung at a man's eyes. From then on I kept these two pieces always within reach.

Some of our friends were home on leave and some on holiday in northern China or Japan. Such normalcies constantly imposed themselves against the surrealistic backdrop of this incredible war. The Bakers were now in a large apartment on the edge of Frenchtown, and every time she phoned Fran urged that there was room for us. But if we went, what would happen to the Downstairs Missy and her children? Or Amah and the Pidgin and the coolie amah? Or all our furniture and belongings?

Among others who phoned was Nellie Friedman, wife of Morse of the Baker Agency. They had no children and Nellie focussed all her love on Morsie. Now Nellie told me that Morsie was on duty with the American Volunteers near the North Station. Every night she walked to his post to give him a clean handkerchief, dry socks and a packet of home-made cookies.

"But that's at least two miles from your place. You walk there and back? Alone?"

"Of course. There are no buses or taxis and the rickshaw coolies are all scared."

"I'd be scared, too."

She pointed out that there were no planes at night and, she thought, less shell fire. "It's not as brave as what the men are doing." I was astonished at her courage...

Other friends were leaving for Singapore or San Francisco—if they could find bookings.

Ruok's disc jockey told us that the Japanese had strafed the biggest dairy's herd of Canadian Holstein cows, again mistaking the herd for Chinese calvary. I drove to Mr. Ho's and bought a case of milk produced and canned in the Fraser Valley of British Columbia.

The Japanese had taken over all of Hongkew, and Settlement Defence was withdrawn to Soochow Creek. The Transport Company to which Jim belonged was now constantly in army-occupied outside territory, evacuating foreigners—nuns and their pupils; hospitals and rest homes; the School for the Chinese Blind, run by an elderly English couple in a red brick compound on Hungjao Road. All were being quartered somewhere inside the Settlement boundaries.

Station RUOK told us that foreign consulates were waiting for the British to move: if the British evacuated their nationals, others would follow suit.

The British evacuation announcement came at about two in the morning. I was sitting by the radio—hammer on one side coat hanger on the other—when the request was aired. It was not an order. In view of the need to conserve food in the Settlement for those on defensive duty, the authorities asked that women with children and men whose presence was not essential in the Settlement should evacuate. Arrangements were being made to take them to Hong Kong or further by the British liner *Rajputana*, leaving in about 36 hours, and the Canadian *Empress of Asia*, due to sail three days later.

I made plans. The Trouble was already a week old. These Japanese wars never lasted more than about two weeks, so this one should be nearly over. If we waited for the *Empress*, which was to sail in three days, we would probably not have to go at all...

The American announcement followed swiftly on the heels of the British. Their nationals would go to Manila. Then came the others. At that time the consulates in the Settlement or the French Concession included those of Guatemala, Cuba, Finland and Greece. The Swiss acted on behalf of all those nationals who, like the Germans and Italians, did not have consulates in the city.

Jim telephoned at six. Had I heard the evacuation notice? Yes, but we had a case of milk.

He said, "For my sake go. I cannot rest for worrying about you and the children." Put this way, there was no argument. "The papers will be issued at the Shanghai Club at eight. That's in two hours time. I'll meet you there and bring your passport. Oh—is the baby vaccinated?"

"I called the hospital because our doctor's away on holiday, but they said it would be difficult to get anyone, all the doctors are so busy with the wounded since the bombing. But they'll try. I picked up some vaccine and it's in the refrigerator."

"Have a new pen nib handy, if necessary we'll do it ourselves."

Other friends would take the Downstairs Missy, Mrs. Laine, to the Shanghai Club. Her sons' baby amah and our Amah would look after her two boys with our children. I wondered what would happen if a bomb fell nearby, or the Japanese army, now fighting on the edge of Jessfield Village, came this way. Some weeks before a young white woman had walked ahead of me along our road and entered a house in the British army's married quarters nearby. I ran to the house and knocked.

Mrs. O'D, a Scotswoman, was an army wife with no children and would therefore not be evacuating. She would be happy to come and stay with the amahs. "I was wishing there was something I could do for someone."

The Shanghai Club on the Bund had always been a man's domain. Members boasted of two things: theirs was the longest bar in the world, and no woman had ever crossed the threshold of the big front door. I parked the car two blocks away to protect it from possible "pixies" and met Jim at the sacred door.

At first Jim agreed to compromise. We must evacuate, but we would wait for the *Empress*. I sat on one of the long wooden benches provided for those of us waiting for the turn of the *Empress* passengers. Those who were to leave next day on the *Rajputana* had their papers issued first. Jim prowled away to compare notes with the other men.

Cabin space on the *Rajputana* was soon booked up, but still applicants stood in line for "deck space only."

Jim came back. "The situation does not look good. I think you should go tomorrow."

"But the *Raj* is all booked up. We'd have to go deck space."

"All the same the lid could blow off here. I wish you would try to get the children home."

I would be allowed "what luggage could be carried in the hand." With twins of two and a baby eight weeks old, how much was that?

Jim had arranged to get some money. All the banks were closed but he had enough to pay the servants well and still have some left for the babies and me. He drove home with me.

Mrs. O'D and Amah had things well under control. A doctor had come, the baby was vaccinated—the pen nib was not needed.

I made only one phone call and that was to Fran. She said they were leaving in three days on a French ship bound for Europe and England.

All that afternoon and most of the night Jim and I organized and sorted out possessions. Everything collected in one corner was precious, to be saved if possible. Furniture in this other room would be nice to have. Everything else could be sacrificed if necessary. After we left, if he could, Jim would arrange for storage.

The baby would travel in the wicker basket, diapers and clothing folded under the small mattress. The twins' clothing tightly rolled, was jammed into a small suitcase around and in two small potties, which they could use in an emergency. A small flight bag held necessaries for myself.

I saw Jim's haunted eyes following the twins as they played and I read his thought. It bothered me too and had to be brought into the open. The *Rajputana* was carrying a quota of round-the-world cruise passengers who would have to double up as far as Hong Kong to make room for Shanghai refugees. She was anchored twelve miles downriver near the Woosung forts and could not come up the battle-lashed river to the Shanghai docks. We would have to travel the twelve miles by tender.

A truce had been arranged between the Chinese and the Japanese from 11 A.M. to 2 P.M. to allow the foreign women and children to pass down the river. But I did not trust this temporary agreement. The time of quiet could bring with it a strong temptation to make a quick, unexpected blast...

"One thing bothers me, Jim—that twelve-mile run down the river."

"Honey, you know a truce has been arranged."

"But will they keep it?"

"I know," he said.

At eight exactly the big brown army truck called for us and we were ready. The amahs and the Pidgin were to drive downtown with us in the truck, then make their own way home. They were all from the same village in the hills above Hangchow, where "no Japanese-man have got."

Only one moment of emotion marked our departure. In the last minute I pulled a second set of underclothing over what I was already wearing, abandoned the flight bag and grabbed my typewriter.

From the open back of the big truck we saw the familiar streets in new perspective, not rolling towards us as they usually did but receding from us. Thousands of foreign flags sprinkled the Chinese crowds on the sidewalks. Union Jacks and Stars and Stripes were turned out on demand at little stalls on street corners doing a brisk business in coppers. Some were square, some long as pennants—green where they should have been blue, purple instead of red. This did not matter to those who carried them, expecting from them somehow a vague protection.

We dropped off Amah, the Pidgin and the coolie amah and saw their sad faces wedged among others jamming a crowded street car. Soon we were lining up in the corridors of the Municipal buildings. For the next two hours we stood in line, moved forward slowly, were queried at desks, sat in a hall, lined up again. Foot by foot we passed through officialdom.

"So slow!" I was almost in tears. "Oh *why* do the British always have to be so slow!"

By eleven we were ushered into buses, two or three dozen at a time, and driven between barbed-wire barricades where throngs of Chinese pressed with yearning on their faces. British sailors and Volunteers directed us until, at last, we were on the tender's deck looking down at Jim on the wharf below. I had the baby over my shoulder, the twins each holding two fingers of my free hand, luggage around my feet.

Suddenly, three small dots in the sky grew bigger—three planes flew swiftly overhead, others rushed at them like angry bees, guns on the ships in the river burst

This amazing device is an "up-to-date sound-detector" to locate aircraft from a distance. Probably employed by the Japanese in the conflict at Shanghai. They were better equipped than the Chinese.

into fire, the flower clouds bloomed overhead and shrapnel peppered the water further out. Then I understood how steady British slowness can help in an emergency. Of all those on the deck around us, of the long line of women still shuffling from the buses to the wharf, not one cried out or hesitated. As quiet settled over us again, Jim was grinning at us from the wharf and a grizzled man stationed near a shallow flight of steps commented, "You're proper soldiers now."

There was a new commotion on the wharf. My name was being called. Jim took a note a sailor waved and had it passed up to me... "Rush vivid story," the magazine at home had cabled. "What it means break up home about 1200 words."

I crushed it in my pocket and forgot about it.

23

EVEN THE SEA, GREAT AS IT IS, GROWS CALM

-Italian

S OME SAID IT WAS WHEN the planes made their unscheduled attack that the British Navy changed its plans. Our tender began to move, but not downriver. As easily as a crab on its home beach it backed and crept forward, edging sideways across a narrow strip of swift-flowing river towards a small destroyer lying parallel to the wharf. In a very few minutes the tender pulled alongside and we were lined up again and helped down a sloping gangplank to the deck of H.M.S. *Falcon*.

A sailor carried our baggage and disappeared with it. I sat hip to hip with other women on wooden lockers around a low small room. Wooden tables were pushed together in the centre with just enough room between them and us to allow the children to move around a little. My baby was on my lap, the twins pressing against my knees. It was very hot and close, and when a sailor came in someone asked if we could have a window open. He pointed out that the port holes were already wide open. "This ship was designed for a crew of 80. There are more than 1800 of you on board at this moment... "

Once again the guns began their shuddering threats. Through the open portholes we saw spurts of water, only feet away, as shells hit the river. Hip to hip, homeless and husbandless we sat, but the navy made us laugh several times as we moved downstream.

An officer poked in his head and looked at us severely. "Through this door," he announced sternly, "and straight

ahead there is another door with a paper pinned to it that says 'Ladies'." He looked at the floor, smiled and added softly, "I'll be around."

An obviously overworked seaman burst in demanding, "Any more bibies?" He pushed a wet, curly forelock off his forehead, growling disgustedly, "Single men 'ave bin mixing biby food for an hour."

One felt it was not for this that he had joined the navy.

The *Raj* was a small liner anchored just off the Settlement or western bank of the Whangpoo near its entrance to the Yangtse Kiang. A barge was moored alongside, and to this barge the *Falcon* was tied up. To board the liner we refugees had to cross the barge and step through an opening low in the ship's side. Because I had so many small children—three under three—I was asked to wait until the end of the transfer. The water was rough, the barge heaving, the *Raj* rolling slightly. On the barge deck were coils of rope and other sea-going paraphernalia... I carried the baby but a seaman was beside me with a firm grip on my elbow. Two others carried the twins and a fourth followed with our baggage.

As the unsteady craft heaved and rolled a gap of ugly water widened between them, closed again, then widened. The little boy was the first to be handed over. As the seaman who carried his sister held her towards the liner, the man on board was momentarily distracted and the child's cotton rompers, which fastened at the bottom with dome fasteners, came undone.

"Quick," called the seaman, "it's coming unstuck." The child was looking down at the water and her small face was terrified. Then strong arms from the liner took her aboard. My escort passed the baby over, I was helped across and we were all together again.

We left our baggage where we could collect it later and went on deck.

Seen from twelve miles away the city, which usually showed a skyline of white towers and domes, appeared as a thick smudge of black smoke. The guns made a constant thunder, and a voice on the loudspeaker asked everyone to keep down until we had passed the Woosung forts. We found an empty corner and settled on the deck, the twins quite content to sit quietly beside me.

We were on the Woosung side of the ship. I saw the Captain standing not far away, about four feet in from the rail, facing the shore, arms folded across his chest. Of all the more than three thousand people on that crowded ship, his must have been the only figure visible from shore. I did not know if the forts were held at that time by Chinese or Japanese, but if anyone had wanted to take a shot at the foreign vessel the Captain would have been the target.

His presence had a paralyzing effect on the whole deck. No one moved or uttered a sound as the battered old mounds slipped past us and were left behind. After the Captain left the deck, stewards came among us with trays piled with sandwiches or glasses of lemonade, and some sort of organization began taking shape on deck. Members of the ship's crew had given up their mattresses for deck passengers to sleep on, but of course there were not nearly enough to go around and we were the last to arrive. All the canvas deck chairs were set aside for smaller children who could curl up in them, but all these were already claimed. Leaving the baby with the

Indian woman next to us, and telling the twins to guard our corner with her help, I went below to fetch the baby basket, and met a friend. It was Mrs. Mac, the wife of a Scottish inspector in the Chinese Customs whom we had met on a holiday in Japan. She was booked with her two children all the way home to Glasgow. They had only a one-berth cabin—one bunk and a couch—for the three of them, but she insisted that we share it. I moved in with gratitude and left the littlest there asleep in her basket while the twins and I went to interview the Purser.

He was a weary man. When he told me the minimum fare to Hong Kong and I opened my purse to pay it he laid down his pencil and sat back in his chair. "I have seen 400 passengers so far and you are the first to pay a fare." I paid it anyway.

Then I asked if I could send a cable ashore to tell Jim that I had found a friend. He said it was impossible: "The cables have been blown up and we are out of touch with Shanghai." But we could still see the smoke above the city across the flat land.

Down in the cabin I cried. I pictured the bullets in the tattered streets, yellow bullets winging back and forth like dragonflies. There was a body lying on the dirty wet asphalt wearing the shirt and shorts of the Volunteers. Comrades turned it over to see the face...

211

Mrs. Mac had the right words to reassure me. "He is much too handsome to be hurt," she said.

That was undeniable fact. Courage took hold again. Half an hour later she was crying and I consoling her, and so continually we helped each other.

Mrs. Mac was a small woman and shared the bunk with her two children that night. We put the twins feet to feet on the narrow couch. The basket was on the floor and I stretched beside it where I could quiet the ship's youngest passenger if she stirred. The carpet was prickly and I thought uneasily that cockroaches were not far away. It was my seventh sleepless night in a row.

I was up on deck very early. It was a gray morning and we were well out to sea, pushing through fair-sized waves. Spray splashed over the railing and spattered the feet of the women who were sleeping side by side along the deck, some with tears on their cheeks.

We followed the normal routine of the day as well as we could: baby bath at ten, the twins' nap after lunch. Just before the two o'clock feeding time I stood on deck and heard a booming sound. It couldn't be, I told myself. We were much too far away.

"Isn't it silly?" I said to a stranger next to me, "I still imagine I can hear guns." She looked startled and hurried away, and soon I realized that what I was hearing was the sound of big waves meeting the ship.

As the youngest passenger battled with her meal, Mrs. Mac came into the cabin. She said she had met the Downstairs Missy, well-cared for by the ship's doctor and now the centre of a bevy of women. Mrs. Mac remarked casually that the Downstairs Missy had told her I had been at the Shanghai Club in plenty of time to book a cabin: Mrs. Laine thought it cheap of me to save money by imposing on Mrs. Mac.

"I told her I was glad to have you share with me, we helped each other."

I thanked her and explained to her that we had planned to book for the *Empress,* but I was hurt by Mrs. Laine's assumption.

Later, with all of us on deck again, another woman asked if I had heard the news: it was awful. The Japanese had overrun the Settlement, and all foreigners were

slain or imprisoned. Now a mammoth fleet was swooping down the coast on its way to attack Hong Kong and might even reach the British colony before we did.

As I stared at her, numb with horror, I suddenly remembered that we were out of touch with Shanghai. How had this news reached us? The stranger I spoke to had scurried away with such a frightened face—could this story be a rumour seeded by my thoughtless remark about hearing guns? Up went Baby to my left shoulder, two small hands clasped two fingers and we paraded down to ask the Purser.

At least it made him laugh. Not a shred of truth, he said—undefiled imagination.

He turned his tired sunken eyes to another passenger. She was on the world cruise with her daughter and they had given up their larger cabin to the refugees. Now they found their single berth cabin much too small: was there nothing better? After she had left I asked the Purser if, in the event that the woman moved out of her cabin, we could move in. After all, there were seven of us sharing Mrs. Mac's single berth.

He made a funny face. "I'll let you know."

Half an hour later the ship's boy found us and took us to a first-class cabin on the cool side of the ship, same deck as the Purser's office, two bunks and sofa, outside porthole. For the first time in several days I saw myself in a mirror. Dreadful sight: eyes as sunken as the Purser's, lips pinched, cheeks hollow. My dress, usually snug-fitting, hung in folds.

Whoever it was who gave us that cabin, the twins put on a show that night which I hope our benefactor saw and enjoyed.

In their two years of life they had known only small spaces, and the canvas-covered foyer before the bulletin board by the Purser's office intoxicated them. At bedtime they escaped naked from the cabin and fled shrieking with laughter down the corridor, chased each other madly around the canvas, threw themselves down and rolled over and over across it.

Too weary to carry both at once, I took them back one at a time. But every time I returned to the corridor, the child left in the cabin would pass me, a pink streak of bubbling joy, racing back to run and strut and roll in the circle of delighted passengers gathering for the before-dinner news bulletin. They thought it too funny to offer me help, but finally I did manage to grab both at once. Soon they were washed and sleepered and settled in for bed.

It was the baby's turn. I planned to share the sofa with her but was too tired and sat on the floor to feed her. Just before midnight Mrs. Mac, wanting to be sure that we were all right, found me still there. Three of us in the cabin were fast asleep, but the youngest, who had obviously been asleep and roused again, was wide-eyed, looking for a late snack. Mrs. Mac gave her a drink from a bottle of boiled water I had prepared and settled her easily in her basket. Then my friend flattened me out, put a pillow under my head and a blanket over me. I had fallen into such a deep sleep that I knew nothing of all this until the next morning.

24

WHAT MAN
HAS MADE,
MAN CAN DESTROY

-German

Mrs. MAC AND HER CHILDREN stayed on the *Raj* and went home to England. Our children and I spent three very difficult weeks in Hong Kong.

At that time, according to reports, there were 10,000 British living in Hong Kong. Almost overnight, they found themselves hosting 5,000 fellow-British refugees, nearly all of them without money.

A camp was set up at the Hong Kong Race Course, where large rooms were divided by sheets into cubicles containing two or sometimes three cots. A cholera epidemic was raging among Asiatics in the city, and on the day of our arrival, deaths for that day alone totalled 1800. Arrangements had to be made to give anti-cholera vaccine to arriving refugees. A camp kitchen was set up, food supplied, sanitary facilities provided. Rooms in private homes were quickly taken up by residents' own friends.

A decision was made by somebody in authority that the camp accommodation was not suitable for my small charges. We were kept on board overnight in our deluxe cabin and not permitted to go ashore until after breakfast, a kindness I deeply appreciated. With the help of friends we knew in Hong Kong, a young couple with an apartment too small for us all, we found a room in a boarding house halfway up the mountain towards The Peak. It was actually the dining room of the boarding house, but after our arrival boarders took their meals on trays in their bedrooms. Tables were cleared away and a double bed and cot were installed for the babies and myself.

The price charged seemed high, but the landlady explained that the staff had to be paid extra to carry the trays upstairs and there were other expenses, too. I had no choice.

The two windows of our room faced the back of the house about ten feet from the sheer rock wall out of which the site had been blasted from the mountain face. It was breathlessly hot and all the children instantly showed the rash of prickly heat. The kitchen was next door—dishes rattled and the Chinese staff talked from five in the morning till eleven at night. Getting the twins to sleep on anything like routine was a major problem.

The eight-week old baby was fretful and restless; her food did not agree with her. I was trying hard to breast-feed her and it took me two or three days to realize that I was the cause of her discomfort. With the twins Jim had diagnosed me as "not a dairy breed" and now my contribution was worse than negative. Fortunately I had brought synthetic baby food as a supplement, and when I gave her nothing but that, life was easier for her.

"Get the children home," Jim had said to me before we left Shanghai, so I made the rounds of the shipping companies. But all tourist accommodation was booked out of Hong Kong for months ahead. Some first-class fares might be available, but I did not have money enough and hesitated to charge or borrow it. For all I knew, we now had nothing but what was in my purse and Jim's very small savings account in Vancouver. Then, too, the "perhaps" hung in the air—perhaps everything would calm down and we could go back to Shanghai.

Wherever I went, the two-year-old twins came with me. The uphill streets were so steep that I felt the two of them and myself were too big a load for a rickshaw puller, and I would not allow us to travel in separate rickshaws. We walked down endless flights of stairs and took taxis up again. A hired baby amah stayed with the littlest, but I would not trust the feedings to her. Every four hours, the twins and I were back to look after that. Walking down the endless flight of steps, Twin Sister sat down one day, rubbed her short shins and begged, "No more up-ty Mommy!" But Hong Kong was all upties.

Baking on its rock that August of 1937, Hong Kong was infested with enormous black ants. Through the rash of the prickly heat the large red bites showed on all three children.

Surprisingly, a cable from Jim; he had found a way to get a message through to us via Nanking, and gave a return address. The twins and I had been to the cable office to send an all-safe message to Toronto, so the cable company knew where to find me. Jim also forwarded a request from a Toronto newspaper asking for the names of all Canadians who had arrived safely in Hong Kong. This proved extremely difficult, for no kind of registry was kept of the refugees anywhere. At a two-year-old's pace we crawled from office to office. Every now and then an urgent request was made for a bathroom. There were no public places in Hong Kong where I could take them; it meant finding someone who had a key and threading our way through endless hallways, and often by the time we got there, the twins had changed their minds.

Finally an official high up in Hong Kong's administration arranged to have a recurrent announcement made on the radio asking Canadians to telephone the boarding house number and ask for me. In this way I gleaned some names to send to ease the anxieties of relatives in Canada, but the cable company refused to send anything collect. Messages had to be paid for. This meant more trips over the upties to the cable office.

Nobody told me, least of all the newspaper, that they already had an accredited representative in Hong Kong who could have done all this much more easily.

The *Empress of Canada* came into port bound for Kobe, Honolulu and Vancouver. Then came an electrifying cable from Jim. "Leave granted, meeting *Canada* Kobe." She was sailing next morning. There was no way to tell him we couldn't make it. I booked third class, and we were asked to be on board by six P.M.

It was a nightmare. I hesitate to remember the abominable conditions in our tiny cabin. It was on D-deck, four narrow wooden shelves holding rough straw-filled pallets. There was no air-conditioning, no portholes, for we were below the water-line, and no stewardess service. The bathrooms were two flights up.

The children's skin was raw with heat rash and insect bites. All night I sat on a folding stool in the narrow corridor outside the open cabin door.

At six the next morning, I took the children up to the Purser's office. (Navigating a ship's stairs and corridors with three small children requires technique; for those who might be called on to do it, here is some advice: hold baby on left shoulder with left arm and hand, have todlers on right side, one holding index finger, one holding little finger on right hand; use left hip to steady self against stair rails or walls of rolling vessel.)

"My husband would never forgive me if he saw where we are," I told the Purser. "I'll have to cable my family for money and go first class."

He said, "Can you stick it for three hours? We're due to sail then. In port the ship belongs to the office; those fellows have never seen where you are or they would never have put you there. Once we're under way the ship is mine and I can put you where I like."

We found a patch of shade on the third-class deck under a lifeboat. The ship did not sail in three hours. We sat in the stifling harbour until noon. Once a seaman, obviously British, came by and peeked into the baby's basket. He asked if he might take the baby for a walk; I told him that as long as he stayed in sight, okay. He carried her tenderly, cooing sweet somethings, and when she went to sleep, put her gently back in the basket.

A woman passenger from the tourist class came to visit saying that she had heard about us. "Everybody's interested." She too asked if she might take the baby for a little while. Glad to get the little one away from the glare of the third-class deck, and feeling I could trust her, I consented. While they were gone our seaman came back, tiptoed to the basket, all a-grin, then looked shocked. He turned a horrified face to me. "Somebody's taiken our baiby!" I explained, but he shook his head disapprovingly. The sun rose higher and hotter, the shade grew smaller. We peregrinated down into the still heat of the bathrooms, where all the twins could do was play with the water taps—

Then—oh, then—we moved! The ship backed from the dock, edged into the open channel. There was a breeze and we lifted our faces to it. Our seaman came and told us that the Purser wanted us. He carried the basket with the baby in it again. We were given a cabin with four large berths and a couch, an outside porthole— open. Three stewardesses crowded around us. One took the baby, one took the twins for a splashy bath. One insistently put me to bed and brought tea in a flowered teapot.

The voyage to Kobe took about five days. Heat rashes vanished, bites became only scars. Two days out from Hong Kong a cable arrived which we should have received before the one we had. It said, "Am trying for compassionate leave doctor helping try to book *Canada*."

Normally the *Canada* would have called at Shanghai but because of the fighting there it did not. The *Canada* and the *Empress of Japan* were the two luxury ships of the *White Empress* fleet. Other shipping schedules, too, were disorganized, but Jim was at Kobe, two burning eyes under a sun helmet and a big hand to hold. He had made it on a Japanese fishing boat, crouching on his heels with the crew to have water-cress soup for breakfast.

It was a fair weather voyage after that on the big *White Empress* through Hawaiian seas home to Canada. At Honolulu there was time for us to walk the sands of Waikiki Beach and drive among papaya and pineapple plantations around the northern head of Oahu Island.

As we entered the cool Vancouver atmosphere and the new little baby neared her third-month anniversary my body suddenly healed itself from her birth.

The train took us from Vancouver to Jim's home in the Okanagan Valley depositing us almost on the doorstep. Beside an enormous black tree stump seven miles north of Kelowna the puffing black locomotive came to a stop and we de-trained. There was no station but the two-storey log farm house where Jim had spent his boyhood stood close by. We learned that the train often made an unscheduled pause here because Jim's mother, renowned for her good butter, left cool fresh butter-

milk in a big bottle among the stump's roots for the train crew. Now the crew were saying "Thank you" by delivering her elder son and his family home from China.

In three or four weeks we were on the move again by train through mountain tunnels and passes, over the prairies and past the northern forests and lakes to Toronto.

The winter in Toronto was a happy one. We found a small apartment on the beach, without furniture, and sat on the floor to talk to old friends. At Christmas time I walked with my sister through large, slow-falling snowflakes to a candle-light carol service in the local library.

Jim had to go back to Shanghai in March when his leave was up and I packed, determined to go with him. But on the day we were to leave, Hitler's troops marched into Czechoslovakia and NO confronted me again. "The whole world may explode," said Jim. "We just can't risk it." He went alone.

The intervening weeks were difficult. The apartment already had new tenants but two friends gave up the lower rooms of their small house to us and improvised living quarters for themselves upstairs.

Mail crossed the Pacific via the U.S. *President* liners and Manila every three weeks. Sometimes the vessels ran into trouble and there was a six-week span of waiting between letters. Newspapers at home were little help.

Now that the fighting between Chinese and Japanese had "passed inland", there was no longer interest in the Settlement at Shanghai. Occasional small stories ran on inside pages with agonizing headlines: "Cholera in Shanghai", "Foreigners Under Fire". No names were given.

The fighting "inland" was only a mile or two from Settlement boundaries, and Jim's letters swung between hope and hopelessness. Things seemed to be settling down, it might be possible for us to return; then, no, there had been another international incident, relations were too brittle. Soon food was trickling back down the creeks, markets looked almost normal; again, no, the battles were swinging back towards the Whangpoo.

The Japanese seemed to have decided that this part of the world belonged to them. The High Command announced that when passing a Japanese sentry, anyone of any nationality must not be smoking, must remove his hat and bow to the sentry as the representative of His Imperial Majesty the Son of Heaven. Jim's work often took him into Japanese territory and I could not see him obeying this command. Failure to comply, the official announcement said, would lead to serious consequences.

At last I asked him what he did about the sentries. He said, "I'm careful not to smoke when approaching a sentry box and I've stopped wearing a hat altogether. That takes care of that."

"But do you bow?"

"I do not." He smiled his impudent Irish smile. "I grin at them."

221

In these weeks of acute anxiety during our winter in Toronto, something happened to me which I have learned since has happened to many others. My sister had loaned me a small radio on which I listened to the news broadcasts. As I was scrambling eggs for the children's lunch, a brief story was reported from Shanghai. A foreigner's body, riddled with bayonet wounds, had been recovered from the Whangpoo. Police were investigating. The "foreigner" could have belonged to any nationality other than Chinese, the wounds could have been inflicted for any of several reasons. Was it Jim? Had his smile for the Japanese sentries not been enough? His work with the Council and also the Volunteers took him often into Hongkew and other Japanese occupied territory. Foreigners who transgressed the Japanese rules were held for questioning in the new high-rise apartment building called Broadway Mansions on Soochow Creek near the Astor House. Their "cells" were small concrete-floored cubicles in the basement designed for storage. Often they were bound. Our friend Bloomie, Jim had written, ran into this kind of trouble and died in his cell. The uncertainty seemed more than one could bear—and then the load was lifted.

From somewhere beyond myself the words were stamped on my consciousness as though they had been clearly spoken beside me: "He will come through safely." The statement was so positive that it could not be questioned. There was a God and He had spoken to me.

I went on stirring the scrambled eggs, suffused with gratitude and the elation of praise. The children were called, washed, fed and put to rest. I wanted to tell them, but the time would come later. The rest of the day moved by and the weeks followed, but now I knew what I had so often asked to know. The knowledge brought an infinite strength.

August was always our lucky month. One evening a stranger appeared in front of the small house asking if anybody at our address knew anyone in Shanghai. He said he was a ham radio operator and had picked up a message from the mid-States which had been picked up in California from a ham in the Fiji Island who received it

from Shanghai.

The message had been dictated by Jim to Sergeant O'D of the British garrison regiment, now Jim's good friend. Scrawled on a torn scrap of paper, it went like this: "Taking house West End Gardens September mxgwlns mingnons vsf sending love all well love Jim."

It was enough. West End Gardens was a pretty compound of small houses off Yu Yuen Road. I booked passage on the *Empress of Asia*, which sailed from Vancouver on September 3rd and followed the cheaper northern passage to the Orient excluding Honolulu. Two letters from Shanghai arrived in the mail, but both were written before the radio message and said nothing about West End Gardens. However, both were encouraging.

The train to Vancouver left late at night. My sister and her husband drove us to the station. On the train I planned that if "No" caught up with us now I would pretend it hadn't reached me. Jim was likely to be overly cautious about us, but the Bakers and other friends had returned to the Settlement—it should be safe for us too. Fortunately, no "No" arrived.

When at last we reached Shanghai, we anchored at the usual *Empress* dock across the river and Jim came with the tender to meet us. His arms were the circumference of the world.

We drove into the familiar streets, up Nanking Road, around the Race Course, on to the Bubbling Well and the Temple of Tranquil Repose. There were no rice lines, no machine guns. The people of the Settlement went about their normal business.

The tiny garden of our little house in West End Gardens was bright with flowers. The front door opened and there was Amah, smiling. A tall boy behind her she introduced as her son, who was to be our new Pidgin. In the shadows of the hall shone another smile, the coolie amah who had been with us the year before, after Ah Zee had left.

Through one of Jim's foremen and the incredible bamboo wireless, word had filtered through to Amah in her mountain village that the children and I were returning to Shanghai. At his office one day Jim was told that a Chinese woman wished to see him. It was Amah.

"My flen' talkee me no go Shanghai," she told us. "My

flen' talkee plenty Japanese men have got Shanghai. I talkee my flen': suppose Missy can go, *I* can go."

"Oh, Amah, I'm so glad you came."

Behind the kitchen there were rooms for the staff and our little organization was functioning once more.

Before the Trouble Amah could reach her home in one day, starting early. Coming back to Shanghai now took six days, passing through two army lines ("have all times catchee paper, plenty paper") and sleeping overnight in open boats, sometimes in the rain, or in small sheds on the creek banks.

In addition to our three house helpers we had a part-time gardener who supplied all the plants (we grew no vegetables) from a "big garden" where he was also employed.

The children were enchanted. "Mummy, mummy, come and see this wonderful thing we've found in the garden." It was a double petunia and they had arranged their three small wicker chairs in front of it so that they could sit and look at it.

These chairs were important, for the delta soil was infested with flukes and the children must never sit on the ground. We had a sandbox built on legs and arranged with the Public Works Department to have sand brought down by barge from cliffs well up the Yangtse River. It arrived at about five o'clock one morning in great baskets slung on poles carried on the shoulders of grinning coolies. It costed us a lot of money. For a few days the children played there happily. Then Amah reported, "Please Missy I think-so this play box no good for baby. I think-so plenty kitty too much likee."

She was right. The sand was carted away by more coolies, the sandbox scrubbed, more sand imported from the Yangtse Kiang, and a strong cover hooked in place at night. Again the children played happily until the day their play turned to filling their small buckets and carting them upstairs to be dumped in toilet and bath tub. It took several hours to find a plumber to undo that caper and again the cost of the sandbox soared higher. We banished sand but kept the box. It quickly became a submarine with the children's three wicker chairs aboard and a flag which Amah helped to contrive.

Public relations: a friendly Japanese soldier giving candy to Chinese children behind the lines outside Shanghai

The war was not far away. Our house was at the end of a terrace, and beyond our garden fence of woven bamboo was a vacant stretch of land. Then came the high stone walls surrounding the home of Wang Ching Wei, long-time political rival of Chiang Kai Shek and now the Japanese-recognized head of the Nationalist government. Gun turrets on the high stone wall housed guards with machine guns, and we often saw the long noses of the guns following the children as they played: the guards were amusing themselves. In 1938 Japan was not at war with Britain and would not want to provoke an International Incident. Every day a detachment of British troops marched smartly through the compound, always to the end of our terrace, as a reminder to the guards and every one else, that we were under extra-territorial protection.

A local collaborator paints over a painted British flag on a building.

Beyond the compound open trucks filled with Japanese soldiers patrolled the Outside Roads because they now controlled the areas outside the Settlement. Every now and then the soldiers lifted their rifles, which were bayonetted, and fired into the sky.

At night, machine guns chattered in the darkness. These were Chinese guerillas harrassing the occupying forces. Jessfield Park was no longer safe for us. When one family moved back to their home on Hungjao Road, a stray bullet killed their son as he slept on a sun porch. Other homes remained empty.

Jim drove me through Chapei, a Chinese district where we had often walked in the "cocktail hour", stopping to watch artisans at work or chat with the proprietors of stores. Now it was a shambles of burned and gutted houses, street after street of stark, corpse-like walls without a sign of human life.

"We did a lot of clean-up here," said Jim. On his return in March he had been assigned to help supervise the disposal of 300,000 dead the war had left around Shanghai. None of this had been mentioned in his letters home.

It was important to the Chinese to be buried in the fields of their fathers, where sons and grandsons could make annual sacrifices during Ching Ming. In such a holocaust as that which struck Shanghai in 1937 this was impossible. From shattered houses, ditches, ponds or fields where they had lain for weeks bodies were gathered up, stacked with timbers or other burnable debris, doused with crude oil and burned.

At the request of the Japanese authorities mules and horses left behind by their army were similarly garnered.

In one continuing pyre, in one day, Jim and those with him burned more than a thousand bodies with 60 mules and horses burned in a similar pyre nearby.

This work was finished but the crematorium smell still hung over the city, especially when it rained.

Chinese from other parts of China who died during this period were embalmed in coffins and stacked one above the other, regardless of wealth and position, in large bamboo go-downs along the Settlement's western fringe. When one go-down was filled another was built alongside—macabre apartment houses for the dead.

25

A WEAPON
IS AN ENEMY
TO ITS OWNER

-Turkish

ON OUR VOYAGE BACK from Canada the children and I made friends with an elderly Englishman and his nineteen-year-old daughter. He was the Superintendent of the School for the Chinese Blind, previously housed in a fine group of buildings in pretty grounds behind red brick walls on Hungjao Road. At the outbreak of hostilities the Transport Company had evacuated the school to the Settlement, where they were given quarters in St. Luke's Refugee Hospital on Brenan Road. The Superintendent's wife had died in England during the following winter and he and his daughter were coming back to try to re-establish the School in its former quarters.

The wide barbed-wire barricades, which British troops had put up around the western fringe of the Settlement and Outside Roads before the evacuation, was still in place. It was possible to drive through it at openings guarded by sentries. Twenty feet beyond the British barricade was now another barricade equally as wide and also negotiable through openings guarded by Japanese sentries. One had to have passes and papers to satisfy both sentries.

When we were invited to tea at the Blind School, our friends said they would send their own car and chauffeur for us and he would drive us home again. He had all the necessary papers. Jim was not able to come with us but felt it was quite safe for us to go. I wore no hat and was a non-smoker. Neither did I bow.

In the preceding months both warring armies had occupied the Blind School buildings, and both armies had shelled it. There were large holes in walls and windows, craters in the gardens, breaks in the paved walks. Ugly black pits gaped indoors where bonfires had been kindled on the floors, with doors, window frames, cupboards and furniture used as fuel. All this the elderly Superintendent, his nineteen-year-old private school daughter and their dedicated Chinese Boy were setting out to repair with whatever help they could entice to come out to the devastated Hungjao area.

Not even the Chinese had returned to Hungjao. The small villages where children had played, geese patrolled and rosy-cheeked country women gossiped were only heaps of blasted rubbish. Here and there corners of what had once been small homes still stood, bare and empty, like fragments of eggshells on vacant ground.

Trees in the Blind School grounds put out new leaves on the stumps of their branches. Beneath them in the long grass lay limbs and torsoes of dolls the blind children had played with, twisted tricycles or wagons they had learned to propel around the paths. Before one doorway was a pile of broken china, evidently smashed in sport. Grieving, the young girl identified pieces of an heirloom tea set of her mother's and mugs her school in England had donated.

Most senseless and tragic was the wanton destruction of Chinese braille printing equipment in the small print shop. Establishing this print shop had been the Superintendent's lifelong labour. Now it seemed quite irreplaceable.

One did not think, "The Japanese did this" or "The Chinese did that." Somehow it was beyond such narrow limits. One only thought, "War did this."

We ate jam from England with tender tea biscuits Young Missy had made herself and drank tea or milk from new cups as the smiling Boy moved quietly in and out, supplying what was needed. It did not seem safe for these three living there, where not one door could be securely locked. But they would not for a moment consider leaving. When not teaching at the School on Brenan Road they spent their time cleaning, shovelling debris, hammering and painting, collecting what they could, hastening, they hoped, the homecoming of the Chinese Blind.

Like our friends at the Blind School, those of us who lived inside the barbed wire barricades were holding a brief for the future. The 99-year lease, under which the broad streets were laid and the big buildings erected on swampy ground, would expire in three or four years time; but so much money had been invested, so great was the bulk of shipping in the port, so important the volume of business to both China and the foreign powers that it seemed inevitable that the lease would be extended for another 99 years.

The spirit of international comradeship had been temporarily shattered. At the outbreak of war, like rats to their holes, we had retreated to the safety of our own nationalities. The Chinese street population no longer carried little foreign flags. The Americans were confidently all-American. We Canadians were not only Canadians, we were also British; the British troops and navy whom everyone acknowledged as invincible belonged to us as much as to our English friends. The Dutch and Swiss were virtuously neutral, the Japanese aloof and arrogant.

The tub-shaped German Chemist from whom we bought our aspirin and baby supplies jubilantly supported Hitler. From under the counter he brought a bottle of Schnapps and urged us to join him in a toast to The Leader. When we refused, he poured our drinks anyway and told us to toast whomever we liked—each other maybe?

Most serene of all were the stateless White Russians. If nobody wanted them, neither were they anybody's enemy. No threatening army or belligerent government stood behind them. Whoever was top man in the foreign settlements, their status would remain unchanged.

As far as possible the Settlement's social routine was maintained: the cards and cocktail hours at the clubs; the movies and cabaret; the three big annual Balls on their appointed days—St. George's, St. Andrew's and St. Patrick's.

We had our little home dinner parties, saw the Russian

Ballet, and heard the Cossacks' Chorus at the Opera House, went to movies and slapped our knees in the dance of the day—the Lambeth Walk.

But it wasn't the same.

In the night, machine guns would suddenly rattle as guerillas harrassed the occupying forces. Whenever we went out Jim wished to take his pistol with him, but I wanted it left at home. "If there is trouble and you have your pistol you'll be in the thick of it. If you haven't your pistol, you'll have to stay out of it."

He complained that half an hour after we left home I started worrying about the children and wanted to go back again. I denied this but knew it to be true.

Strict curfew was maintained from midnight until six A.M. Those who danced or visited beyond midnight had to stay where they were until daybreak. Passes could sometimes be obtained but if stopped on the streets without a pass the night was finished at a police station. Once we were challenged.

"Oh, officer," exclaimed the gentle Russian woman we were driving home, "please don't stop us. I must get home to feed my baby." We were allowed to drive on. Next day she telephoned me. As soon as she and her husband were in the house, she said, she poured a glass of milk and hurried upstairs to waken their 14-year-old daughter. "She was so surprised and said she didn't want it, but I made her drink it. She is the only baby that we have, and I didn't want to be a liar."

Our friends Sergeant and Mrs. O'D still lived in the terrace of houses where we had first known them. She had been warned by doctors that having a child might cost her her life, but the O'D's were taking the risk and we shared the experience with them.

One day about noon she telephoned me. She was supposed to stay in bed, she said, but an old beggar was lying just outside their kitchen door, moaning terribly as he died. She wanted to help him, but her Chinese Boy refused to touch him and would not even take him water. Because of her pregnancy she hesitated to try to help the old man herself: what could she do?

I had to tell her that, even if she weren't pregnant, I

did not think she could do anything. Among other things, she had the devils to contend with. The working classes of the Chinese would believe that the devils had the old man in their powers and could quickly transfer to anyone who interfered, which explained her Boy's reluctance. Also under Chinese codes, if she aided the old beggar and he died, numerous relatives could claim compensation from her husband. I promised to telephone a friend in the Police and ask what should be done.

My friend pointed out the legal complications. Since Mrs. O'D lived on an Outside Road the street in front of her house was under Municipal jurisdiction, but the alley behind her back door was Chinese territory. For Settlement authorities to give assistance would be an infringement of Treaty Rights. He said he would contact the Chinese Police in that area but doubted that anything would be done—because of the war, death was commonplace in and around Shanghai.

Nothing was done. Nothing was done. Hour after hour the tattered beggar moaned in the alley. Passing Chinese stopped to look at him but nobody helped him. Even after Sergeant O'D came home that evening the situation could not be altered.

At last, in the night, the groans dwindled to silence. Sergeant O'D and the Boy passed a rope under the dead man's arms and dragged the body to the street in front of the house. There, before dawn, a Settlement patrol gathered it up and moved it to a main street where the Chinese Benevolent Society took over.

The Benevolent Society was formed by well-to-do Chinese businessmen to help the very poor. There were always many Chinese poor in the Settlement, but under the Land Regulations their welfare was the responsibility of the Chinese community. The point had not been covered in the original Treaty since at that time the foreign communities were taboo to Chinese. When Municipal authorities applied to the Chinese Government to have it incorporated they were refused, for the Central Government was still determined not to extend in any way the power of the foreigners.

Deaths among the poor greatly increased when the war refugees flooded the Settlement. Their families were too destitute to arrange for burial. Around dawn every morning a van provided by the Benevolent Society made a circuit of the main streets to collect these bodies and arrange for satisfactory burials.

Visiting journalists, not knowing this background and seeing bodies on the streets in the early mornings, wrote scathingly of the callousness of the "Foreign Devils".

To keep our minds from brooding on the local problems, Fran and I began studying Chinese cooking. Under Amah's guidance I chose the simple Shanghai style, but Fran, who had to entertain her husband's business associates, took up the more classical and fashionable Mandarin or Pekinese. Both Pekinese and Cantonese cooking seemed to favour a combination of ingredients and sauces, but in the Shanghai style each ingredient was cooked separately and served in its own bowl in the centre of the table. Guests who had lived a long time in China referred to my Chinese fare as "coolie chow", which at first I thought referred to its economy. However, Mrs. Dolly Chiu, author of a reference book on Chinese cooking, stated that "coolie chow" referred to the average daily meal Chinese families enjoyed at home. At such meals all the main course dishes were served at once instead of the more formal serving of only one dish at a time. Serving all the food at once but in separate bowls was the way Amah taught us, and Jim and I preferred it this way.

The Chinese were proud of their cooking and different regions had their own specialties. The North (populated chiefly by Moslem non-pork eaters) was famous for its duck. Ningpo, just north of the Yangtse Kiang, was known for good soup, and tong-kwai or soup bowl was the nickname applied to all men from that province. Soochow claimed superiority in tea because of its delicious water, and it was said that the great Emperors always had bottles of Soochow water to ensure good tea when visiting the lesser Warlords.

Dr. Wang of the Municipal Health Department, well educated and always friendly, taught me many interesting things. He said that the Chinese had long recognized that man is what he eats. In early days rich men greeting

each other did not ask, "How are you?" but, "How is the health of your cook?"

Once a week we had a Chinese dinner, often sharing it with guests. I learned to use green ginger with fish, a dash of gin or other spirits when cooking pork cubes. Amah or I chose vegetables for their colour—the *bah-tsei*, a chard-like plant with bright green leaf and broad, snow-white stalk; or *cong-tsei* a red-purple creeper which at home is regarded as a ground weed. Amah shyly charged that "this English Missy" spoiled such foods by boiling them in water. She said boiling weakened flavour and made the vegetable tough. Better to chop the greens and add them to hot fat ("makee dance, this oil") with only the water they were washed in adhering to them. Prepared this way, and steamed tightly covered over low heat until all liquid was absorbed, even prosaic home-style cabbage had a bit of glamour.

I learned that to gourmet Chinese there should be three qualities in every dish: flavour, colour and contrasting texture. The bright pink roots of spinach give both colour and contrasting crispness to the dark-green

234

velvet of the leaf. Bamboo shoots and water chestnuts, besides having a delicate flavour that is usually lost when canned, retain their whiteness and crispness through cooking. So does does celery to a lesser degree.

Chinese custom in Shanghai also decreed duck soup or fish served after the main courses, just before dessert.

With our dinners we served Chinese wines in exquisite small cups. These wines were fairly strong, and two cupsful seemed enough to last the meal. Mr. Ho, the grocer, had many varieties and told me that the flavours—orange peel, herbs, plums or flowers—were always added after they were distilled.

For dessert we stayed with dates or oranges or, as a change from sweetness, *tzo-ih-dau* or tea-eggs, peddled and sung of by street vendors. We made our own, lightly hard-boiling eggs, then gently rolling them so that the shells were cracked. The eggs were then simmered in tea for about ten minutes, peeled and served hot, with fresh-brewed tea in pretty Chinese covered cups.

Amah now enjoyed answering the telephone, and this had become one of her duties. In the overcrowded conditions of the wartime Settlement, wrong numbers were frequent and roused her to furious invective. She would never hang up as long as the caller was on the line and for some reason callers were hard to convince. Her shrill tirades, literally translated, went something like this:

"Hullo? Who man you? No mind who man me, who man you? Wrong number. Wrong number, Pig. What number you want? No mind what number me, what number you? Pig! Devil! Wrong number, who man, who man, pig, devil, who man?"

These verbal encounters convulsed our guests and apparently intrigued the callers, for Amah would no sooner be back in the kitchen before the phone rang again.

Jim found the solution. In Japan we had heard hotel boys answer the phone with a high-pitched *"moshee-moshee."* Now, if the phone rang a second time, Jim would answer. In a shrill voice he intoned, *"moshee-moshee?"*

This induced a long, stunned silence. Then the receiver at the other end of the line would go very carefully back on its hook.

26

DON'T PULL
HARD ENOUGH
TO BREAK THE ROPE

-Portuguese

ALTHOUGH WE TRIED to pretend otherwise, the Settle-ment had somehow lost its meaning. We were no longer a community of many people existing at peace with each other. Instead we were becoming fragments of the old embattled world outside, on guard against each other, defensively maintaining our individual free-dom.

We saw aggression on the faces of the Japanese, poli-tics in the smiles of the Chinese, smug self-interest in the blandness of the neutrals. Every glance, given or re-ceived, contained a threat.

Fred Baker decided he could operate his business bet-ter from London than from the war-encircled city and he and Fran went back to England for the last time. Basil suffered a stroke and was invalided home in a wheel-chair. Our circle of friends dwindled and changed.

Bullets flew astray in and around Jessfield. A young Chinese was killed there. It was no longer safe for the children.

The gardener planted the garden with perennials but the spring rains flooded them out. He planted again from his seemingly inexhaustible supply and as they were coming into bloom a wandering typhoon dumped rain from its outside edges on Shanghai at the peak of high tide. Downtown streets were flooded and so were West End Gardens.

A municipal chauffeur called for Jim each morning

and brought him home in the late afternoon, the car spreading sheets of water on either side of the roadway. In the garden dozens of green frogs swam. The children watched them from the sunporch windows and made paper boats to launch from the doorstep.

The nearest open space where I could take the children to run inside Settlement boundaries was the foreign cemetery on the corner opposite the Temple of Tranquil Repose. Four life-size stone angels draped their wings at the corners of a rich man's burial plot just inside the high iron gates, inspiring the name 'The Angel's Garden'. The children ran on the wide gravelled walks, hid behind monuments and tombstones and stayed off the graves except when they tenderly rearranged bouquets of real or artificial flowers blown awry by wind or rain. We avoided Baby Row. Before driving home we always peeked into the Bubbling Well in the middle of the street.

The paper often carried stories of indignities heaped on foreigners in the north; how they were forced to strip in public or mercilessly detained for long periods of time for no apparent reason. When we were again asked to tea at the Blind School on Hungjao Road I was uneasy about the sentries at the Japanese barbed wire barricades.

Again our friends' chauffeur called for us with all the necessary papers. Along the road, weeds and grass grew in the ruins of the villages and softened their starkness. At the Blind School progress was remarkable. The Superintendent's living quarters, the big dining room and one long dormitory were completely repaired. Grass was cut under one group of shade trees and the children played there rapturously.

The Chinese Braille print shop was still a shambles and that to me was the ultimate senseless tragedy. What possible purpose was served by its destruction?

A new Japanese sentry was on duty when we were driven home, a thin, sullen man with narrow, hooded eyes. He examined our papers slowly, in great detail. The great emptiness of the derelict countryside stretched around us. The sentry on the British side of the barbed wire barricades was not in sight.

At last the papers were handed back, the car began to move forward, then a sharp command stopped us. The car backed up. What now? Were we to be another International Incident? I felt as stiff as a granite statue, the smallest child sitting on my knee, the twins crowding close on either side, my arms enclosing all three. The Japanese was groping in his shelter just behind him. He held his rifle with its bayonet in front of him. What was he groping for? Without the faintest change of expression he thrust a wilted bunch of zinnias through the open window onto my lap and motioned the chauffeur to drive on.

The British sentry was in front of his box, and the delay here was barely long enough to stop the wheels of the car from turning, no time even to smile. We gathered up the wilted flowers and rushed them to water when we reached home. I would tell Jim they were a gift from His Imperial Majesty. But why?

We suffered from inflation in the Settlement. Bread, which had been 20¢ a loaf, was now $1.20, coal leapt from $10 a ton to $250. Children's leather sandals, which the cobbler had once custom-made for us for $12, went up to $50. Then the cobbler disappeared and we could find no other who made children's leather sandals. Amah made prettily embroidered cotton slippers and kept the children shod.

"It used to be," said Jim, "that living here one could save something. Now it takes all we have just to keep going, so what's the point?"

The point was that in about three year's time he would qualify for a lifetime pension and that was worth trying for. We did not own the house, but we could sell the lease. Families leaving the Settlement for home usually sold their major furnishings by auction, but Shanghai in 1938 was a buyer's market, and the buyers were few. Precious possessions could be packed, stored and shipped by professionals, but the packers were Chinese and no Chinese wanted to come out to West End Gardens. The sensible course for us was surely to wait it out.

"There will be no war in Europe," our German chemist assured us. "Our great leader is dedicated to achieve our ends without war."

"What are your ends?"

"Our just deserts."

A shipment of small denominational currency due from the Chinese National Bank in Nanking did not arrive and we had a coin shortage. If you gave a one dollar bill for 20 cents worth of cabbage, you received back a scrap of paper with some hieroglyphic pencilled on it. Nobody else would honour this scrap of paper, and if you took it back to the man who had given it to you he would disclaim all knowledge of it. The whole situation seemed totally out of control. Nobody could assume tonight what tomorrow's expenses would be.

When we knew that our fourth child was coming, Jim wrote out his resignation but kept it in his pocket. However, I was never any good at the baby business. In August the doctor said that the children and I must go home within three months and must have either Jim or a registered nurse with us. The resignation was handed in on August 4th with a petition urged by the doctor that Jim be allowed to leave in two months instead of the required six.

We considered bringing Amah home with us, but after many discussions, with her and others, we decided against it. Most of the Chinese in Canada at that time were Cantonese, and it would be hard for Amah to find a countryman who even spoke her own language. Dialects in the different regions of China were so different that a Shanghai woman married to a Cantonese had to converse with him in Pidgin English. Amah's staple foods would be hard to find in Canada and the climate would be difficult for her. Shanghai was sometimes cold in winter but was classed as semi-tropical, and Amah's home village was ninety miles further south. In the end, we found Amah a place with a Canadian friend of ours, but she left after a month.

We took with us envelopes addressed in both English and Chinese to her at her home so that I could write and tell her about the new baby. (Amah foretold correctly that the baby would be a boy. Her reason: my last baby had said "da-da" before she said "ma-ma".) I did write to Amah, sending the letter to her village in Chekiang pro-

vince and the letter reached her after six months. One
year later we received Amah's reply, written in a fine spi-
dery script, perhaps by her son or by a professional letter
writer. Amah was at home and apparently safe and
happy. Because of the conditions reported in China at
that time we did not dare to write her again.

27

THE BEGINNING
OF HEALTH
IS SLEEP

-Irish

WAR WAS DECLARED on September 3rd, 1939, and the British Consulate issued an appeal to all British men to stay at their posts in the Settlement. Jim had already resigned and felt that under the circumstances he could not retract.

Among the rumours that flew around us was one that a fleet of German submarines was already at Vladivostok vowing to clear the Pacific of the proud white *Empresses*. All information about the *Empresses* became 'classified'. Nobody knew when they would arrive, when they would leave or by what routes they would travel.

Jim booked passages for us on a Japanese liner leaving for Vancouver from Kobe. We would make connection by taking the 20,000-ton regular ferry between Shanghai and Nagasaki, travel by train to Shimonoseki on the north coast of Kyushu Island, cross the narrow straits on a small barge for standing passengers only, then take the night train to Kobe.

Because of the war with China, the Japanese army had priority claims on all trains, and reservations for seats as well as berths had to be made well in advance. Jim's head foreman, Chang, found a crew of Chinese and saw to the packing of our precious possessions, which then departed by van into oblivion. When the *Empress of Canada* appeared in the Whangpoo one morning, Chang got our barrels aboard and the ship sailed 'for ports unknown' as suddenly as she had arrived. We received the barrels

241

about six months later. Not long afterwards the *Canada* became a troop ship and was torpedoed in the Red Sea.

Most of our personal baggage was sent ahead to Kobe, but we carried a motley assortment of hand luggage with us which baggage authorities would not accept. The twins carried their big Teddy Bears and the smaller girl a beloved rag doll with home-made checked pants. Two suitcases contained the children's overnight things and the individual "conveniences" which always had to be ready. My portable typewriter was never accepted as baggage and had to be carried. We also had two violins, my own and one for the children. There was a four-foot-long wooden box containing quantities of cotton wool safeguarding the tube of the huge thermometer that had stood in front of the best-known bookstore in the Settlement—we had acquired the thermometer along with the house in West End Gardens. All these, with our coats and personal night bags, made a formidable heap in the cabin. They were all checked and ready and we had our passports, cholera certificates and other papers demanded by Japan-at-War. The train for the four-hour trip to Shimonoseki came to the dock and our ferry was due to arrive in plenty of time for us to make the transfer to our reserved compartment.

The Japanese port doctor at Nagasaki refused to accept the anti-cholera inoculation certificates signed by our Shanghai doctor. As we entered the harbour small bottles were issued and every passenger ordered to produce a "sample" which the port doctor could test himself. Passengers were dismayed. The children refused point-blank to oblige, although we unpacked the conveniences for them and coaxed them to be good. Out in the corridors tempers were seething. Through the porthole we saw our train arrive on the dock and stand, hissing and waiting.

Miracle of miracles! One of the three co-operated. Joyfully we filled our bottles with the one sample: there was a knock on the door and a kindly gray-haired lady conspiratorially whispered that she had some sample to spare if we needed it. We thanked her but said we were all fixed up, and she knocked on the next cabin door.

We moved the heap of hand luggage to the deck near the gangway to be ready for speedy transfer to the train, but officials at the gangway said we could not leave. The port doctor was not satisfied with the sample from a third-class passenger and wished to conduct another test.

"Oh no! Not us again!"

No, only the third-class passenger. But we must wait. We explained that our train was due to leave, reservations had been made weeks before, we had to catch a ship that was sailing from Kobe next morning. The official's face was quite impassive, as he said, "So sorry."

We took the hand baggage back to the cabin to wait. After all the excitement the children napped. Our train pulled away without us—then came the glad tidings that the third-class passenger did not have cholera, and we were now free to disembark.

We stuffed ourselves into a taxi and went to the railway station, but there was no way to get to Kobe that night. Railway officials were "so sorry", but apparently unmoved. Then someone suggested that if we came back next day the same train that we had missed today would take us on to Tokyo, where our ship would call before starting for Vancouver.

"We'll do that. Can we make reservations?"

"So sorry. No reservations left."

"Not even for seats? We can't stand all the way to Tokyo. My wife— "

"So sorry."

So much for that. We decided to have our loaded taxi drive us to Mogi, the small fishing village six miles away where we had spent a happy holiday two years before. We would enjoy ourselves, the children could play on the beach next morning and then we would come back and try again.

Next day we boarded the train and an Englishman on the teaching staff of Tokyo University took us into his private compartment as far as Shimonoseki. We stood on the crowded ferry across the darkening straits with a porter who had promised to put our luggage on board the Kobe train. We stood in the aisle as the train pulled out and Jim disappeared. A sweet-faced Japanese woman insisted I take her seat. Then Jim came back with a guard whom he had bribed generously to allow us to sit in the observation car—on condition that not even the children settle to sleep until the last privileged passenger had gone to his berth. We settled there, our suitcases, thermometer, typewriter, Teddy Bears and violins heaped in a corner.

One passenger, a portly uniformed Japanese soldier whom we thought a General, sat sipping his drink until midnight. When he at last went to bed, we pushed together four big chairs to make beds for the twins. The littlest child slept in my lap and Jim stretched out in the General's big over-stuffed chair. The lights never went out.

Six in the morning brought us to Kobe and a two-hour stop. We headed for a hotel, and I took the children to a washroom where we cleaned the soot from our faces. Then we ordered breakfast in the dining room, but Jim was still at the desk asking questions. Four or five of the hotel staff were insisting that the ship had sailed the night before, but a porter said he had heard she had been delayed 24 hours and was still at the dock.

"Call me a taxi!" said Jim.

"But sir! Even if the ship is still there you cannot go aboard until two this afternoon. There will be nobody at this hour to admit you."

"Call me a taxi just the same."

We wrapped toast and fruits, jam and boiled eggs, knives, forks and spoons in table napkins, collected the thermometer, typewriter, violins, coats, Teddy Bears and suitcases from the train and pushed them all into a taxi with me and the children on the back seat, and Jim with the driver. The taxi sped downhill to the docks, horn bleating urgency all the way.

The ship was still there, the gangplank and boarding steps in place. No one was there to admit us, nor was there anyone to stop us. We found our cabins, and the steamer trunks already there confirmed our ownership. We washed again, ate our eggs, toast and jam and fruit, stretched out on the clean bunks and had a sweet warm nap.

At noon the children were hungry again and a surprised cabin boy answered the bell. Jim asked, "What time lunch?"

"No lunch, sir."

"Why no lunch?"

"No passengers until two o'clock sir, so no lunch."

"*We* are passengers. We want lunch."

The boy brought to the cabin a whitecovered table, a large platter of several kinds of sandwiches, oranges, milk and coffee.

At two o'clock we heard the passengers come aboard. There were not many. The engines quickened their rumble, on deck the breeze freshened, the blue and green waves boiled and bubbled to a rich cream in the wake and....

AFTER PEARL HARBOUR the Japanese officially occupied the International Settlement and the French Concession and interned the nationals of their enemies. Some of our friends died during internment; others suffered mentally and physically and never really recovered. When the 99-year lease on the piece of swamp land and adjoining concessions expired, neither Chinese nor Westerners had any rights in Shanghai to re-negotiate, and the dream of a multi-national community ceased to exist.

MANCHURIA

AMUR R.

CHAHAR

MONGOLIA

JEHOL

LIAOTING PENINSULA

KOREA

JAPAN

YELLOW R.

⊙PEIPING

TIENSIN⊙

SHANSI

HOPEH

YELLOW R.

SHENSI

UNGHUANG

SHANTUNG

KYOTO⊙

CHANGAN⊙

LOYANG⊙

KAIFENG⊙

YANGTZE R.

SIAN

HONAN

ANHWEI

YANGCHOW⊙

HUPEH

NANKING⊙

CHINKIANG

ICHANG⊙

HANKOW⊙

WUCHANG⊙

SUI

SHANGHAI

HANYANG

KIUKIANG

HANGCHOW⊙

NINGPO

CHANGSHA⊙

KIANGSI

CHEKIANG

HUNAN

HANGCHOW

FUKIEN

LIU CHIU ISLANDS

KWANGSI

TUNG

CANTON⊙

PESCADORES ISLANDS

FORMOSA

KWANG

⊙HONGKONG

MACAO

HANOI

HAINAN

TONGKING

PHILIPPINE

ISLANDS

247

AFTERWORD

BY
PAT
CARNEY M.P.

S HANGHAI, CITY OF MY BIRTH, shimmers in a haze beneath my hotel room in the former French Concession. I am staring at the red tile roofs outside my window, listening to the horns hoot and howl through the
streets below. I am wondering why I feel so frustrated in
this enigmatic country, source of so many future expec-
tations.

I did not come here to shop, apparently the activity
most encouraged by our Chinese hosts, nor to view children dancing "How Happy and Sweet Our Life." I came
on a purely personal odyssey, to compare the China of
Today with the China of the Thirties when my parents
lived here.

I did not consider the possibility that I might not like
the People's Republic of China when I planned my trip.
For nearly sixty years, China has been the bright thread
in our family tapestry of adventure, romance, births and
upheavals ever since my father and mother arrived in
Shanghai.

My tour group is staying at the Ching Chiang Hotel; I
am obviously in the converted living room of an apartment known to my parents as the Cathay mansions.
There is a false fireplace behind the sofa and the walls
are painted a shade of robin's egg blue I had forgotten
existed. On the night of our arrival I had explored the
building in a state of high excitement, barging into
rooms allocated to our tour group, wondering whether

my mother came for tea here, what liaisons whiled away the hot, humid afternoons, whether in his bachelor days my father's French mistress entertained him in rooms now billeting an American banking group.

Through the trees below shines the white domed roof of the French Club, now closed, where my parents and their friends danced and drank and celebrated the glittering jazz-filled nights and days, oblivious to Mao Tse Tung's Long March to Liberation and the war clouds over Europe, or the Depression dust bowls sanding the gears of the American economy.

I want to walk the Bund, that park-like embankment bordering the Whangpoo River and lined with the abandoned citadels of trade and finance, shipping and embassies, built by the Europeans on a marshy bog to create the International Settlement, granted to foreigners under 19th century treaty rights, and now gone, vanished, to be replaced by—what? I want to see what *is* compared to what *was*, when Shanghai was the Sin City of the Orient and where, my father told me, one really did part the beaded curtains and plunk one's foot on the brass rail of seedy bars.

We are being swept through China in groups of "Foreign Friends" from all corners of the world: Japanese and Koreans, Mexicans and Americans and French and Germans all wearing our lapel badges, searching frantically for our tour buses, tripping over each other's luggage in the elevators; while China itself, vibrant, crowded, noisy and exciting, remains out of reach—a series of blurred images and sights and sounds interpreted mainly through polite and often uncomprehending guides seemingly programmed to supply every necessity but information. I have yet to learn whether the China that fascinated my father for nearly twenty years and colours many childhood memories still exists; or whether it was myth, dissipated by civil war and the Liberation and the exodus of Westerners; or whether some essence of that earlier era would evolve in the new rapprochement with the West sought by Vice-Premier Teng Hsiao P'ing and his colleagues in their New Long March Toward the Four Modernizations—the ambitious attempt to simultaneously improve agriculture, industry, science and technology, and defence.

We tourists are an essential element in that strategy. We supply some of the foreign currency to finance Teng's international shopping list of chemical plants and oil rigs and communication equipment and computers. In legendary Hangchow, where temple bells once echoed through the velour-soft hills on my parent's honeymoon, airport billboards now exhorted us to buy Marlboro cigarettes, Hennessey cognac, Seven-Up and something called Tiger Wok. In Peking we would augment the traditional cups of fragrant steaming tea with Coca-Cola.

We find ourselves endlessly bused to Friendship Stores, and department stores and curio shops. "Come and buy," urges a sign in one handicraft store. "Come now, shake a leg," our Chinese guide will exhort us as we rush through the Ming tombs almost at a dead run—into the souvenir shops where we will obligingly part with our yuans for good silk and cheap jewelry and posters and assembly-line prints. "Another few years and it will be Coney Island," says one Canadian whose business takes him to China regularly.

My memories of China are the random images of childhood. Our house and garden. Amah, our nurse. Riding in a taxi through flooded streets. A refugee family camped under a yellow beach umbrella. My father in his tropical whites and my mother in silk prints and bobbed hair. The rickshaws and beggars in the crowded streets. A Japanese sentry at the end of the lane, and the bewildering confusion of the evacuation; seeing my twin swung across the water by a sailor to a waiting British ship. Standing in our living room sun porch watching airplanes. (Chinese? Japanese?)... The Bund, viewed from a great height. Going with my father to visit the family of his Chinese foreman.

Most of the familiar names have vanished from the maps of the city. Our tour bus has deposited us at the Shanghai Museum and we look over the city from the third-floor windows. I know that Yenan Street below was once called the Avenue of King Edward VII, built seven carriage-widths wide to mark the boundary of the International and the French concessions. I pointed to where the bronze Angel of Mercy once stood on the Bund, and identify the imposing Customs Building Tower. Across the street is a turreted building decorated with laundry and pots and bamboo baskets; through the open window we can see non-political posters on the walls. Below us, three men, one working and two watching, are rebuilding the curbstone. The streets are packed with bicycles and pedicabs and pedestrians and the odd truck honking through the crowd. Leaving the museum, we pause to watch two men squatting on a curbstone with baskets of live shrimp and fresh slopping fish. In a back alley, a woman washes her hair in a bowl.

On the Bund at last, we walk along the embankment, beside the Whangpoo River with its skittering sampans and junks and ferries. As a child I remember watching Japanese airplanes attempting to bomb a Chinese warship; two former American warships are berthed in her place. We soon attract a very large crowd, who circle us in claustrophobic fashion whenever we stop. A school of children in white shirts and smiles run up to clap Hello! Goodbye! in an increasingly louder chorus and then dance off to meet us farther along.

"Good evening," a gray-haired Chinese says in perfect English. I ask him how he had learned his English. He worked for the Shanghai Light Company in the old French concession, he replies. My mother had written the utility's advertising copy; I wonder if they had ever met. Another man, spotting my flight bag, asks me if I am from Hawaii and gives me the address and name of his brother in Honolulu.

A very nervous young man in a green suit explains he is a middle-school student on his day off. He introduces every sentence with the phrase, "By the way." At my request, he identifies the Seaman's Club, which I believe to be the old British Consulate where my parents were married. At the end of the Bund we come to Wang Po Park, still with its iron fences, one of the two places in the old Settlement banned to Chinese because of their rampant spitting catarrh; the other place was the race track. Today the park is filled with Chinese exercising with slow, graceful, martial arts movements. The race track, now used for parades and demonstrations, is called the People's Park.

Escorted by a huge crowd, I am isolated in a maze of memories and the echoes of legends. Surely that is the Astor House; I thought it had been bombed. And what was this building, with its imposing British crests in the glass doors, now guarding a flock of bicycles within its tarnished tiled interior? When Mao's armies took over the Settlement in 1949, they did not know what to do with these bizarre buildings with their columns and crouching lions. Searching for clues to their original identity is like looking for a lost city, buried not by sand, but by people who choose to obliterate the history behind these blackened walls.

A Japan Air Lines guidebook records how Shanghai developed largely as an enclave for Western commercial interests after the former fishing village surrendered to the British in 1842. It advises: "Questions about the old days are usually met with an awkward silence as if the visitors were probing into the sooner-forgotten misdeeds of a wayward child." The foreigners of the 1930's are presented as colonial exploiters and oppressors. But it did not seem that way to my father, as he inspected the slaughter houses along the Whangpoo River and worked to improve health standards. There are still a handful of Westerners absorbed like invisible aliens into the urban jungle: I hear of a doctor who would know my father. What was life like for a Westerner caught in the thirty-year diplomatic freeze between China and the United States, which finally thawed last year with U.S. recognition of China? We can only guess.

With the help of the China Travel Service, we engage the services of a taxi driver old enough to remember the shape of the city before Liberation. He is a dignified, gray-haired gentleman with bad teeth called Mr. Shu. I want to locate the bubbling well that stood in the middle of Nanking Road, across from the Temple of Tranquil Repose at the western edge of the International Settlement. Mr. Shu draws over to the crowded curb, stops the car and imperiously waves all traffic to stop in order to usher me into the centre of the street, where he points down at the pavement. The famous bubbling well has been paved over.

The house I remember as a child was in West End Gardens, a compound of terraced houses off Yu Yuen Road in Chinese territory beyond the Settlement. All morning we explore the entrances and alleyways of busy neighbourhoods under the protective eye of Mr. Shu. But the houses either have no garden or they have a tree but the wrong porch and we honked our way through the crowds to Chungshan Park where we played as children.

We knew it as Jessfield Park and adored the stone lions, perfect for scrambling and playing hide-and-seek. The usual red and gold Chinese characters blare their obscure messages above the open gates. An old lady with gray hair and once-bound feet sits at the entrance. The park is very dusty; the grass looks dry and gray. Lovers sit holding hands, screened by private little bushes, and adults exercise in concentrated oblivion. As we wander down the paths past the stream and little pavilions, every rock looks like a lion. For one group of laughing Chinese I try to draw a lion; the result looks like a pussycat. The lions have left the park.

A ruddy-faced worker approaches us and announces he has studied English in evening school for four years. He gives us permission to take pictures of a sign with a goose, chickens and an earth satellite. "Sheyasheya-ni," I say. "Thank you." "No, no," my friend corrects me. "That is Peking dialect. In Shanghai you say "Sheyasheya-nung." I clap my hands and say "Sheyasheya-nung." "In your country, are men and women equal?" inquires the ruddy-faced man. I paraphrase Mao's quote: "Women hold up half the sky, but it is the heavier half." The crowd laughs.

Afterwards we eat a Western-style meal in the ornate dining room of the Peace Hotel, the fabled Cathay Hotel of the Thirties; the tile ceiling is cracked and the stained glass broken, but a potted palm still stands before the net-curtained revolving door like a 1930's stage set. I look out on a view of the Bund I have seen before on some family outing in China Past. I think: if I turn my

head fast enough, I can see my parents holding hands in
the corner. Haven't I heard their voices echoing through
the Chinese music and traffic in the wind-cooled, tree-
shaded streets?

Always there is nothing there.

I can't find my China Past; I wonder what I can relate
to in China Present, whether there is, in fact, any point
of contact between the West and the East to be made. In
1978, more than half a million Western tourists came to

China. Some come because China is chic; last year the pyramids of Egypt, this year the Forbidden City. Some come to learn. Some come simply to shop. Hopefully, it is a beginning, one we will be pleased to look back on.

As our plane bounces through the warm, turbulent air and the green hedges and red fields fall away, I reflect that I have left China three times, once by sampan and destroyer, once by night train and ferry, and now by air, but I have always come back. My seatmate on the flight is a Chinese woman my age, also born in Shanghai. I learned that her father was an officer in Chiang Kai Shek's Nationalist army, which Mao's Communists forced off the mainland to Taiwan.

Fellow exiles, we clink our brandy glasses. We may return to our birthplace while the Chinese Gate is swinging open to the West, but she will always be an Overseas Chinese and I will always be a Foreign Friend.

We know that neither of us can ever go home again.

A longer version of this piece first appeared in City Woman Magazine, September/October, 1979.

上海

ABOUT THE AUTHOR

Dora Sanders Carney was born at Capetown in September, 1903, moving to England in 1909 and to Canada in 1911.

Before leaving for what she thought of as a short trip to China in 1933, she freelanced for *Macleans, Saturday Night*, the *Manchester Guardian* and other periodicals, and occasionally contributed poems to the *Canadian Forum*.

En route to Hong Kong, she met Jim Carney, who convinced her to forget her plans and explore the wonders of Shanghai. This book is a memoir of her Shanghai experience.

At the end of October, 1939, the Carneys came home to raise their four children in Canada. Because of the War and contract obligations, they left behind almost everything that Jim had earned in 18 years of service to the International Settlement. Jim entered Veterinary College to obtain the degree which would enable him to carry on the work he had been doing in China. Dora wrote occasionally for *Saturday Night* or the *Family Herald* in Montreal, and also gave talks on China to raise money for the Red Cross.

After graduation, Jim joined the B.C. Government staff, and they spent four years in Victoria, then ten years on a ten-acre farm outside Nelson in West Kootenay.

In 1958 they moved to the Fraser Valley and Dora returned to writing as Women's Editor and feature writer for the Abbotsford, Sumas and Matsqui *News*. After three years she resigned to help Jim build a retirement home on Saturna Island. Since Jim's death in 1976 she has divided her time between Saturna and Vancouver.

Foreign Devils Had Light Eyes is her first full-length book, completed in 1980.